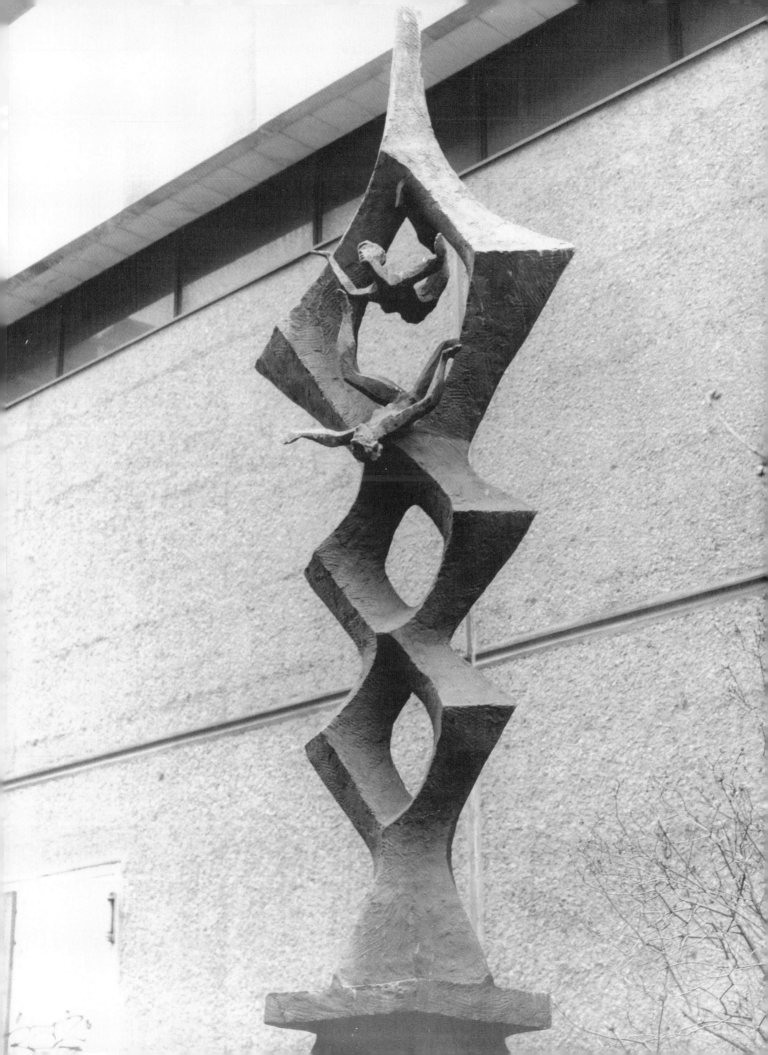

Pace Downtown Theater
Schimmel Center for the Arts, NY

Previous Page:
Chaim Gross Sculpture
"Heaven and Earth,"
NYC

One Pace Plaza

PACE MARKETING SOCIETY

ICAN MARKETING ASSOCIATION
presents

CREED of LEVER BROTHERS

THE GLOBAL MARKETING of NUGGLE FABRIC SOFTENER

ESDAY, MARCH 27

ALL WEST (2nd FLOOR)

0 TO 7:30 PM

PACE AMERICAN MARKETING ASSOCIATION
presents

MR. GREG CREED of LEVER BROTHERS

THE GLOBAL MARKETING of SNUGGLE FABRIC SOFTENER

WEDNESDAY, MARCH 27

LECTURE HALL WEST (2nd FLOOR)

6:00 TO 7:30 PM

PACE UNDERGRADUATE MARKETING ASSOCIATION
PRESENTS:

Study Abroad Workshop for Pace Students

FEATURING:
Dean Mary Handley of
THE AMERICAN UNIVERSITY OF ROME

This informative and entertaining event will take place on Monday March the 11th. from 12:00 - :00p.m.. in the Student Union.

oin P.U.M.A

Pace Players

PACE PLAYERS PRESENT

PACE PRE - MEDICAL SOCIETY

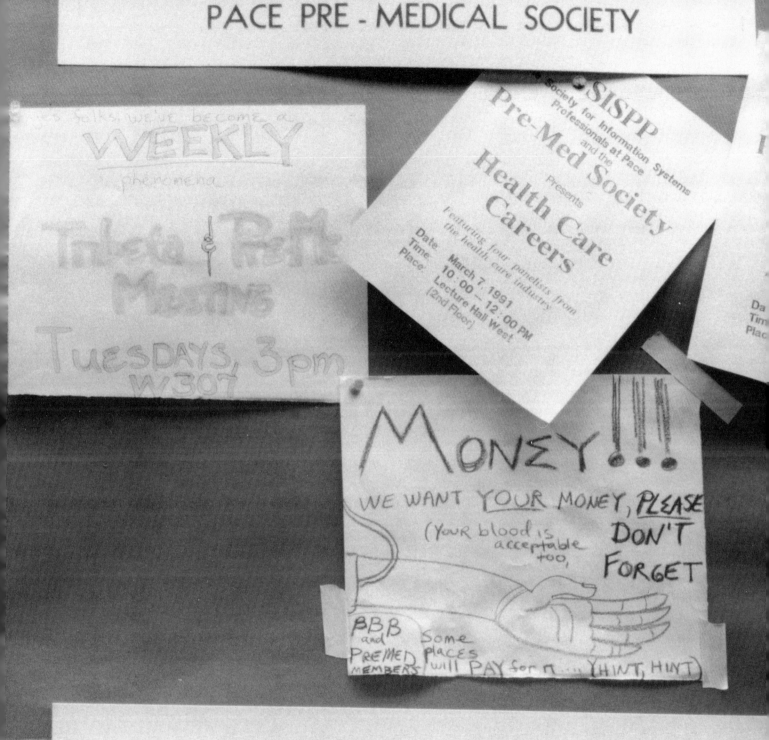

yes folks, we've become a
WEEKLY
phenomena

Tribeta & PreMed
Meeting
TUESDAYS 3pm
W307

SISPP
Society for Information Systems
Professionals at Pace
and the
Pre-Med Society

Presents

Health Care
Careers

featuring four panelists from
the health care industry

Date: March 7, 1991
Time: 10:00 - 12:00 PM
Place: Lecture Hall West
(2nd Floor)

Da
Tim
Plac

MONEY!!!
WE WANT YOUR MONEY, PLEASE
(your blood is
acceptable
too, DON'T
FORGET

BBB and some places will PAY for it... (HINT, HINT)
PREMED
MEMBERS

PHI BETA SIGMA

George Washington Carver (1860?-1943)
Agricultural Chemist
George Washington Carver won international fame for

One Pace Plaza
Henry Birnhaum Library, NY

Overleaf:
Entrance of Schimmel
Center for the Arts, NY

OPPORTUNITAS
The History of Pace University

Text by
Marilyn Weigold

Photographs by
David Finn

Pace
University
Press

Left: Bas Relief,
Choate House, Pleasantville

Previous Page:
Chaim Gross Sculpture
"Acrobat in the Ring,"
One Pace Plaza, NYC

Distributed by arrangement with
University Publishing Associates, Inc.

4720 Boston Way
Lanham, MD 20706

British Cataloging-in-Publication Information Available

Library of Congress Cataloging-in-Publication Data
Weigold, Marilyn, E.
    Opportunitas: The history of Pace University/text by
Marilyn Weigold: photographs by David Finn
    p. cm.
    Includes bibliographical references.
    1. Pace University — History, I. Finn, David, 1921 -
II. Title.
LD4455.W45   1991
378.747'1 -- dc20   91-26872
                                      CIP

ISBN: 0-944473-06-7 (pblc. alk paper)

DESIGNED BY RUDER·FINN DESIGN

Table of Contents

Chapter *4* From 1960-1975

Chapter *5* From 1975-1991

Introduction

The story which will unfold in the following pages is part institutional history and part biography, for the history of Pace is essentially the story of people. From its founding in 1906 to today, Pace has benefitted from the devotion of countless students, faculty, staff, alumni, administrators and trustees. Most visible in shaping an institution which has endeavored to remain faithful to its motto, Opportunitas, have been the five Presidents of Pace. Given Pace's long history of preparing students of all ages and backgrounds for challenging careers in business, particularly accounting, it seems quite natural that the institution's chief executive officers have been successful business people who fine tuned their skills as entrepreneurs, corporate executives or administrators at other institutions of higher education before coming to Pace.

The first President of Pace, Homer St. Clair Pace, who with his brother Charles Ashford Pace, an attorney, founded the institution in 1906, had gained managerial experience in the transportation industry before becoming a C.P.A. and establishing an institute to train accountants. Homer's son, Robert Scott Pace, served a lengthy apprenticeship as his father's assistant before becoming Pace's second President. The third and fifth Presidents, Dr. Edward J. Mortola and Dr. Patricia O'Donnell Ewers, were administrators at other institutions before coming to Pace, while Dr. William G. Sharwell had a long career at New York Telephone and AT&T before being named Pace's fourth President. As organization people, Pace Presidents have been keenly aware of budgets, balance sheets and enrollment statistics. Had they not been, Pace would hardly have evolved from a business institute into a comprehensive university.

Just as important in the development of the institution has been the ability of the different Presidents to relate well to students, faculty, staff, alumni, trustees and friends of the University and to plan intelligently for the future while tackling present problems with verve and circumspection. In large measure, every President of Pace has been successful in these areas because he or she has been much more than a capable manager. Indeed, each has been a humanist, artist or visionary. Evidence of this is Homer Pace's early career as a journalist and his later work as author of inspirational articles; Robert Pace's attainments as an artist whose medium was photography; Edward Mortola's youthful success as a musician and his later achievements as a visionary who dreamed big dreams and set out to make them happen; William Sharwell's artistry as a film producer with an unusual ability to combine visual and musical images; and Patricia O'Donnell Ewers' contributions as writer and English scholar.

Like Superman, whose real identity and work clothes were hidden, each Pace President has been something more than what meets the eye. In essence, each of the five individuals who have shaped the institution's destiny since 1906 has been a poet in a three-piece suit. Doubtless the artistic side of the institution's chief executive officers accounts for the marvelous serendipity which has characterized Pace from its inception. One eye on the bottom line and the other on a vision of the future makes for interesting management. In a changing environment, it can be an indispensable element in institutional survival and success. How Pace has adjusted to changing times in a turbulent century while remaining faithful to its vision of providing opportunity, with a capital O, to a highly diverse urban and suburban population is an intriguing tale of calculated risk, hard work, good luck and, above all, extraordinary people from Presidents on down to the newest freshman who uses his/her Pace education to climb the socioeconomic ladder and who one day returns to alma mater as trustee and benefactor.

Poets in three-piece suits - there are lots of them at Pace, always have been and hopefully always will be because a Pace education is so much more than training in business subjects; it's a broadly based liberal education for business, the professions and, most of all, for life. How this came to be so will be recounted in the pages which follow.

Foreword

The history of Pace University is, as history must be, an account of the dreams and labors of many people. The Institute that became a College and then a University was the creation of two brothers, Homer S. Pace and Charles A. Pace. The characteristics they instilled into their fledgling school — quality, professionalism, respect for the individual, openness to opportunity — persisted through the growth to the present day Pace. Faculty and administrators contributed enormously to this history through their loyalty, their devotion to the progress of the school and their determination to lead students to academic success and fruitful careers. Today we value the past as the foundation for an even more significant future.

Our historian, Dr. Marilyn Weigold, has searched archives, extensive correspondence, written and oral history documents, and the memories of scores of associates. She has been a faithful reporter of Pace's history and in that reporting she has shared with all who care about Pace a pride in the past and confidence in the future.

Dr. Edward J. Mortola
Chancellor Emeritus
Pace University

Pace University, whose mission is expressed in its motto, Opportunitas, has played an essential part in the fulfillment of the individual dreams of success of its students. The history of the institution demonstrates that the University's story parallels the success of its graduates.

Founded in 1906 by the Pace brothers, Homer St. Clair and Charles Ashford, Pace was a business school for men and women who aspired to a better life. Pace Institute began its transformation into a modern university with emphasis upon the liberal arts and sciences under Robert Pace in 1948. With the dynamic leadership for twenty-five years of Dr. Edward Mortola, followed by the steadying managerial stewardship of Dr. William Sharwell, Pace has grown from rented facilities and few resources into one of the largest universities in the state of New York, with multi-million dollar physical plants on three campuses, an endowment of over $27 million, and a reputation for strong academic programs, excellence in teaching and talented hard-working graduates.

As Pace University begins its eighty-sixth year, the present leadership pledges itself to build upon the institution's historic commitments and strengths. The platform that is available to us came from the exercise of the American Dream. Although it is a different time and the stage is set differently, Pace will continue to embody the theme of Opportunitas for waves of economic and ethnic immigrants and a newly attracted population of second-generation college students who see at Pace a primary interest in student success. The tradition of excellent teaching and service, the diverse locations, the New York area as an intellectual resource and the economic enterprise of the region are a foundation that the creative people of Pace will convert into an unique educational enterprise: Pace University.

Carl H. Pforzheimer, III   Patricia O. Ewers
Chair, Board of Trustees   President
Pace University   Pace University

Dr. Patricia O'Donnell Ewers, President, Pace University
and past Pace Presidents Edward J. Mortola (left) and William
G. Sharwell (right)

ACKNOWLEDGEMENTS

The chapter notes indicate not only the source of the data utilized in preparing this history, but also the range of material found in the superbly organized Pace University Archives. Throughout this project, the author benefitted from the expertise, professionalism and genuine helpfulness of Ellen Sowchek, University archivist. Antoinette Wallace, Central Files assistant, also provided invaluable assistance with primary sources for Chapter 5. For earlier periods, the late Dr. Robert Pace, with whom the author conducted lengthy interviews, was most helpful. At every juncture, Dr. Edward J. Mortola provided guidance and useful insights.

The author would also like to acknowledge Dr. Joseph Sinzer, University historian, who laid the foundation for a University history in the 1970s by gathering and evaluating primary sources and writing at length about different periods of Pace's development. Dr. Sinzer also reviewed the author's manuscript and offered excellent suggestions for enhancing it. The following colleagues and administrators reviewed the manuscript and, in a series of interviews with the author, clarified various points, thereby ensuring the accuracy of the history: Dr. Joseph Pastore, Dr. Joseph Houle, Dr. Thomas Robinson, Bob Hoffstein, Professor Irving Settel, Dr. John Flaherty, Dr. George Shanker, Dr. Marilyn Williams, Dr. Alfreda Geiger, Dr. Donald Ryan and Professors Bernard Brennan, Richard Matthews and Marie Eckert.

Lastly, the editorial committee of the Pace University Press was extraordinarily helpful. Without Sherman Raskin, Allan Rabinowitz and Mark Hussey, the Pace history would not have assumed its final form. In addition to the expert guidance provided by the committee, Allan Rabinowitz researched and wrote the article on the history of the accounting profession which appears in the history and also acted as illustrations editor. Mark Hussey devoted countless hours to the difficult task of editing the manuscript, and Sherman Raskin, director of the Pace University Press, coordinated the work of the committee and that of Ruder and Finn, who did the layout. As his contribution to the project, David Finn, internationally acclaimed photographer, visited the Pace campuses and took the contemporary pictures which appear in the history.

The author also owes a debt of gratitude to Zania Byrd, departmental assistant, who performed many useful services ranging from photocopying to the compilation of data for the appendixes, and to Linda Bathgate, graduate assistant for the M.S. in Publishing program, for her work in preparing the manuscript.

1

Chapter From 1906 to 1921

OPPORTUNITAS

America has long been regarded as the land of opportunity, and one U.S. city, more than any other, has been perceived as the place to be by those anxious to scale the heights in business, the arts, fashion, communications and other fields. As the song says, if you can make it in New York, you can make it anywhere. In the late nineteenth century, countless European and Asian immigrants to the United States settled, whether by choice or by chance, in the great metropolis and set out to make new lives for themselves and their families. Native-born Americans, frequently from small towns in rural areas, did the same thing. Ironically, one of those U.S. citizens by birth who left his mark on his adopted city, a cultured Midwesterner named Homer St. Clair Pace, had an aversion to big cities. Only six years before Homer Pace and his brother Charles Ashford Pace established the Manhattan accounting institute which would evolve into Pace University, Homer, who was then thinking about a career in law rather than accounting, wrote to his boyhood friend Casper Ramsby, with whom he was considering opening a law office, "Casper, I have about concluded that we will settle in a smaller town than New York or Chicago when we begin the practice of law. I don't like the looks of it very much in a city. It seems to me that a fellow could pay rent on a 10 x 12 office in the top of one of the modern skyscrapers for years without getting a client, or attracting any more attention in the world than one of the cornices under which he has retired. I believe it would be better to locate in a smaller town, where we could be heard when we spouted."[1]

According to Homer, career advancement was only one reason for choosing a smaller municipality for, as he told Casper, "In a social way, too, one would cut more figure in a comparatively small town. A real good singer, for instance, could go begging for recognition in a city like this, while in a town like Manistasee, Battle Creek or Kalamazoo, he would be a Crackerjack. It would be well, it seems to me, to hunt up a town of moderate size in a new and developing farming country, and stay right by it. It seems foolish to be considering this matter before we go to school, but nevertheless it is quite an important part of the scheme, and I am going to be on a still hunt for a town that suits me."[2]

Homer was a great planner, but his careful approach to the challenges of business and life was not rigid. There was in his makeup an element of flexibility which enabled him to appraise every opportunity correctly, and Homer was not the sort of person who would allow a fine chance for advancement to elude him. If it meant relocating to New York City, so be it, although even after a few years in the metropolis, he was anything but enamored of large urban areas. As he told his Aunt Elmira Pace, "The city life wears on my nerves...."[3] Confiding a bit more in his friend Casper Ramsby, Homer declared, "...and what is a success in a city like this? A chance to live in a flat and pound the darned old asphalt streets with burning feet for the remainder of my life, or else live out in the mosquito districts and spend an eighth of my early life...or three hours a day, traveling ....Spiritually a man does not count at all. I sized up New York in a spiritual way and gave up as a bad job."[4]

Despite his harsh criticism of New York City, Homer decided to remain in Manhattan, initially as an employee of the Chicago Great Western Railroad, and then as an educational entrepreneur. Although Homer St. Clair Pace would achieve recognition in a service field, his rise to prominence was not unlike that of the industrial giants of the post-Civil War Gilded Age. Contrary to the "rags to riches" theme pervasive in the Horatio Alger stories and other literature of the period, successful businessmen of this era rarely started from scratch. Most were native-born Americans from middle-class families. Some, like John D. Rockefeller, Sr. (who would acquire a country estate at

Pocantico Hills, just down the road from the Pleasantville campus of the school founded by Homer Pace), had financial help from parents to launch their first business enterprise. But even those who lacked such assistance were in a better position to become successful businessmen than the average American of this period because they possessed more education than the typical citizen.

At a time when few Americans completed elementary school, the Gilded Age entrepreneurs were, for the most part, high school graduates. Some, like Rockefeller and Frank W. Woolworth, the retailing genius whose impressive Gothic-style office headquarters stands just across Broadway from Pace's Civic Center campus, rounded out their education at business schools. Armed with training in bookkeeping and other subjects helpful to budding entrepreneurs, these men set out to make their mark in the business world. For a few years they usually worked for someone else, but once they had gained experience, they struck out on their own, usually trying several different businesses before settling on the one which suited them best. Along the way, these men moved from rural areas of New England, upstate New York, or the Midwest where they had spent their childhood years. Whether it was Connecticut-born railroad magnate Collis P. Huntington dividing his time between San Francisco and New York, or Rockefeller moving from Ohio to Manhattan, the Gilded Age entrepreneurs abandoned the country for the city. Usually the city was New York.

Homer St. Clair Pace had much in common with the business moguls who changed the face of the city by erecting skyscrapers to house their corporate offices and altered the course of the nation by transforming it from an agrarian country to an industrialized giant. To begin with, there were the rural origins. Homer was born in a log cabin, in the small town of Rehoboth, Ohio, on Easter Sunday, April 13, 1879. His parents were John F. Pace and Elizabeth Ellen Hamilton Pace. John Pace, who pursued careers in public education and journalism after serving in the Union Army during the Civil War, was the descendant of

John and Elizabeth Pace - 1910, Parents of Charles and Homer

an Alsatian immigrant who had settled in Pennsylvania in the eighteenth century. John's father, Palmer Pace, relocated to Perry County, Ohio, in the early nineteenth century. There he married Mary Allen, whose ancestry was English. Homer Pace would be the first family member to stray very far from open fields and lush farmland but his childhood was decidedly rural and filled with the kind of adventures city boys only read about. One of them was so exciting that he had vivid recollections of it a half century later. Of this experience, Homer said, in a letter to a friend:

> Your story of the rattlesnake in the bird's nest reminds me of a somewhat similar incident during my youth. There was a small spring of perfectly good water, about as big as a skillet, in a railroad cut near my home. It was our habit to climb up the bank and take a cooling drink out of this spring when we were

walking down the track. One dark night we were going through the cut, and thought we would have a drink. Just as my companion was about to lap the water up...he thought he would take the precaution of lighting a match. The spring was completely filled with a snake, cozily coiled. I am sorry for the sake of the story that it was not a rattlesnake or copperhead, but the shock was quite worth while for all that.[5]

When Homer wasn't exploring the great outdoors, he was toiling away in public school. At age six, he was literate to the point of printing a charming little note to his cousin David in which he declared that David's father was "the best uncle I have."[6] A surviving report card reveals that Homer was a fine student, in terms of both academics and deportment. He was also an ambitious lad who wanted to learn something which would enable him to earn a living. It was this desire which prompted him to enroll in the Reed City Commercial School where he studied stenography for a few months in the spring of 1895. For the next two years, he helped his father publish the *Pere Marquette Journal*, a weekly newspaper in Chase, Michigan. A surviving issue of the paper, from December 4, 1896, contains articles directed towards the weekly's agrarian readership. In addition to "What the Farmers Want," "Manures for Onions," and "Weeds as Fertilizers," the issue contained pieces on Chinese self-reliance and Joan of Arc. Inscribed in the newspaper's account book was a wonderful motto which is quite applicable to the career of Homer St. Clair Pace: "Treat all with respect, confide in few, wrong no man."[7]

Following his father's death in 1896, the newspaper folded and Homer Pace enrolled in Ferris Institute, Big Rapids, Michigan, for some additional training in business. He remained at the school for the spring term of 1897. After that he was off to a job as a stenographer with the Ludington, Michigan, law firm of G. H. Blodgett and C. G. Wing. When he began working in Ludington, on July 3, 1897, Homer's salary was $6 per week, not a fortune to be sure, but in view of the fact that the United States was then in the fourth year of the second worst depression in the nation's history, merely landing a job was an achievement. Knowing when to leave even a good position was also important. Thus, as Homer himself pointed out, "After working in these law offices for two years and studying law during that time, I received a civil service appointment and was assigned to duty in the War Department with headquarters at St. Paul, Minnesota."[8]

Homer's friend Casper Ramsby was also thinking about a civil service position and beyond that, establishing a law practice with Homer after they had both completed their legal studies and had been admitted to the bar. The plan, which did not get beyond the talking stage, was for Homer to concentrate on the more practical, business side of the law and Casper to focus on the theoretical. Homer thought that this "will make a combination that will not only win us shekels, but will land us in Congress as well."[9]

Homer had it all figured out. He and Casper would squirrel away part of their salaries every month so that "by the time we are ready to make a start in the cruel world, we will not only have funds to buy books and office fixtures, but enough to tide us over the 'freeze-out' period, so much dreaded by young lawyers."[10] Although Homer admitted that "my ideas may be hazy," he told Casper " we are young enough and have sufficient gray matter and spinal column...to enable us to do most anything we set about."[11] He continued: "With your lack of self confidence, and my overstock of conceit, I think we would make a pair that would weather the storms of life and public opinion...."[12] To overcome any reservations Casper may have had, Homer, who was already demonstrating talent as a promoter, said, "A combination like we would make, after a few years of additional packing of our already well stored brains, would be a power in a thrifty and growing community. If you think you would like the law, and I know you would, I think it would give you a greater chance to do good than any other profession excepting the ministry and possibly the medical profession. You are not solemn enough for a parson, and you like your rest too well of nights to be a physician."[13]

Excerpt from 1892 notebook of Homer Pace - Age 13

Convinced that law was the only sensible career path at the time, Homer said, "It opens up so many and varied lines of work, insurance, real estate...that it would be strange if we did not find something suited to our tastes. It 'stands us in hand' to be picking up some profession...for we were never cut out to be satisfied with being clerks. There is a class that clerkships will satisfy; their normal condition, as a rule, however, is below a clerkship, and it is, of course a somewhat elevated position. We started as clerks and in order to be contented must rise to something... higher."[14] But what was that something higher? As Homer saw it, nothing short of boss would do, for, as he told his friend, "It would be no particular glory for us to 'hold down a job' in an ordinary office; the only surprise would be that we would be contented to be an 'understrapper,' especially when we feel it in our bones that we are equal, or superior, to the 'boss.'"[15]

TO TEXAS AND BACK

The determination with which Homer St. Clair Pace was planning his legal career was attributable, at least in part, to a highly unsatisfactory experience as an employee of Wm. Cameron & Co. at its lumber mills in Angelina, Texas. Always eager to improve his situation, Homer had fired off a letter to William Cameron inquiring about employment at their various facilities. Within days, he was informed about a position for a stenographer at one of the company's more remote locations. Homer was one of two finalists for this position. The other man (who, like Homer Pace, had studied at Ferris Institute) was actually chosen, but despite the $60 per month salary which was luring him south, he did not have enough money for rail fare to Texas for himself and his wife. With his good sense of humor, Homer explained that his rival "could not raise enough of the coin of the realm to pay the freight on himself and better half, so the plum (?) fell to the lot of your humble servant."[16]

Homer was quite correct to place a question mark after the word "plum" because the four months he spent in Texas, in the fall of 1898, turned out to be dreadful. Throughout this time, he corresponded with Casper Ramsby, who was spared no detail concerning rural Texas. To begin with, there was the heat wave which greeted Homer upon his arrival in dense fog at 3 a.m. of a September morning. "You may have seen hot weather in your time," he told Casper, "and it may be that you will see hotter, but I doubt if you ever saw anything equal to this south Texan climate."[17] Then there were the health problems. Homer told Casper:

> The town is situated on the Angelina river, a stream so dead you cannot see that it has a current and as yellow as yellow can be even now, and they say it is clear this time of year. The people are afflicted with the chills and fever, and honestly, I have seen more sickness in my brief stay here than I ever saw in my life before.[18]

No sooner had Homer taken up his duties in Angelina than malaria decimated the mills. According to Homer:

> This forenoon the bookkeeper was taken with the fever and I am running the whole office. He was too sick to talk when he left. The mill is not running because the head sawyer is sick. He was sick yesterday, and all the men who are not sick are losing time. It is no uncommon thing to have as high as six quit the mill in one day, sick with the fever and chills. It beats anything I ever saw.[19]

As for his own health, Homer told Casper:

So far I have escaped, but today I begin to feel rather queer, and I may expect an attack of it. I am careful of myself and coming so late in the fall, I hope to escape. The bookkeeper, however, has only been here six days longer than I have and he is down today. May the saints be with me! Also large quantities of quinine.[20]

What troubled Homer even more than the possibility of contracting malaria was the fact that the bookkeeper was "not our style of man....In fact he is not honest."[21] The bookkeeper, whose attack of malaria had initially evoked compassion, was not the sort of person with whom Homer cared to associate. "He has different ideas from what we have on virtue," Homer said, "he believing in gratifying the lowest appetites without any regard to the resulting harm on himself or anyone else."[22] When Homer first arrived in Angelina, the bookkeeper attempted to initiate him but the newcomer flatly refused. According to Homer, his co-worker insisted that "a fellow with my ideas would be laughed at here in this society, or almost, any society...."[23] Still, Homer was not persuaded to stray from the straight and narrow path. He informed Casper that, "I gave him to understand very distinctly that I would not participate in his pleasures, and that I would not accompany him on a certain trip to one of our neighboring towns. He made the trip — alone however. A fellow here is supposed to do more or less of this immoral work, but if

Homer Pace in Texas, leaning against pole

Homer Pace in Texas, standing at right

they find out that anyone says 'boo' to their sister, then there is a shooting match. Such honor as that makes me sick. Honor? No more honor about that than there is about the lowest criminal."[24]

Homer was also very troubled by the exploitation of African Americans. He told Casper, "They look down on a negro and will hardly speak to one, yet these same fellows sneak around after dark and do things of which we would blush to speak, with these same negro women, that they say are no more than cattle. What kind of honor do you call that? I tell you, Casper, the north is so far ahead of the south in everything that makes life worth living and the world better, that there is no comparison."[25]

Despite his abhorrence of the situation in Angelina, Homer made the best of it, telling Casper, "I try to do a little good as I go along, and I have more than once had an opportunity since I have been here to sympathize with the suffering and say kind words to ears that were more used to curses than blessings. If I have increased the faith of one person in the unselfishness of mankind, my work in Angelina has not been in vain."[26]

As for his official work for Wm. Cameron & Co., Homer said, "I keep the time for the mill, planer, kiln, yards, etc., do the stenographic work, invoice the shipments of lumber, make bills [of] lading, assist on the books, rent and look after 98 dwelling houses, and most of the time have enough to keep me out of mischief. Never

have a night to myself, and would have to work Sunday if I would allow it. I draw the line there."[27]

Although it was not in his job description, Homer decided to accompany three railroad cars filled with lumber to a railroad junction about eight miles from Angelina. "I went to see the country and enjoy the air," he told his friend, adding, "When we were nearly back just before twelve, we crossed a bridge or trestle which gave way. The cap was rotten and the rail sunk with the engine...When the engine went down it nearly threw us off, but the engine drove ahead and went on to the rails again....The next thing I saw was a cloud of dust and a boxcar went off....The engine ran on the wheels on one side for an instant and seemed to hover over the ravine. If it had gone over I would not be writing this letter in all probability."[28] Homer escaped without a scratch but his close call may have triggered some thinking about his own mortality and that of others. Despite the prospect of a $10 pay increase to $70 per month for assuming additional duties at the mill, Homer was thinking seriously about leaving Texas only two months after he had arrived. Concern for his widowed mother was one factor in his decision to head north. "If it was not for my mother I would not be back to Ludington for a good long while," he told Casper.[29] In a handwritten postscript to another of his typewritten letters, Homer said: "Mother has kept writing for me to come home and my heart is not as solid as a brickbat so I have concluded to take this step."[30]

If Homer had second thoughts about his decision to leave Texas, they were quickly forgotten the moment he became an unwitting participant in some Texas mayhem. Homer described this incident as follows: "A man rushed into the commissary this morning while your humble servant was purchasing 26# of pecans for home consumption this winter, and started on a dead jump down the store yelling 'WOW, WHOOPEE, give me a gun, a gun, WHOOPEE, I want to shoot the sunofagun, WOW, Ten dollars for a gun. WOW.'"[31]

Later that same day, Homer witnessed "a fellow stab at

another."[32] He told Casper, "Two fellows have been drinking and started a quarrel. One...struck at the other fellow's head. He ducked and stabbed with his knife. They separated them. They are still quarreling and I keep one eye out the window watching."[33]

On another occasion, an employee who had been dismissed threatened the bookkeeper who shared an office with Homer. The disgruntled man used a tree outside the office for target practice and shot up his own home, but the bookkeeper and Homer were spared. Homer treated the incident quite humorously. Referring to the gunman, he told Casper: "When he poked his head in I assured him that he had my moral support, but as I was busy with an invoice I would prefer to have the doors closed so the shooting wouldn't disturb me."[34]

Describing yet another incident involving a gun, Homer said: "The bookkeeper and I had to chase a fellow out with a gun a week or two ago."[35] In view of these experiences, it is no wonder that Homer fled Texas, but not before he had lined up a job in Michigan. Moving north meant taking a substantial pay cut, amounting to about $20 per month, but this did not deter Homer. Although he rejected one offer at a salary of $40 per month, he decided to accept a position paying $43.33 per month with the law firm for which he had previously worked. Convinced that he could pick up some additional stenographic work in the evening, enough to boost his monthly income to $50, Homer was content to return to the old firm, albeit temporarily. By living at home, he would keep his expenses to a minimum and, equally important, he could increase his shorthand speed, which had diminished because of his more varied duties in Texas. Homer outlined his plans for Casper Ramsby, saying, "I will not bargain to stay with Wing and Blodgett any length of time, but do my work well and improve all I can in speed and accuracy. You know the difference between law office work and lumber office work as regards shorthand work. If I stick by stenography any length of time, I cannot help but think that the road to success lies along the line of fast work, and I have

Homer S. Pace - December 1898 - Age 21

my misgivings about the lumber office work."[36]

Not long after Homer returned to work in Ludington, one of the principals in the law firm died. Mr. Blodgett's passing, together with the decision Homer had made a bit earlier to increase his speed and then move on, accelerated the young man's career timetable. Thus Homer began applying for other positions and sought recommendations from C.G. Wing. Very supportive of the young man's efforts, Wing wrote that Homer Pace "is worthy of a better place and finer work than this town affords," adding, "Mr. Pace can do better than any stenographer that has been here in Ludington within my knowledge, and I have tried them all one time or another. Besides he is quite a man in his own right and capable of conducting private business with fine discretion."[37] In another letter, Wing asserted that "of all expert shorthand writers that have been in my employ in the past twenty years, he is easily first and best equipped for doing a great deal of work. Both in quality and quantity he is up to the highest mark."[38]

One of the recommendations written by C.G. Wing was addressed to the University of Michigan at Ann Arbor. Homer Pace was evidently thinking about enrolling in the university, provided he could find a position which would enable him to support himself while he pursued a degree. His employer, therefore, said, "He wishes to take a course of study, and whenever there may be an opening for him to employ his art in such a manner as to pay his way at the University I wish you would send me word....his antecedents are the best, and prospectively he is worth educating. The ordinary work of a law office does not afford him time for study under competent teachers, as would be the case perhaps if some part of each day could be given to him at the University. When there is an opening for such talent please write."[39]

Homer St. Clair Pace did not enroll in the University of Michigan. Instead, he accepted a position as manager of the Mason Telephone Pay Station Company. His compensation was $60 per month, the equivalent of what he had been earning in Texas, and the working conditions were considerably better. Yet Homer remained with the company only six weeks. The reason for his short tenure was the sudden appearance of a better opportunity, a civil service appointment with the War Department in St. Paul, Minnesota, at an annual salary of $l,000. This represented a one-third increase in income for Homer, and the additional money was indeed welcome because in the summer of 1899 he had taken a bride, Mabel Evelyn Vanderhoof. By September 1899 the newlyweds were living in "a fine little house."[40] They had six rooms "three up and three down...some four or five closets, a pantry, good cellar and bath room with water closet."[41] The rent was $12 per month and according to Homer "it is worth it to have all

the conveniences of life."[42] Homer enumerated some of them in a letter to his friend Casper Ramsby, "I am about two miles and a half from the business center, and pay five cents carfare each way and take my lunch down town. I can get an excellent 'square' (meal) at my former boarding house for 20 cents, or I can spend anywhere from a nickel to a dollar at a lunch room. So you will see that with carfare and noon lunches I spend nearly $10.00 a month besides my rent."[43]

Homer had no complaints about the quantity, variety and price of food in St. Paul. He told Casper, "Everything but fruits can be purchased to better advantage than in Ludington. The best creamery butter costs 26 cents the pound - dairy about 18 or 20. Flour costs, the best grade, 60 cents for 25 pounds."[44] Other items in Homer's budget were also eminently affordable. As he told Casper, "My fuel during the cold weather (hard coal) costs me somewhere about $8.00 to $10.00 per month. This runs the grand total of rent, street car and lunch expenses, and fuel up to about $30.00 per month. In summer I ride a wheel and save on the street car expense, and the fuel costs less than half."[45]

Biking to work in nice weather could not have been too burdensome for a healthy young man, but the advantage of living closer to his workplace was apparent to Homer, who confided: "From my experience I think it would be better economy to live down-town and save street car expense and the time spent going to and coming from work."[46]

Now that he was happily situated, Homer could set goals for the immediate future. One, as he told Casper, was to perfect his knowledge of the Spanish language. Already able to converse in Spanish, Homer planned to spend the winter "going after the language of Cervantes with a determination that will make me look like a native of Aragon by spring, and I am going to sandwich it with all sorts of lighter study."[47] This, as well as other things, had to be postponed when Homer's bride fell ill with "lung fever."[48] Although she made a complete recovery, the medical bills must have been a heavy burden for the young couple. To pay them, Homer was compelled to appeal to his friend, Casper, also a newlywed, for a loan. "I have been undergoing extraordinary expenses for several months," he told Casper, adding, "You don't know how much your favor will relieve the 'pressure,' and if you are in no particular need of it for a month or so, it will aid me that much more."[49]

Perhaps it was the increased financial pressure, or maybe it was merely a persistent urge to improve his situation which caused Homer to tell his friend, at the very time Mabel Pace was ill:

> Don't prepare for the civil service...with the idea of making it a life work. My idea of the civil service was, and is, a place where one can have plenty of time for study and at the same time receive comfortable wages....As to my law aspirations, they are stronger than ever and even now I am arranging to attend the evening lectures at the University of Minnesota....I am going to make up the deficiencies in my education as I go along, complete my law course, and then see where I am "at." If the government service is paying me what I will be worth at that time, I will stay with my Uncle Sam; if I am still receiving $1000 a year, I shall sever my connection....At present I very much doubt whether I am worth the $1000 that I receive, and I am going to be contented. Think of that—contented. That is a surprising state to find yours truly in.[50]

Despite his assertions, Homer did not remain contented for long. In November 1899 Homer's boss, Lieutenant Colonel Arthur L. Wagner, assistant adjutant general for the department of the Dakotas, received an unexpected transfer to the Philippines and departed almost immediately. Understandably concerned about this sudden development, Homer confided, "His successor has not been appointed yet, and of course I don't know whether I will profit or lose by the change. It is very unlikely that he will be succeeded by as able a scholar, however, and in this respect I am almost sure to lose. On the other hand, my work will be still lighter, allowing me more time for

study."[51] One option available to Homer was a transfer to the Philippines but perhaps because of his unhappy experience in Texas, he was reluctant to move to another remote area. The fear of contracting disease also seems to have played a part. "The Colonel's chances for living in the Philippines are hardly as good as they would be in the United States proper,"[52] Homer declared. Since two of Homer's former employers had died, he was quite concerned about Colonel Wagner's well being. He told Casper, "It is a sad fact, but a 'true fact' nevertheless, that my employers do not thrive well. In my scrap collection I have the obituary and picture of my Texas employer, Mr. Cameron, and he was worth millions; I also have poor Mr. Blodgett's obituary....Please to not mention this remarkable coincidence to anyone else, as I hardly have enough saved to retire on. If it should become known that I am a Hoodoo my prospects for 'jobs' would be slim."[53]

In all truth, Homer St. Clair Pace did not have anything to worry about. In January 1900, two months after Colonel Wagner had sailed for Manila, Homer resigned from government service to become private secretary to A.B. Stickney, president of the Chicago Great Western Railroad, at a salary of $l,200 per year plus expenses. Homer secured this position by answering a newspaper ad. In the subsequent interview he managed to outshine college men who had applied for the position. But after he had been in the job for ten months, Homer may have had some misgivings. His Methodist upbringing made it difficult for him to endure the boss's cursing, and there were other things he didn't like about the job. He told Casper, "This being cooped up in an eight story stone building has its disadvantages, especially to a farmer like myself. I am afraid I will never get over the liking I formed for the woods and nature...."[54]

But green fields did not lie in Homer's future. At age 21 he had adult responsibilities which precluded forfeiting a good position for the unknown. His mother had moved in with him, and his wife had given birth to a daughter. Homer took genuine delight in telling his friend Casper about the little girl named Helen. Describing what a later generation would call "quality time," the hardworking Homer said, "Our daughter is waxing strong and the point of a tooth may be felt which as yet has not become visible. If you could look in on us some night and see Mrs. Pace holding her on my back, while I am down on all fours doing the elephant act, you would wonder if it was the same sedate old Pace who used to attend to legal matters and conveyancing in a Ludington law office."[55] Homer added a handwritten postscript to his typed letter. It said, "I have got a vote this year - think of that!"[56] Homer St. Clair Pace had truly come of age.

NEW YORK, NEW YORK!

Three months prior to his twenty-second birthday, Homer received an offer he couldn't refuse, a chance to relocate to the east coast as manager of the railroad's New York City office at 31 Nassau Street. He arrived in the metropolis in the middle of January 1901. By March l, his salary had increased by one half of his original earnings. He was now receiving the munificent sum of $l,800 per year. In 1901 Homer became Assistant Secretary of the Chicago Great Western. A year later he acquired a new title, Secretary of the Mason City and Fort Dodge Railroad, an affiliated line. In 1903 he was earning $3,600 per year. By that time Homer was considerably more than a first-rate stenographer.

In his years with the railroad he had acquired expertise in the financial area. In 1904 he was "auditing the construction accounts of the various Syndicates" and was preparing for the New York State C.P.A. examination.[57] "I am busy, busy, busy," he told Casper Ramsby. "Besides," he said, "I am a commuter, if you know what that means and spend three or four hours a day on the cars and boat."[58] The Pace family was residing in the pleasantly bucolic community of Hollis, Queens, but the commute, which entailed a ferry ride across the East River, was not to Homer's liking. In one letter to Casper he detailed how he traveled home, saying:

I can start by boat, trolley or elevated as I choose. The nicest way is to walk to the foot of Wall Street (ever know it had a foot?) and take a Long Island Railroad Annex boat, a snug little steamer called the Sagamore, and sail up the East River three miles to Long Island City. I will then take a train for a fifteen mile ride out into Long Island. Or, I could go across the Brooklyn Bridge on a trolley and get a train on another branch of the L.I.R.R. in Brooklyn. Or, I could take an elevated train uptown three miles, cross over to Long Island City in a ferry and then take the train. Or I could take a trolley at the bridge and by transferring twice make the whole trip by trolley. But they don't run sleepers on the trolleys, so that is not practicable. A commuter runs like an electric clock, by jumps.[59]

A handwritten postscript to this letter stated, "New York life is pretty strenuous for a quiet fellow like me."[60]

An additional burden was business related travel. Homer had to journey frequently to the railroad's home

Park Row - Newspaper Row in the mid-1800's

office in St. Paul, even in winter. "I was in Saint Paul for six weeks this winter," he told Casper, lamenting that he had "missed the January examination which I planned on taking."[61] Homer's next opportunity to sit for the C.P.A. exam would be in June but, in the meantime, he declared, "I am busier than the proverbial two men chasing one snake."[62] The number and variety of projects Homer was directing at the railroad made him feel overwhelmed at times, but besides the tasks which were directly related to his job there were other things which consumed his time. He enumerated them for Casper: "I have had to spend two hours and a half to three hours a day on the hike between my house and the office. I have had to make garden, beat carpets, mow the lawn. I am putting the finishing touches on a two years' course of study in accountancy and cramming for the examination."[63] Fortunately, all of this agreed with Homer. Physically he was able to stand the strain. He told Casper, "I got weighed the other day, and imagine my surprise to find I tipped the beam at an even 150 — the most I ever weighed. I cannot account for that. Theoretically I ought to rattle when I walk. Practically, I am disgustingly fat and feel podgy. But don't worry, I'll get rid of some of it during the hot weather."[64]

Extra weight wasn't the only thing Homer would abandon. In 1906, he left the railroad where he had risen to Corporate Secretary. Bailing out with a golden parachute consisting of deferred compensation of $1,200 per year through 1909, Homer used this cushion to launch his C.P.A. practice. Having passed the New York State examination, Homer opened an office at 154 Nassau Street on October 11, 1906. The road from Michigan to Nassau Street, by way of Texas and St. Paul, had not been an easy one. Along the way Homer had seriously considered several different types of careers before making his final decision. As late as 1904, though he was diligently preparing for the C.P.A. examination, he was thinking about purchasing a Midwestern newspaper and printing business. He asked an aunt residing in Michigan to keep him "in touch with the situation."[65] He also requested that she be very discreet, saying, "I rely upon you to say nothing about these things, for their success will depend upon keeping a close mouth. I wish you would return this letter when you write, that I may be sure it does not go astray, or destroy it and tell me you have done so."[66]

After getting the important things out of the way,

Homer provided details of his life in the East. "Our garden is a wonder," he told his aunt, adding, "We have already had lettuce, radishes and onions. Our yard must contain twenty or thirty trees and the air is heavy with the odor of lilacs...the finest I ever saw. How I wish we would use some of them Decoration Day on the graves of pa and baby. I will depend upon you to see that some flowers are put there."[67]

Referring to an upcoming C.P.A. examination, Homer said, "I am busier than ever. Examination comes the 21st of next month, and as it costs $25 a try, I do not care to fail. I hope to pass, but it is no cinch. I have passed 23, but the last are the hardest of all, and it would not be strange if after passing twenty-three straight, I should come a cropper on this one. But I hope not."[68] As for his job, Homer betrayed his dissatisfaction by confiding, "Things are moving along about so so in a business way....Sometimes I long for a chance to do things where I would know the people and could make myself felt....Of course the salary is good and that is a consolation."[69]

One of Homer's greatest fears was that he would become accustomed to a high salary and would never strike out on his own. "The more salary one gets the harder it is to quit," he admitted.[70] Yet he was determined that this would not happen to him. "I have been considering several things," he told Casper.[71] One of them was a printing business. Homer figured that if he could establish such a business in the Midwest, where wages for printers ranged from $12 to $16 per week, compared with $22 per week in New York City, he would be able to keep his production costs low. Since many of the railroads, including east coast lines, had their printing done in the Midwest, Homer hoped to attract their business. He felt that he knew enough "influential people in New York and in Chicago and St. Paul" to make this feasible.[72] Once the printing business was on a solid footing, Homer planned to "acquire a line of good newspapers."[73] He told Casper, "My idea would be to make every paper entirely local, manager live in the town and run it strictly on local lines.

The job work, however, could be done better and cheaper at the principal office, wherever that might be. Now all these things could not be done in a minute. The thing to do would be to get a paper and run it awhile, and keep branching out as opportunity offered."[74] Homer's brothers, one of whom, Elmer, was a union printer, were not so sanguine. They said the plan wouldn't work but Homer was not deterred. He insisted that "they cannot conceive of a man with the daring and nerve to carry it to success."[75] The self-confident Homer believed he was that man. To Casper Ramsby he said, "I have had my nerve educated in the last five years, and I know conditions in that Michigan country just as well as if I had made the country. I did not pick up potatoes for a living and board myself at Ferris's for nothing. I know nearly every fellow from Reed City and Ludington. I could start with a prestige worth something. I have a large following...who would welcome a paper run by me. The banker at Scottville coaxed me last summer to take the Enterprise."[76]

Here we have Homer the budding entrepreneur. Like the industrialists of the Gilded Age, he was determined to be his own boss. A successful business was his goal. The nature of that business was less important than Homer's burning desire to be an independent businessman. To achieve this goal, he had worked out a strategy, one which called for the utilization, under certain conditions, of tactics employed by the big industrialists. One can only wonder whether his friend Casper was shocked to read the following words, which flowed from Homer's typewriter: "There is one more little point, which will perhaps make you think that my industrial training has wrecked my morals, but it would not have to be used except in emergency. Supposing we wanted a paper, and they would not sell at a reasonable price. We would work on Mr. Rockefeller's plan. We could keep what one might call a portable outfit, army press, case of type and a traveling devit, which we could run into a town and run a paper at a loss, if need be, until the owner saw things differently....But this perhaps would not be necessary."[77]

In contrast with the tactics required to create the newspaper empire, Homer hoped to do some good once he was well established. "The success of the newspaper scheme," he told Casper, "would make me a power for good, and a terror to evil...."[78] At the same time it would ensure an adequate income. On that subject, Homer felt that owning a chain of newspapers, perhaps in partnership with Casper, if he could be persuaded to come into the business, would be preferable "than to make a success of a thing where my only reward would be the money gained, as would be the case in New York."[79] When he wrote these lines in the spring of 1904, Homer was anything but bullish on New York. He confided to Casper, "I have a few friends here, but frankly I get heart sick of the whole thing. The monotony of it all, the grind as you call it, the absence of a chance to do things, tires me, and Mrs. Pace and I long for a little town, a little business and a little home. I have had my city experience and I am glad of it, but I can hardly reconcile myself to serve a life sentence. Pretty soon I must decide. If I once embark on the accountancy line it will be a long, hard struggle, and I won't turn back. It will mean city life for me for good."[80]

At this juncture, the choice was between the newspaper business and a multi-faceted accountancy practice, which would include an instructional component designed to prepare people for the C.P.A. examination by studying at a school similar to Koehler's New York School of Accounts. When Homer himself was getting ready for the exam, he discovered "that New York afforded very little and very poor instruction along these lines, and I found that the accounting literature in the United States was practically nil."[81] Homer, therefore, spent $75, a huge sum at the time, for British accounting publications. He then "prepared literature on different branches of accounting and with a lawyer friend of mine, have prepared lectures on various law matters."[82] Before long other students were using this material, and Homer was doing some tutoring. One of the people who became interested in Homer's work was an English accountant who was anxious to pass the

PUBLIC ACCOUNTING PRACTICE AND EDUCATION IN THE UNITED STATES THROUGH 1906

New York City served as the first home for accounting in the United States. It was here, in the early decades of the nineteenth century, that sole practitioners began to offer accounting services to the public, and that the nation's first self-styled accounting school taught bookkeeping and mathematical science for a brief time beginning in 1818.

Public accountants appeared in greater numbers during the 1850s in both New York City and Philadelphia. By the 1880s their work had become increasingly professional in nature by providing more than the routine accounting functions. There were 155 public accountants in New York City in 1886 and accounting firms in partnership form existed there from as early as 1866. Philadelphia's Wharton School of Business was established in 1881, and began to teach accounting in 1883.

During the last quarter of the nineteenth century business and industry flourished throughout the nation, with New York City as the principal commercial center. Industrial concerns incorporated and their securities were publicly sold; there were financial panics in 1873 and 1893; monopolies were created; labor unions emerged and strikes took place; Congress enacted an Interstate Commerce Act and the Sherman Antitrust Act to regulate business.

As business organizations and regulation grew so did the largest New York public accounting firms. At first there were imports from England, namely Barrow, Wade, Guthrie + Co. in 1883, and Jones, Caeser + Co. (now Price Waterhouse and Co.) in 1890, but then American firms were founded - Haskins & Sells (now Deloitte & Touche) in 1895, and Lybrand, Ross Bros. & Montgomery (now Coopers and Lybrand) in 1898. Large organizations, prominently U.S. Steel in 1891, engaged the larger CPA firms to audit their records. In 1902 U.S. Steel began the practice of having auditors elected by stockholders and publicly issuing an audit certificate signed by the CPA firm.

The first U.S. accounting organization was the Institute of Accountants and Bookkeepers formed in New York City in 1882 and later known as the Institute of Accountants. Many of its members engaged in public practice and one class of them needed to pass difficult exams. It focused upon pioneering accounting education and providing accounting literature.

In 1887 the first national organization of public accountants was incorporated as the American Association of Public Accountants. Today its name is the American Institute of Certified Public Accountants. It had been founded at 45 William Street in downtown Manhattan and most of its early members practiced in New York City. In 1892 it was granted a provisional charter by the New York State Board of Regents to start a college for accountants; however, the school was not successful.

CPA exams were first given in December 1896 when New York State gave the profession of independent certified public accountants its first legal recognition. An exam candidate had to be at least 25 years old with 3 years experience, at least one of them in a public accounting office. The initial exam and its early successors dealt largely with today's basics but reflected public accounting practice of that era.

Two years and two exams went by before six CPA certificates were finally issued as a result of the third exam in 1898. By 1906, after 10 New York State exams, only 188 certificates had been granted based upon examinations although 185 were granted based upon waiver of the exam for persons who had practiced public accounting for at least one year before the passage of the 1896 CPA law. Throughout the United States only 617 certificates had been issued by 1906, half of them in New York.

During the first decade of the twentieth century the CPA profession grew rapidly in prestige and an increasing number of larger corporations chose to retain CPAs to perform periodic audits. The need for properly educated accountants was growing much more quickly than the supply.

In 1900 only 12 colleges and universities offered accounting courses, and only 4 of them included auditing courses. New York University started classes in the first department of accounting in 1901. In 1902, evening classes sponsored by the Pennsylvania Institute of Public Accountants began to prepare students for the CPA exam. Those classes were turned over to Wharton in 1904. Accounting literature was almost nonexistent at the time.

This was the educational and professional environment in public accounting when the Pace brothers embarked upon their educational venture in 1906.

by Allan M. Rabinowitz

New York State exam. He felt that Homer's materials "were as good as the ones he used in London. This particular fellow passed fourth in a class of 300 at his Chartered Accountant examination, that is to say only three fellows outstripped him in all England."[83]

Buoyed by the praise of the Englishman, Homer began considering "the advisability of opening up a school in New York for coaching in accountancy and also for teaching the real, genuine bookkeeping that the accountants consider the best, and which cannot be found in the commercial schools."[84] In addition to this, Homer was thinking about a correspondence course while, at the same time, doing "regular accounting work."[85] He knew this wouldn't be easy. "The disadvantage of this is that it will take a prodigious effort," he told Casper.[86] "I will have to give of my very life to make it a success...."[87] And that is precisely what Homer would do.

He sat for the C.P.A. exam on June 21 and June 22, 1904. "I believed I passed easily," he told Casper in early July.[88] He had other news for his friend as well. "A great big boy arrived at our house yesterday morning, and we are all feeling finer than silk over it," said Homer.[89] The new baby was Robert Scott Pace, who would one day succeed his father as President of Pace Institute and preside over the institute's transformation into a college.

A month after the birth of his second child, Homer told Casper, "To be entirely frank, I have such an exceptional opening before me in a business way, in carrying out the accountancy work and publishing my writings, that I hardly think it likely that I will take up the work in Michigan. As I told you, it is a time of choosing with me. My better judgment tells me to stay with the city where there are suitable fields for exploiting my meagre talents. My longing is for the country—the woods and the fields and independence. I detest columns of figures and musty ledgers. But there is money to be found in them, and I guess I had better stay and corral it, getting what pleasure I can as I go along....I am going to take a decided stand very shortly—city or country—and stake everything on the

throw. I have a good many city habits lately, and I sometimes doubt whether I would ever again fit well in country environments, even if I tried."[90] The handwritten postscript, squeezed in along the left hand margin of this typed letter is especially revealing. It said, "My friend Seatree, C.A., C.P.A., manager of Price Waterhouse & Co. N.Y. office (40 accountants) just called. He says my writings are the finest ever on accounting, and that they entitle me to be called the pioneer in accountancy literature in America. It is hardly so good as all that but as the Texans say 'they are not so pokey.'"[91]

The die was cast. In December 1904 Homer declared: "My teaching procedure is progressing nicely - I now have students of my own - charge them $150 each, and they seem to think it is worth the price. Maybe I will float a company soon to push the teaching business!"[92]

In another of his famous handwritten postscripts, Homer said: "I am working from 7 A.M. to 11 P.M. and have been for a long time, the extra work being spent on my teaching procedures. It amounts to half a dozen large text books."[93]

Without a doubt, Homer was on his way. By September 1905 he was fully committed to his new endeavors. "There is no prospect of my going back to St. Paul," he told Casper, adding: "Little old New York is good enough for me. I have tucked the newspaper scheme away carefully in the cobwebby chamber of my head-piece where repose dreams of western cities made clean and good and prosperous by two young Michigan chaps, dreams of law, of politics, of goodness, and of wealth which would entitle one to a pair of suspenders for each pair of trousers. Each carried its pleasure, each served its purpose, each is a comfort now. And I am making new ones."[94]

At the age of 26, Homer had found his life's work. To succeed in his chosen field, however, he had to cultivate an image of maturity way beyond his years. Homer was the first to admit that "I am a boy, and will always be a boy. I can get just as excited over a new target rifle as ever, and when I am having my films developed I can hardly wait."[95]

His wife teased him about this, reminding him of his prematurely graying hair, something which helped in renting a new home for the Pace family in Flatbush, Brooklyn. The day Homer rented the house, the real estate agent and several other men were speculating about his age. One man thought he was 36, while the others were sure he was at least 40. Homer, who, admittedly, did look quite mature, told them he was 50 and they believed him! This would have made Homer older than his brother Charles Ashford Pace, ten years Homer's senior, who, in 1906, became a partner in an educational enterprise which was unique from its very inception.

PACE AND PACE

Before joining Homer in the educational enterprise which would one day become Pace University, Charles had had several careers. He had taught school and had clerked in a general store by day while studying law at night. A part-time position with a Cambridge, Ohio, law firm was followed by a full-time job and a partnership in the Cambridge firm of Rosemond & Pace. In the fall of 1898, while Homer, whom Charles characterized as "a hustling youth" who "deserves to be successful," was in Texas, Charles was considering entering politics.[96] He informed his mother, "I am building up my boom as much as I can for prosecuting attorney, and if I am successful in getting that nomination next spring it will fix me up in good shape financially. Politics is an uncertain quantity, but my friends seem to think that I must succeed in the race. Judge Campbell has been after me a half dozen times in the last month to form a partnership with him the first of year, but I think I shall stay with Mr. Rosemond....I am getting so I feel at home when trying a case, and like the work very much."[97]

Despite this assertion, Charles abandoned trial work and journeyed to New York where he became a court reporter. After two years, however, he returned to the Midwest as private secretary to Frank B. Kellogg, later Secretary of State in the Coolidge administration. But Charles did not remain long with the St. Paul law firm of Davis,

Mabel Vanderhoof and Helen Pace - wife and daughter of Homer

Kellogg, & Severance. Instead, he returned to New York City where he again worked as a court reporter and then joined Homer in the educational enterprise.

In 1906, with $600 borrowed from Ansel Oppenheim, the treasurer of the Chicago and Great Western Railroad, Homer and Charles Pace established the partnership of Pace & Pace to prepare candidates for the demanding New York State C.P.A. examination. They rented an office and one classroom in the Tribune Building at 154 Nassau Street. The Pace Civic Center campus now occupies the site where the New York Tribune used to be published.

Between Charles's lectures on law and Homer's on accounting, plus the materials prepared by the brothers, the first class, consisting of a dozen students, received excellent instruction. The original course lasted 66 weeks,

Letter of Recommendation for Homer Pace - Age 18

H.S. Pace Employment History in his own words

or two school years, and it included applied economics as well as law and accounting. Classes were held two nights a week. The Pace brothers were continually revising and updating their lectures and the materials distributed in their classes. Forty lessons, called lectures, in accounting and applied economics and forty-six lessons in law comprised the original material.

What the Pace brothers offered their students was truly state of the art, and the word spread quickly. The brothers' materials were already being used in a course at the 23rd Street Y.M.C.A. Under a five-year arrangement which began in September 1906, the Paces supplied faculty and texts for accounting classes at the Y.

By June 1907, less than a year after they had opened for business, the brothers' operation had expanded, on the basis of word-of-mouth advertising. Homer described the growing operation in a response to a query from the Midwest about a Pace correspondence course. He told the prospective student who had written to him, "Yes, I have passed all of the New York C.P.A. examinations, and have been actively engaged since last October in preparing in the neighborhood of one hundred men for our examinations. We have enrolled eighty men in our Y.M.C.A. classes, which we operate under a percentage contract. This Autumn we will install another large school in Brooklyn."[98]

As for a correspondence course, although Pace & Pace would offer one from 1909 to 1933, they were not quite ready to proceed with this type of instruction in 1907, all of which prompted Homer to say, "We have not given a mail order course yet, and may not do so. We have it under consideration. We give a long, rigid course which requires two years' work. We charge for it $150....Commencing entirely unknown we have, in eight months, built up a school of 100 students, solely on the merit of the work, and in the face of long established schools here."[99]

The rapid expansion of the Pace educational operation, which had already begun, took two forms, that of the Extension Schools, at different Y.M.C.A.'s, and that of the Private Schools, owned and controlled entirely by Pace & Pace. The same year that they began personally instructing students on Nassau Street, the Paces established the New York Institute of Accountancy at the 23rd Street branch of the Y.M.C.A., in conjunction with the Educational Department of the Y.M.C.A. A year later the New Jersey School of Accountancy was founded. It also offered the Pace Standardized Course in Accounting at the Newark Y.M.C.A. In 1907 the Accountancy Institute of Brooklyn also began offering the Pace Standardized Course at the Brooklyn Central Y.M.C.A. The course utilized textbooks authored and published by the Pace brothers, but the

January 1906
- Winston Churchill is elected to Parliament
- British suffragettes prepare to use violence to win the vote
- Tsarist Russia is reported to be hindering distribution of $3,000,000 donated by Americans to assist Russian Jews
- Largest individual taxpayer in U.S., merchant Marshall Field, dies at age 70

February 1906
- President Theodore Roosevelt's daughter, Alice, marries the Speaker of the House of Representatives
- British launch world's largest battleship
- Cyclone kills 10,000 in South Pacific
- N.Y.C. police begin using fingerprint identification

March 1906
- Susan B. Anthony, American suffragette, dies
- Algeciras Conference concludes with agreement on foreign involvement in Morocco
- Census of the British Empire reveals Great Britain controls 20 percent of the world
- Harvard University physical director concludes that contact sports, especially basketball, endanger health of women

April 1906
- San Francisco is devastated by earthquake
- Mount Vesuvius erupts

May 1906
- Alpine Tunnel connecting Italy and Switzerland opens
- Russia's first democratic parliament meets

June 1906
- Pure Food and Drug Act becomes law

- Architect Stanford White is shot by his lover's husband
- Antitrust suit against Standard Oil begins

July 1906
- Captain Alfred Dreyfus is fully exonerated of spying for Germany, and receives the French Legion of Honor
- Russell Sage dies, leaving a fortune of $80 million
- Pacific Express derails into the Hudson River, killing 45 passengers

August 1906
- Chilean earthquake kills 5,000
- Brooklyn Rapid Transit Co. increases fare to ten cents

September 1906
- Peasants attack Russian estates
- Race riots occur in Atlanta, Georgia

October 1906
- Paul Cezanne dies
- SOS is adopted as a warning signal at first conference on wireless telegraphy
- Tidal wave in Florida Keys kills 2,500

November 1906
- U.S. troops land in Cuba
- President Theodore Roosevelt embarks upon first official visit by an American Chief Executive to a foreign nation
- Head of Mormon Church is charged with polygamy following birth of his 43rd child

December 1906
- Theodore Roosevelt is awarded Nobel Peace Prize
- Racial rioting erupts in Mississippi

instruction was conducted by others. Homer and Charles Pace, however, got around to the different schools. In 1909 Charles wrote to James F. Hughes, who had been Homer's first student before going on to a stellar career in accounting which included serving as president of both the New Jersey and New York associations of Certified Public Accountants and establishing his own firm. Charles' letter read, "Homer left yesterday for Baltimore and Washington to round up the prospects for those schools, which open Monday and Tuesday evenings of next week. I am here

taking care of the work at this end but will leave Monday morning for those cities and assist in the openings. The outlook is pretty good."[100]

Charles had more news. "I suppose Homer has told you that we are also putting the course in at Los Angeles," he told Hughes, adding, "They write us that they have had many inquiries and expect to start with a good enrollment. The Y.M.C.A. there has had a night law school giving a three years' course. They have decided to cut it out entirely and have made a contract with me to insert my course instead."[101]

HOMER PACE'S NEW WORLD: LOWER MANHATTAN IN 1906

Openings are usually marked by considerable fanfare. The debut of a new building, retail outlet or Broadway show invariably entails lots of hoopla, but that wasn't the case in October 1906 when the educational institution which would one day evolve into Pace University opened its doors. Located but a stone's throw from New York City's first theatrical district and the site of Barnum's Museum, whose founder was the nineteenth century's undisputed master of hype, the new school began operating during the first decade of the city's consolidation. The unification of the outlying boroughs with Manhattan in 1898 created a city of 3.4 million people, second in size only to London. A city as large as New York was the perfect site for an educational institution specializing in training for business because from the Dutch colonial period onward, New Yorkers have been interested in piling up the guilders, shillings and dollars. At the very time Pace was founded, the citizens of the metropolis were eagerly devouring newspaper articles about the rich and famous of that day, just as later generations would take delight in the ups and downs of the Trump empire. The New York Times, for example, which, together with the other major daily papers, was published in the Printing House Square area, now Pace Plaza, kept its readers up-to-date on railroad magnate James J. Hill's sale of his iron properties to U.S. Steel. William Randolph Hearst's quest for the Democratic Party's gubernatorial nomination also made headlines and just as the younger members of the Kennedy clan would not be able to escape the glare of publicity towards the end of the twentieth century, in 1906 a Rockefeller's every move was scrutinized. When John D. Rockefeller, Jr., failed to attend a Sunday school picnic on a damp Saturday in October, the Times devoted an entire column to this non-event, captioning the story: "John, Jr. Was Afraid He'd Catch Cold and Didn't Go."

In 1906, as today, financial news was very important. Whether it was London's soaring taxes, the $2.8 billion U.S. debt, which averaged $35.49 per person, or the financial success of American baseball teams, whose best season in history had just ended, the newspapers provided their readers with all the details. The installation of a record number of telephones in New York City in the autumn of 1906 was also deemed newsworthy because of the increasingly important relationship between improved communications and business volume. On the whole, business in the city was good and almost anything imaginable was available in Manhattan, including $20 imported men's suits stocked by a retailer on Nassau Street. Perhaps a bit harder to come by was the "monkey millinery" worn by a female passenger who disembarked from Hamburg on October 6, 1906. The lady was wearing a panama hat topped by a small live monkey!

Not all of the news stories were as amusing. Killer tornadoes in the South, a Pacific earthquake, the collapse of a bridge in Wisconsin and the lynching of two African-Americans in Alabama were reported at the time Pace opened. Closer to home, cyclone-like winds in New York and the deaths of spectators at the Vanderbilt Cup automobile races on Long Island absorbed the public's attention, as did allegations of patient abuse in one of the city's largest hospitals and the incredible story of rioting by parents of students at public schools in Brooklyn. A rumor that Health Department doctors summoned to the schools to check students for eye and throat infections were going to slit the children's throats sparked the rioting. Since few of the parents understood English, attempts by school authorities to disabuse them of the absurd notion that their offspring would be harmed failed. The police were summoned and the parent protesters were forcibly ejected from the schools, some of which had to be closed for a time.

While rioting was taking place in Brooklyn, over in Manhattan, alumni of City College gathered to mark the anniversary of the birth of Townsend Harris, founder of City College and America's first envoy to Japan. Presumably Homer and Charles Pace read about the impressive gathering at the City College Club in midtown Manhattan and who knows, perhaps they dreamed of a time when Pace would celebrate an anniversary. What the future held for the little school they had established was very much a question mark but in the vibrant New York of 1906, anything seemed possible. Given the intelligence and diligence of the two young men from the Midwest, success was only a matter of time.

The good news didn't end with this. Charles went on to say, "Everything points to a record-breaking enrollment in the two New York schools this fall. We never had so many inquiries and personal interviews with prospects, and we have already enrolled twenty or twenty-five men. I would not be surprised if we had 125 new men on the opening nights, October 11th and 12th."[102]

The previous year had also started off very well. The *Bulletin* of the New York Institute of Accountancy and the Accountancy Institute of Brooklyn declared in October 1908: "The school year opens with such a heavy enroll-ment that it has been found necessary to double the lec-ture-room space in each institute."[103] The *Bulletin* also extended a cordial invitation "to practicing accountants, prospective students, and others interested, to attend any of the class sessions and observe the instruction...."[104] Visi-tors were assured that "prospective students will not be unduly urged to enroll, but every effort will be made to make their visit enjoyable."[105]

By 1909, when enrollment in the New York area schools exceeded 300, Homer was forced to ask students wishing recommendations to speak with him or Charles before using their names as references. "Before we will undertake to recommend a student we must have a knowl-edge of his ability," Homer insisted, "and we will then base our recommendation upon the facts without regard to our personal relations with him."[106]

In 1910, when Homer was not only teaching but was also "working on a system of accounts for the Monmouth Beach Inn, which operates garage, stables, casino, cottages, etc.," he told James F. Hughes about plans for additional expansion of the Extension Schools.[107] Homer was partic-ularly enthusiastic about the possibility of awarding degrees for the work done at the Y's. He said, "Confiden-tially, the Y.M.C.A. expects to obtain a charter to grant degrees this autumn, and when it is secured, our work will be used as the basis....There is little doubt but that we will be in Boston within a short time with a full fledged degree granting course. The present Y.M.C.A. school in Boston

1907 Pace Text
First Lecture in Accountancy -

Notes by Homer Pace - 1917

has an enrollment of 2,200, which includes a Law school of 400 students, and the annual teachers' pay-roll is $80,000."[108]

Although the hoped for degrees did not materialize, by 1919 more than 4,000 students were taking Pace courses in the New York metropolitan area alone. By 1921 the standardized course was offered at Y's throughout the United States. The Pace name and methodology became famous in Buffalo, Boston, Washington, D.C., Cleveland, Detroit, Milwaukee, Grand Rapids, Kansas City, St. Louis, Denver, San Francisco, Los Angeles, Portland, and Seattle. Administering such a far-flung operation was not easy,

Helen, Homer, Robert and Mabel, Pace Summer home, 1908

however, nor was the maintenance of quality control. The Pace brothers, whose fine reputations as educators were on the line, were especially concerned about maintaining high standards. Therefore, they decided to phase out the Extension Schools. The brothers' arrangements with the Y.M.C.A. ended in 1921. Thereafter, they concentrated on the Private Schools.

The first of the private schools, which opened its doors on Nassau Street in 1906, moved in 1910 to the Hudson Terminal Building at 50 Church Street, and in 1913 relocated to the Hudson Terminal Building at 30 Church Street. It had a number of different names during its first few years of existence: the Pace School, the Pace Private School, the Pace & Pace School, the Pace Institute of Accountancy and Business Administration, and Pace Institute. When the New York school was in its fifth year of operation, Pace Institute of Boston opened its doors. The

first two women to become C.P.A.'s in Massachusetts were graduates of this school. In 1917 Pace Institute of Washington was established.

By the mid-1920s, however, the same concerns about quality control which had arisen in conjunction with the Extension Schools caused the brothers to phase out all of the Private Schools except the one in New York. In 1924 the Boston operation was taken over by its manager and two faculty members who continued to offer the Pace Standardized Course under a franchise arrangement with the brothers. The Washington School was spun off in 1925 and became Benjamin Franklin University. The Paces were in no way involved with that institution. Nor were the brothers linked with Walsh College in Troy, Michigan, or Robert Morris College in Pittsburgh, though both schools offered the Pace accounting course and had a franchise arrangement with the brothers for the use of their textbooks. Having

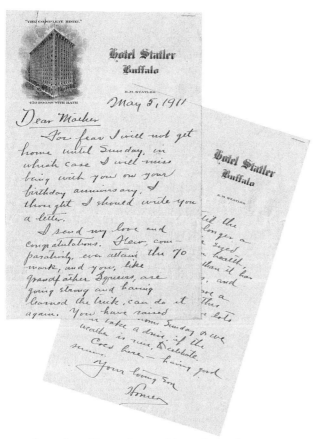

1911 letter from Homer Pace to his mother on her 70th birthday

branched out very early in their careers as educational entrepreneurs, Homer and Charles were now extracting themselves from all of the far-flung operations. It was now time to concentrate on New York to the exclusion of everything else.

Personal factors, as well as sound business principles, may have dictated that the brothers contract their operations. Although they had expanded the original copartnership three times, bringing in Frederick M. Schaeberle in 1910, Horatio N. Drury in 1913, and Charles T. Bryan in 1921, Homer and Charles were active in every phase of the business. As early as 1908, this had begun to take its toll. Writing to James Hughes, Homer admitted: "My nerves are in such shape that I doubt whether I do much work before the first of October, and I expect to put in all my time at Belmar."[109] The Paces had rented a "nice little

FREDERICK M. SCHAEBERLE

Like Homer and Charles Pace, with whom he was long associated, Frederick M. Schaeberle journeyed from the Midwest to New York City in the early twentieth century and decided to remain here. Upon graduation from the University of Michigan, where he received the A.B. degree in 1901, Dr. Schaeberle became principal of the Detroit Technical Institute. In 1910 he arrived in New York City, where he enrolled in the Pace accounting course. Within a year, he obtained a position with Price, Waterhouse & Co. but soon thereafter he joined the auditing staff of the Pace & Pace public accounting firm.

By 1913 Dr. Schaeberle, who was certified in New York, New Jersey and Ohio, was a partner in the firm of Pace & Pace. He also served on the first Board of Governors of the Accountants' Club of America, Inc. and the board of directors of the Lafayette Bank & Trust Company. Besides his association with Homer Pace in the accounting firm, Frederick Schaeberle, in his capacity as President of Business Textbook Publishers, published and distributed the Pace textbooks nationwide.

At the time the Pace schools were expanding from coast to coast, Dr. Schaeberle became comptroller and treasurer of the educational division of Pace & Pace. In later years he served as treasurer of Pace College and was a member of the Pace board of trustees. Until his death in 1977, at the age of 93, Dr. Schaeberle, who was awarded an honorary doctorate in Commercial Science from Pace in 1954, remained vitally interested in the institution he had helped build and mold for more than four decades.

cottage" on the shore, and while Homer was not ill to the point of being confined to bed, he was exhausted and needed a change; "I am going to catch some fish down the coast before I get back," he told Hughes, adding: "They

Charles Ashford Pace

got a sea-bass last week on a line and pole that weighed 44 1/2 pounds. Two or three of those fellows would make a good mess."[110]

A month later, he wrote to his former student about an attack of ptomaine poisoning. "You know I am poisoned through gas or food about every six months and I am getting to expect it just like I do the 4th of July or any other celebration."[111] Homer recovered, but between the business and myriad other things, he was carrying a heavy load. In the spring of 1909, he really had his hands full when his wife, son, and mother, who was residing with him, all became ill simultaneously. This occurred at the very time the family was about to move from Brooklyn to Ridgewood, New Jersey. "I am anxious to get the folks corralled at Ridgewood, and then I think I will be more comfortable," he told James Hughes.[112] Through it all,

Homer retained his sense of humor, telling his former student: "When I was young and foolish, I wanted to leave a salaried position and get into business for myself so as to have a good deal of leisure time. Happy days!"[113]

Homer was not the least bit hesitant in unburdening himself to James Hughes because he regarded him "as the most loyal fellow in the world," as well as "the original Pace man."[114] Moreover, Homer interspersed bad news with good. In a letter written in the fall of 1908, Homer lamented the fact that his sister-in-law had come down with malaria, keeping Charles "away from work during the opening week...."[115] But the same letter reported good news, namely that "out of the possible passes the seven men who have so far sat upon examination we have made 86%...."[116] Three students had passed everything the first time they took the C.P.A. exam. No wonder Homer said, "We are well satisfied..."[117]

Adding to Homer's joy was the fact that "among our new men is a graduate of Harvard..."[118] Another piece of good news was the fact that a "Princeton graduate was in to see us and we really are delighted with the class of timber that we are enrolling at present."[119]

A year later, in the fall of 1909, Homer had some especially good news for his former student. "We have the University on the double jump," he said describing the competition with New York University.[120] Eager to provide "the original Pace man" with all the details, he told Hughes, "Two of our students, who are seniors with Haskins & Sells, and both of whom are University students, one of them having the degree of D.C.S., have been offered $5 a night to instruct at the University this winter. They say they are too busy studying in our Elementary course to accept the offer. We understand the University is going to make a prodigious effort to reorganize the Accounting end of their school. So many of their students are coming to us that we are getting ashamed of ourselves. However, we will continue to receive them without prejudice and hope that they will continue to advertise heavily."[121]

1914 Pace Ad

The Pace Student, monthly publication from May 1918

Word-of-mouth advertising may have been the best kind and surely the least expensive but Homer and Charles knew they could not rely on it to the exclusion of more traditional ways of getting the word out about their educational activities. Advertisements in newspapers, magazines, and even the *World Almanac* were part of the marketing plan. The Pace ad in the 1911 edition of the *Almanac* proclaimed that professional education in accountancy "affords training for the practice of a new and uncrowded profession, and for greater capacity and earning power in private employment."[122] Advertisements in *The Journal of Accountancy* highlighted the Pace Agency for Placements, Inc., which served 6,282 people, both jobs seekers and employers.[123] To prepare their students to be placed in good positions, the Pace schools offered instruction "by practicing attorneys and certified public accountants."[124] In 1915 the Pace standardized course was taught "in 52 prominent schools and colleges throughout the country to approximately 5,000 students."[125]

Other ads in *The Journal of Accountancy* promoted summer study by extension and the Pace Standardized

Course in English for "men and women everywhere - in Business and out of Business."[126] A Pace ad in *Collier's* asked "Do you know your present worth in the business world?"[127] Another ad in the same publication urged readers to "prepare now to be an executive."[128] A *System* magazine ad, which began with the words "Earn More" in large letters, urged readers to send for a free booklet entitled, "What Can You Earn?"[129] Besides advertising in the aforementioned publications, Pace bought space in *The American Hebrew, Cosmopolitan, The Literary Digest, The New York Times, The Brooklyn Eagle*, and high school newspapers, and if all of this weren't enough to bring in new students, the travels and lectures of Charles and Homer would do the rest.

Whether it was Charles speaking on "The Value of Legal Education in Business," in Detroit, or a joint appearance of the brothers at the Buffalo Y.M.C.A. to mark the opening of the second year of their program in that city, such public relations efforts were invaluable.[130] At times, it seemed that the brothers were always on the run. In March 1911 Homer reported that "Monday night I expect to lecture before the C.P.A. Society....On the Tuesday following I will lecture in the School of Philanthropy, affiliated with Columbia."[131] He also had "a date with the Brooklyn Evening High School, and expect to lecture a week in the Y.M.C.A. Training School, Lake Geneva, Wisconsin, in July."[132] In 1916 he taught accounting at the Columbia University College of Pharmacy.

It was not unusual for the brothers' lectures to appear in print after they had been delivered. The Buffalo Y.M.C.A., for example, published the entire text of Homer's 1912 address entitled, "The Efficiency Movement in Business," which concluded with the observation that "progress in efficiency, that is, in the elimination of unproductive effort, means greater material prosperity with more time to pursue the higher and more pleasurable things of life."[133] When *Troy Men*, the weekly publication of the Y.M.C.A. in that upstate New York city, was deluged with requests for an outline of Homer's Efficiency speech, the editor printed the articles on business in general and accounting in particular, plus pieces addressing the quality of life and work. In the former category, one of the noteworthy articles dealt with organization. Like most of the material appearing in the publication, it was written by Homer St. Clair Pace. In view of his experience in journalism going back to the days of the *Pere Marquette Journal*, it is not surprising that Homer was a both a good writer and a good editor. On the subject of organization, Homer wrote:

> The difference between an army and a mob, between an effective, organized industry and isolated units of production or distribution, is almost entirely a matter of willingness and ability to give, to take, and to execute orders.[134]

Homer went on to say: "No executive can feel safe in giving an order, either orally or in writing, without obtaining some evidence that the order is understood by the one receiving it."[135] He then proceeded to explain, in a systematic way, how this could be accomplished.

Helping others perform well was one of Homer's chief objectives. Articles such as "Personal Preparedness," "Accountants as Counselors," "Productive Use of Personal Time," "You and Your Money's Worth," "Cultural Reading," "Character Building," and "Women in Business" showed the way. The last of these articles was published a few months after the United States entered World War I. At the time there was considerable speculation about the role women should play in the war effort.

As co-founder of an educational institution which had welcomed female students from the beginning, Homer had great respect for the abilities of women and urged that they become a major force by taking the place of men in industry and business. To prepare women for office positions vacated by draftees, Pace Institute offered a new course in Emergency Clerical Service for Women. Only a month after the United States entered the war, the National League for Woman's Service, an organization created to "coordinate and standardize the work of women of America along lines of constructive patriotism," sent fifty

Mabel Vanderhoof Pace during World War I

lecture in its entirety.

Since Homer's thoughts were invariably insightful and well presented, even major New York City newspapers took note of both his lectures and writings. The September 13, 1913 edition of the *Tribune* contained a lengthy piece by Homer on the need for better education for business while the October 2, 1915 issue of *The Sun* featured Homer's article on the relationship between the individual and the modern business world. These articles lured prospective students to the Pace courses, and once they had enrolled, a delightful publication called *The Pace Student* helped keep them there.

First published in 1915, *The Pace Student* contained

Business English Class - 1916

women to Pace to take the new course.[136]

At a time when more and more women were flocking to Pace Institute, one woman who had been a mainstay of the Pace brothers' educational enterprise in the early years, Miss Lillian M. Smith, assistant to Homer Pace, left the Institute to join the American Expeditionary Force in France. Miss Smith, a Vassar College graduate and a former Latin teacher at Adelphi Prep in Brooklyn, had been approached by the Young Women's Christian Association. This group was funneling a great deal of money into France for such projects as the establishment of residences for nurses, telephone operators, and other female workers from the U.S. The Y.W.C.A. required the services "of an experienced accountant to organize financial procedures and to install a proper system of accounts."[137] *The Pace Student* noted that "Miss Smith was asked to undertake

this work because of her accounting experience, her knowledge of the French language, and her familiarity with conditions secured by former visits to Europe....Miss Smith sailed last May, and arrived safely at her destination after an eleven-days' voyage. She crossed the ocean during the period in which the submarines carried their attacks to mid-ocean and to the American coast."[138]

Indicative of just how far capable women could go at a time when their services were in demand, *The Pace Student* said, "Miss Smith's work in effect will be that of a controller. She will devise and install accounts for the Hotel Petrograd, which is the name of the Y.W.C.A. hotel in Paris, and for the various centers established by the Y.W.C.A. throughout France. In addition to this work, she will make an audit and verification of the financial transactions that have already taken place. The work will require Miss Smith to travel throughout France, and will afford an exceptional opportunity, not only for a service of a vitally important nature, but for obtaining at first hand a knowledge and understanding of all the American activities in France."[139]

As usual, *The Pace Student* was very upbeat, particularly in light of the fact that Lillian Smith had written to Homer Pace about the piercing sirens which frequently awakened her and the nights she was forced to spend in bomb shelters. Happily, Miss Smith survived the war and resumed her position with what she called the "Pace Organization."[140]

The very capable Lillian Smith wasn't the only Paceite to make an outstanding contribution to the war effort. Homer Pace went off to Washington, D.C., as Acting Deputy Commissioner of Internal Revenue. His responsibilities "related almost exclusively to the development of the work of the Income Tax Unit in Washington."[141] Homer developed procedures and trained the staff, and when his work had been completed, he was praised by Daniel P. Roper, Commissioner of Internal Revenue, who said: "I want to congratulate you...on the prospect that we seem to have of successfully consummating the immense task of auditing in proper manner, and with expedition, the large volume of income tax returns."[142] In closing, Roper declared: "The splendid work performed by you for your Government during a time of great need should be a source of much gratification to you."[143]

No matter how satisfied he may have been, Homer St. Clair Pace did not pause to bask in his newly acquired glory, for it was now time to return to New York City and resume his work of building an even greater Pace Institute. The immediate task was to establish a day program for returning veterans. After this became a reality in 1919, Homer and Charles had to begin planning for the new decade which was almost upon them. The farm boys, turned accountant and lawyer, had laid a good foundation while, at the same time, marching on a broad front with their far-flung enterprises. But it was now time to marshal their resources in the great metropolis which Homer had so disliked years before. Like the Gilded Age entrepreneurs and the late twentieth century "In Search of Excellence" types, Homer had spied an opportunity and had made the necessary adjustments to seize and benefit from the chance of a lifetime. The earnest young lad from rural America who had told his friend, "I don't like the looks of it very much in a city," had certainly changed his outlook.[144]

Indicative of Homer's revised thinking is a delightful little piece he wrote for *The Pace Student*. Entitled "Don't Knock" the article advised:

> Don't knock, boost....Don't knock your town or your city, boost it. It's not the worst place in the world....Don't knock your concern - boost it....Don't knock yourself. If you say you're a failure, feel sorry for yourself, and wish you were dead...other folks will pay no attention to you, and the wheels of progress will crush you underfoot. Boost yourself, not egotistically, but self-respectingly; don't let your chin and your chest sag - hold them up. Knock as a habit, and you will become cynical, pessimistic, and unhappy. Boost as a habit, and you will become mellow, optimistic, and happy - your friends' best friend and your own as well.[145]

In the nearly two decades since he had first set foot in New York City, Homer had prospered by taking his own advice. He had become an educational entrepreneur who, in the next twenty years, would leave an even more indelible mark on the city where he had once been a stranger.

New York Campus

*The New York Campus dates
to the founding of the
institution in 1906. One Pace
Plaza, completed in 1969,
is an 18 story tower and
complex designated the Civic
Center campus. 41 Park Row
is 16 stories.*

One Pace Plaza

41 Park Row

*Pace Downtown Theater
Schimmel Center for
the Arts, NY*

Sculpture,
Henry Birnbaum
Library, NY

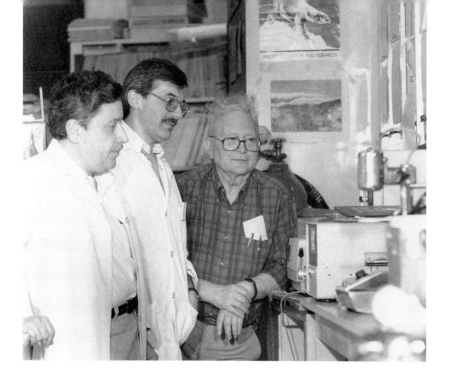

Haskins Laboratories

*Annual Advisory Board
Luncheon, M.S. In
Publishing Program*

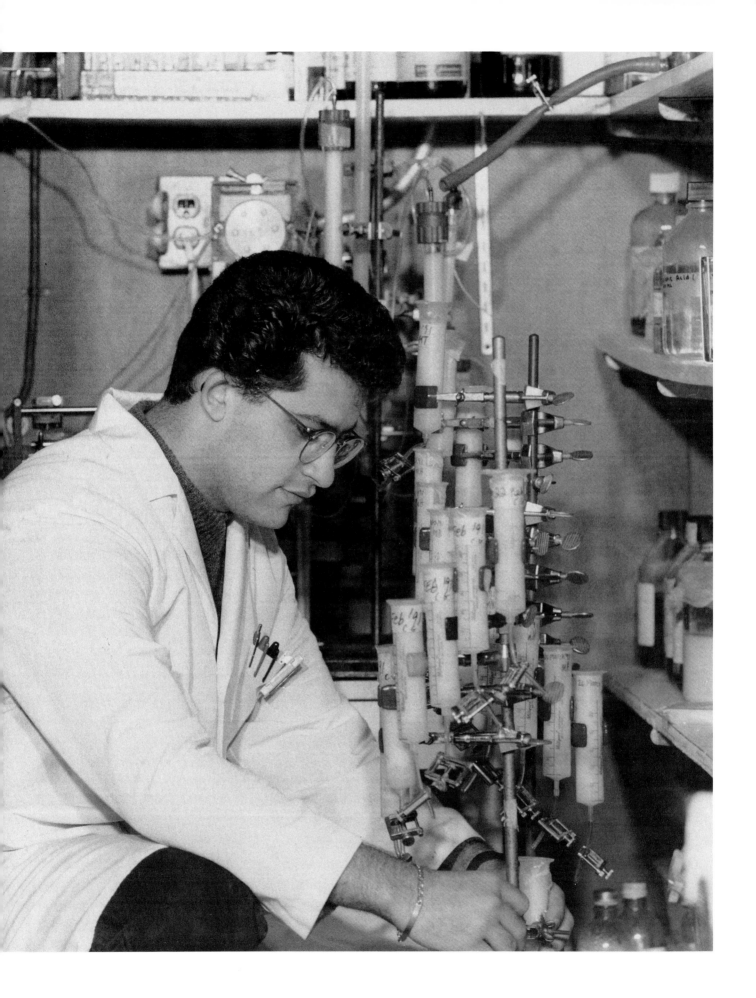

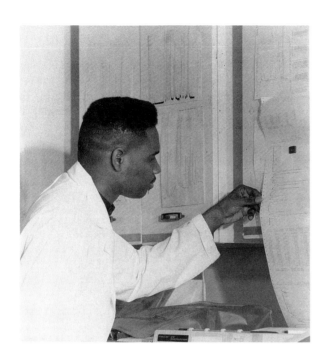

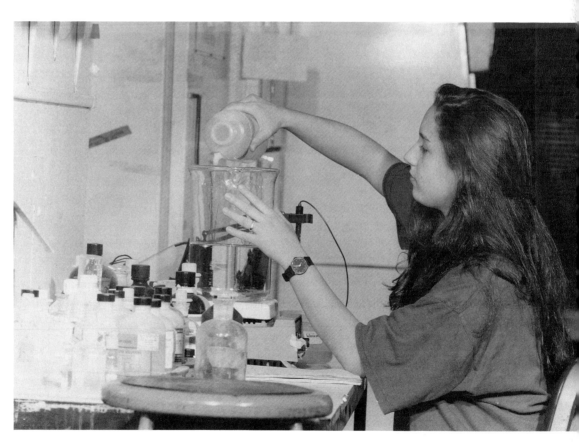

Haskins Laboratories

2

Chapter From 1921 to 1942

POST-WAR EXPANSION AND CHANGE

There is an old saying about good teachers being born, not made, and perhaps that was the case with Horatio Nelson Drury, an extraordinarily popular and effective professor of English and Speech at Pace Institute during the school's foundation period. A Phi Beta Kappa graduate of the University of Vermont, Drury left his native New England to teach at preparatory schools in the Hudson Valley. Later he served as chairman of the English Department at what is now the State University of New York at Cortland. From there it was on to New York City to a teaching position at Stuyvesant High School, and moonlighting as a communications instructor for banks and insurance companies. One enthusiastic corporate student, an executive of the Metropolitan Life Insurance Company, introduced Drury to the Pace brothers and in 1913 the former Vermonter joined Pace Institute.

Besides teaching courses in English and public speaking which he developed and for which he wrote textbooks (published by Pace & Pace), Drury trained new accounting and law instructors "in the distinctive teaching required by the Institute."[1] This entailed formal classes in educational methodology, which Drury conducted several times a year, and an ongoing mentor relationship with new faculty. When he wasn't teaching or helping others improve their performance in the classroom, Drury was assisting with *The Pace Student* by planning issues and writing articles. He also wrote the school's public relations material, including the bulletins. As excellent a speaker as he was a writer, Horatio N. Drury was much in demand on the lecture circuit and frequently addressed business audiences in New York and elsewhere. Commenting on the extraordinary Mr. Drury's many talents,

Facade, One Pace Plaza,
New York City

Horatio N. Drury

The Pace Student noted:

> His abilities were varied, and he did many different
> things; but he enjoyed most of all the actual work of
> teaching. He was never so happy as when in the
> classroom, face to face with his students, elucidating
> some point in grammar, composition, rhetoric, or in
> public speaking.
> Few men have equaled Mr. Drury in vocabulary, in
> beauty of enunciation, in control of voice, in pronun-
> ciation, and in the construction of felicitous phrases.
> It was a rare treat to listen to him, either in formal
> speech or in conversation.[2]

For a man of such talent, a person "of large and impressive stature," who had been quite an athlete as well as an
intellectual, to have been cut down in his prime was a terri-
ble blow to Pace Institute.[3]

Drury became ill a few hours after finishing his regular
Saturday afternoon class at Pace. Nine days later, on
March 7, 1921, he died, at age forty-one. One of his
enduring legacies to Pace Institute and its students, both
past and future, was the creed originated by Horatio Nelson Drury. In many ways, the Drury Creed encapsulated
the essence of the Institute's philosophy by asserting:

I Believe

I BELIEVE in MYSELF, for I have learned that self-
confidence enables me to face life with strength,
courage, and patience.

I BELIEVE in MY DAILY WORK, for I have found
that my doing it contributes not only to my personal
well-being, but also to the well-being of my fellow-
men.

I BELIEVE in MY CAPACITY FOR DEVELOP-
MENT, for I have had ample proof that any man
can train himself to render a larger and a more
exceptional service the older he becomes.

I BELIEVE in PURPOSEFUL STUDY AS A MEANS
OF MENTAL GROWTH, for all my life I have seen
usefulness, advancement, and prosperity come as a
matter of course to men with their perspective
widened and their reasoning ability developed by
means of concentrated study.

I BELIEVE in OPPORTUNITY, for I can name
many men who have achieved success in business
because of their unflagging desire for success, their
earnest efforts to attain it, and their worthiness of it.

I BELIEVE, therefore, IN MAKING THE MOST
OUT OF MYSELF, day by day, week by week,
month by month, for I know I shall thus gain the
most enduring of all rewards - not only increased
earning-power, but peace and satisfaction of mind
and spirit.[4]

The untimely passing of Horatio Nelson Drury wasn't
the only change occurring at the Institute in 1921. In
September of that year, a new law requiring private
schools to obtain licenses took effect in New York State.
Pace Institute promptly applied and received its certificate
of approval for Accountancy and Business Administration,
Cost Accounting, and English from the State Education
Department. For the remainder of the decade there were
no roadblocks impeding the school's expansion. Indeed,
this was a time of rapid progress characterized by such
substantial growth that new facilities were required.

In 1928 the school moved to the Transportation Building at 225 Broadway, but with 3,000 students by 1929,
Pace had to lease 20 percent more space in the Transporta-

tion Building. This happy circumstance had come about because "the past year has been marked by a decided increase in the number of day school classes in the various courses."[5]

Before acquiring badly needed classroom space, the Institute had used a stagger plan of enrollment. Fall semester classes began anytime from August 11 through mid-November and spring classes started anytime from January through May. As soon as sixty registrants had signed up for a class, it began. Although this type of scheduling was unusual, even in the 1920s, it proved attractive to students because it gave them "a wide range of choice as to the time they begin their work."[6] In 1929 the students were provided with still another opportunity, the chance to do the equivalent of a full semester's work during an extended summer session beginning in May. This "time-saver" term, as it was called, was a way of attracting and retaining students.[7]

So, too, was the Pace scholarship program. To heighten its visibility among public school educators, the Institute awarded a half dozen scholarships to its day school to highly qualified high school seniors. Teachers and principals in schools in New York and New Jersey nominated up to six students per school. Following personal interviews with Pace faculty, the Institute selected the scholarship recipients.

Whether scholarship students or working people paying their own way, Pace students received a unique education in the 1920s. Since Homer S. Pace was a firm believer in the old adage that a picture is worth a thousand words, visualization was emphasized in some Pace courses. This took the form of thousands of stereopticon slides, which were prepared for the Institute and made available to its instructors.

Supplementing classroom instruction was a field experience component. Instructors regularly exposed their students to the real world of business by arranging field trips. In the spring of 1924, for example, day school students were given behind-the-scenes tours of National City Bank,

Pace at 225 Broadway - 1940s

the Steinway Piano Company, and the Consolidated Stock Exchange. Describing the visit to National City Bank, *The Pace Student* said: "Relatively few persons, even those of long experience in business, have had the opportunity afforded to the students on this trip."[8] Summing up all three field trips, the magazine noted that they "covered the range of banking, manufacturing, and stock brokerage - a noteworthy series of field studies of the utmost interest and value to the students...."[9]

Evening students also had an opportunity to participate in field experiences. A Saturday afternoon in June 1925, for example, was spent visiting the Treat Company, Inc. in Brooklyn. The students met with the firm's president and learned about the manufacture of potato chips. Many companies visited by Pace students and their professors had a Pace connection. Frequently, one or more of the company's managers or executives had studied at Pace. The trips, therefore, served several purposes. Besides acquainting students with the intricacies of running a particular type of business, visits to banks and companies advertised the Institute, heightened student awareness of the success awaiting Pace graduates, assisted in the establishment of an embryonic "old boy" network which could

THIRD ANNUAL DINNER
AFFILIATED SCHOOLS
PACE STANDARDIZED COURSES
MACHINERY CLUB, NEW YORK
MAY. 17, 1916.

help students find good positions, and enhanced the student-teacher relationship.

This last goal was also achieved by the freshmen/faculty dinners held during the 1920s. These events were no mere cold cut buffets, but enormous banquets for 500 or more people. Typical of the dinners was the one held in 1925 at the Hotel St. George in Brooklyn. Six hundred of the eight hundred students enrolled in the Institute's sixteen freshmen classes gathered for a formal dinner and a speech by Homer S. Pace. The talk was broadcast over radio station WMCA and students attending the banquet were encouraged, prior to the big evening, to invite their families and friends to tune in. The radio audience, as well as those attending the banquet, heard President Pace impart some of his own philosophy and that of the late Horatio N. Drury. Remembering his own early struggles, Homer told the freshmen that they "should acquire and develop the power to visualize achievement."[10] He continued, "If Lincoln had not visualized himself as a practicing attorney,

debating with the Douglases of the future, he would not have been sustained in the lonely hours of study that necessarily preceded his work as a lawyer. Edison visualized the incandescent electric lamp long before it illuminated our homes and streets."[11] Homer's goal was to encourage the freshmen to persevere. Thus he told them: "No other wall or obstacle is as great as the one you build in your own mind. Your mere conviction that you can't do a thing, inhibits your effort and, therefore, the possibility of your accomplishment. If an eight-foot ditch confronts a person, and he is thoroughly convinced in his own mind that he can't jump across it, he will not try."[12] Fully convinced that obstacles could be overcome and that they sometimes proved very useful in spurring one to action, Homer declared, "Poverty and hardship, difficulties of various kinds, do much to help us, for the imminence of starvation...speeds up our power both to visualize and to act. It is truly said that a rich man's son does not have a fair chance because of the lack of spurs of this kind. Let us pay thanks to our hardships - they are often blessings in disguise."[13] One can imagine Homer's youthful audience pondering the big question posed during his talk: "Why may not each one of you...see himself big on the screen of the future?"[14] As for Homer himself, he was definitely thinking big, so much so that provision had to be made for 1,100 students at the 1928 freshmen dinner. Once again, the audience heard a talk by President Pace and did a bit of community singing. Long before Americans knew anything about how the Japanese engender company loyalty, Homer S. Pace had hit upon singing as a way of fostering cohesiveness in a group. As early as 1923 the Institute held a Song Week. *The Pace Student* explained this custom by stating, "It is the belief of the officials of the Institute that community singing, such as that indulged in by many of the leading organizations of business and professional men, is of great value to students, not simply in giving them a bit of relaxation from their technical school work, but in engendering within them something of a community spirit so likely to be lost in the rush of busy metropolitan life."[15]

When they weren't singing or visualizing their way to success, Pace students were acquiring the skills needed to

climb the socio-economic ladder. One of those skills was public speaking. In addition to formal classes in oral communication, the Institute had a Public Speaking Club. Established in 1925, the club held its first meeting on a sweltering June night. Despite an indoor temperature of nearly 100 degrees, enthusiastic club members gathered to hear a talk by Homer Pace, who was tireless in his efforts to get across the idea that finely honed communications skills were a key to business success. In May 1926 readers of *The Pace Student* were reminded of this in an article entitled "Speak in Public and Have a Good Time." The article noted: "If a man expresses himself before a business meeting in a convincing and interesting way on a subject at issue, he immediately commands respect and attention. The man in the same audience who has the opportunity to speak, but who remains silent, may conceivably have better ideas and may be an abler man. So far as the public opinion of the group is concerned, however, the man who speaks commands instant respect and measurably affects action, while the other man does not."[16]

For the person who spoke up intelligently, the potential rewards were great. According to *The Pace Student*, "A man who is...able to speak and who uses his ability in business meetings, in fraternal gatherings, at business conventions, in professional societies, and in community and civic affairs, soon becomes favorably known and is in demand for executive or other positions that require, among other things, the ability to speak in public and to exercise other qualities of leadership."[17]

Good communications skills paved the way to the executive suite for otherwise qualified Pace men in the 1920s, but what of Pace women back then? Despite the fact that women had obtained the suffrage in 1920, equality remained an elusive goal. Getting ahead in the world of commerce was easier for the business man than for the business woman. The same was true of education, though Pace Institute had two female deans, Lillian Smith and Alice Ottun.

After receiving her M.A. from Columbia University,

Alice Ottun held various administrative positions at Pace, beginning in 1929. Early in her career at the Institute, she was Director of the Day School Division and Evening Secretarial Division. By the mid-1930s Alice Ottun had two titles, Dean of Admissions and Instruction in the day school, and Dean of Admissions and Instruction in the evening division of the School of Marketing, Advertising and Selling, the School of Secretarial Practice, and the School of Shorthand Reporting. Lillian Smith was Dean of Admissions and Instruction in the evening school division of the School of Accountancy Practice, the School of Accountancy and Business Administration, and the School of Credit Science in the 1930s.

Besides advancing women employed by the organization, Pace Institute attempted to make opportunities available to its female students. A superior education was regarded as the key which would unlock the door of occupational advancement for these women. As if to reinforce this notion, *The Pace Student*, in 1924, quoted an unnamed woman executive who declared: "A knowledge of bookkeeping and accounting is something that a woman can market immediately at a good salary."[18] The magazine continued: "Accounting work ...offers an immediate vocational opportunity for trained women, but, what is of more importance, it offers a real opportunity for women to develop themselves to fill executive positions."[19]

Pace graduate Florentine D. Goodrich, Director of the Women's Department of the Pace Agency for Placements, and later Treasurer of the Tennessee Valley Authority, reiterated this thought in 1927, declaring: "There is more demand for competent women bookkeepers and accountants than can be supplied, and a greater demand for women with executive ability and training than can be met."[20] This did not necessarily mean, however, that landing a superior position was easy for, as Goodrich pointed out, "as an indication of the lengths to which employers will go in order to obtain the right kind of employees, it is not infrequent for business executives to come to our headquarters for the purpose of giving what amounts to an oral

examination to young women who wish to enter their employ....Fitness for the particular position to be filled is of equal importance to the employer and the applicant. If the particular business, or line of work, under consideration claims the deep, natural interest of the worker, her enthusiasm and ability in performing the tasks imposed will be greatly enhanced. Her keen interest would express itself in increased financial returns."[21]

Of course, to qualify for a highly remunerative position, a woman had to possess superior training, something Pace Institute emphasized in its advertisements directed towards potential female students. Typical of the ads was one appearing in 1924 which declared, "Women who seek business insight, technique, preferment, are invited to attend a series of informative lectures on technical business subjects to be given at Pace Institute. The first lecture 'Fundamentals of Double Entry' will be given by Homer S. Pace, C.P.A."[22] Another ad, from the same period, announced "special accounting instruction for women."[23] The instruction took the form of a "special course in accounting for women," which was designed "to develop additional capacity to earn a larger income."[24]

For women who preferred less quantitative work, Pace offered a secretarial practice course. This program was not sex segregated, however. A 1926 brochure for the program declared that its aim was "to train experienced stenographers, both men and women, to become able secretaries and personal assistants to executives...physicians, artists, writers, and other professional people."[25] The program had two distinct elements: lecture periods for theory, and laboratory periods for practice. The lectures emphasized the development of "personality, initiative, tact, cooperation, reliability, memory and powers of analysis."[26] The lab sessions included "actual office work" in record keeping, taking of minutes, arranging itineraries, and preparing budgets.

Some students who emerged from the Secretarial Practice Course became very enthusiastic alumni of Pace Institute and retained ties to the school through a newly formed alumni association. This organization was an outgrowth of the Pace Club which, in the early 1920s, welcomed both students and alumni. Dues were $1 per year, and for an additional $1.50 members could purchase a ten-karat gold club pin. The club sponsored lectures on business related topics and had its own basketball team whose members donned blue and gold uniforms to compete with other clubs and school teams in the New York area.

In 1922 the club hosted a midwinter dance at the Waldorf. Tickets cost $1.50, and the advance publicity claimed that the music would be "the best."[27] In the spring of 1922 the club sponsored a banquet at the Hotel Commodore. It featured "community singing and musical selections by vocal and instrumental soloists especially engaged for the occasion."[28] Adding to the merriment were "balloons, paper hats, and other novelties."[29] Quite aside from a pleasurable evening, the banquet afforded Pace alumni and students an opportunity to do some networking, or as *The Pace Student* put it: "It is the only time that we get together as a great group to make merry and find out who's who and why in our chosen field."[30]

Pace New York people weren't the only Paceites getting together. Pace clubs were organized in a number of cities where the Pace Standardized Course was offered and there was even a National Federation of Pace Clubs. When the Institute severed ties with the private schools outside New York, however, the Pace Alumni Association, organized in 1925, served as a link between graduates and their alma mater.

PUBLICATIONS

Another potent force binding alumni to the Institute were two important publications: *The Pace Student* and the *American Accountant*. Right through the mid-1920s *The Pace Student* featured serious articles of interest to graduates as well as those preparing for business careers. Included in this category were "The Proprietorship Type of Mind," "The Theatre - Its Organization and Accounting," "Accounting Procedures in Modern Hotels," and

"Accounting Procedures for Contractors."[31] Most issues of the magazine also contained pieces aimed at the self-improvement of the reader. Examples of such articles were "Are You Selfish in Conversation?", "Success through Service," "Make the Resolutions," "If You Don't Like It, Do It!", and "Master Your Moods."[32]

Despite the popularity of such articles and the magazine which published them, *The Pace Student* was discontinued in 1926 in order to permit Homer S. Pace to devote his attention to a new magazine, the *American Accountant*, which was directed towards the entire accounting profession. To be sure, many Pace graduates and students subscribed, but the appeal of the magazine, which made its debut in 1927, was considerably broader. Articles of interest to practicing accountants dominated the publication.

Typical pieces had such titles as "Business Formerly an Art, Now a Real Profession," "Canadian Banker Gives Views on Training for Business Career," "Planning, Budgeting and Control of Department Store Expense," and "When Is a Bank Insolvent?"[33]

Homer Pace philosophized less in the new publication, but each issue did contain an editor's page which showcased his wisdom, common sense and wit. The page contained a little bit of everything: jokes, comments about articles appearing in the issue, and, now and again, a bit of Homer's solid Midwestern philosophy. "Perhaps some of us take our work a little too seriously," Homer told readers of the September 1927 issue, adding, "It is well to think now and again, for the sake of the relief, that it won't matter a hundred years from now. And the hard-driven accountant or business man may profitably bring a little more good nature into his daily tasks. Friendly, helpful words, given or received, ease off the tension, while anger and caustic comments do the contrary. The majority of the big men in the professions and in business know how to relax - they do not take themselves too seriously."[34]

That may have been the case in the 1920s, but once the United States drifted into the economic morass known as the Great Depression, it was a different story. For Homer S. Pace, the depression meant abandoning the wonderful magazine to which he had devoted countless hours writing, editing, and pasting up copy in the Great Hall, a cavernous room occupying a separate building behind the Pace family's home at 40 Montague Street in Brooklyn Heights. He truly loved this sort of work but the economic situation necessitated the discontinuation of the magazine in 1933. Homer explained his decision by saying, "It is quite true that the *American Accountant* did not produce an income more than enough to cover the cost of printing, postage, and clerical expenses. Its editor and contributors have always worked for the good of the cause, and cheerfully....If...the depression had not come, it and thousands of other buoyant ventures would, no doubt, have been riding the bounding waves of prosperity."[35] Had there been

no Great Depression, Homer may still have been forced to discontinue the magazine or turn it over to someone else because of the time and energy required to publish it. Homer himself admitted that "the editorship imposed upon me many days' work each month that I could not very well avoid and that kept me from using my abilities on behalf of 2,500 or more young men and young women who were looking to me for the best I could give in the way of instruction."[36]

It came as no surprise to anyone who knew Homer S. Pace that he fully refunded all subscriptions to the magazine and personally responded to every letter written by readers dismayed by the loss of a favorite publication. Homer was so touched by the mail he received that he saved every letter with the intention of binding it "in permanent form."[37] Most of the subscribers who took pen in hand to lament the demise of the magazine were accountants who used their firm's letterhead to mourn the loss of "the finest magazine that has ever been published."[38] One accountant wrote: "Your editorials alone were worth far more than the subscription price to the magazine, not to mention the excellent manner technical questions of practically every description were treated in the articles."[39] A professor of accounting at Boston University wrote, "I will find it a distinct loss in my accounting work here at the College, as I considered it by far the best accounting publication from the standpoint of the young accountant that was published. Our students showed a great interest in this magazine and until last year we sent you a considerable number of subscriptions from students."[40]

Professional accountants also felt the loss. The C.P.A. Bulletin, published by the Society of Certified Public Accountants of the State of New Jersey, asserted, "In the seven years of its service to the profession of accountancy, the *American Accountant* has attained a pre-eminent position among the accounting periodicals....Its editorial pages were replete with themes of current and vital interest....The technical articles which illuminated its pages constitute a lasting reference library which every accountant, student and practitioner, will continue to use for pleasure, guidance and profit."[41]

The "original Pace man," Homer's first student, James F. Hughes, expressed similar views in a letter to his mentor. He wrote, "The magazine was just one more activity on your part which causes the accountancy profession to be greatly indebted to you for all that you have done in its behalf during the past quarter of a century. Personally I felt that the magazine was a typically Homer Pace product. Others have commented to you, I am sure, upon its high standard, excellent content and pleasing appearance."[42] Turning prophetic, Hughes continued, "My feeling of regret over the fact that the magazine will no longer be published is somewhat tempered by a belief that the time thus released to you will be employed...toward doing further constructive work in behalf of the profession, the substantial growth of which I have enjoyed living through in association with you."[43]

When James Hughes had commenced his studies with Homer Pace, accountancy was still in its infancy in the United States. The professionalism which would characterize the field somewhat later was just emerging but high standards were, nevertheless, being set even in the early days and nowhere more so than at Pace Institute. The students who were trained there, as well as those who took the Pace Standardized Course elsewhere, helped set those standards, much to the delight of Homer who was, first and foremost, the quintessential teacher or, as he said, in his reply to James Hughes, "I have tried over the years, as an incident to my principal work of teaching, to demonstrate a number of things in connection with accountancy. I can say to you that I have undertaken these incidental ventures without thought of profit or personal aggrandizement. These ventures have, I believe, borne fruit and they will continue to bear fruit in the years to come. As I find myself entirely free to work with my students, I feel quite satisfied with all of the expenditures of time and money that I have made."[44]

At this juncture, Homer did indeed need more time to devote to the students of Pace Institute. "The school work with which I am connected is broadening very much in scope," he told one former *American Accountant* subscriber, adding, "We are now teaching, in five different schools, subjects that cover a wide range. It has become increasingly plain to me during the last year or two that I must concentrate all my energies on this work if I am to carry it through to a full measure of success."[45] In his reply to another former subscriber, he elaborated further saying, "Last year we organized the School of Marketing, Advertising and Selling and we are just starting the School of Credit Science. There is so much to do in order to plan the new courses, prepare text materials, select and train teachers, and the like that I found it entirely impracticable to take the time necessary to perform editorial duties."[46] One chapter in the varied and interesting career of Homer S. Pace had closed, but an exciting new one, for which a preface and introduction had already been written, would now begin in earnest.

PACE INSTITUTE IN THE 1930s

The economic cataclysm which was at least partially responsible for the demise of the *American Accountant* was a factor in the dissolution of the international accounting firm of Pace, Gore & McLaren, which Homer had established in 1928 as a successor organization to the accounting firm of Pace & Pace, which had operated from 1906 through 1927. On January 1, 1928, an engraved announcement proclaimed the establishment of the new firm, which operated under the name of Pace, Gore & McLaren for four years. In 1932 the firm was dissolved and the partners in its New York office, Homer Pace, Frederick M. Schaeberle, and Charles T. Bryan, all of whom were officers of Pace Institute, concentrated exclusively on their educational work. Schaeberle was Treasurer of the Institute, while Bryan performed as Secretary, and was also involved in the textbook publishing part of the business.

Although Homer and his associates had hardly

Charles T. Bryan
Secretary, Pace Institute
Chairman, Board of Trustees 1947-54

ing, "Factors that cause the expansion are the steady growth of the entire institute and the increasing popularity of the day school courses....The new space in the tenth and twelfth floors provides several commodious classrooms. They will be filled immediately by the new classes that are being organized on the year-round schedule of the institute."[47]

This assertion proved to be correct. Pace graduated its largest class, up until that time, in 1930 and during the depression enrollments grew by almost l,000 students, in part because Homer Pace took nothing for granted and was willing to make sacrifices for the good of the Institute, such as forfeiting his salary, signing over his insurance, and extending $100,000 worth of tuition credit to students requiring loans to finance their education. The worsening economic climate also required Homer Pace to summon his considerable talents as innovator and publicist. For the foreseeable future he had to constantly think of new ways to attract and retain students. Besides reorganizing the Institute, in 1933, into three distinct and more visible divisions, the School of Marketing, Advertising and Selling, the School of Credit Science, and the School of Accountancy Practice, each with its own advisory board of outside experts, Homer placed renewed emphasis on flexible scheduling. Late starting courses were added during the regular academic year and evening classes in summer were vigorously promoted. Once popular courses, which, for one reason or another, had been dropped were revived. A new version of the World War I era accounting course for women was offered and proved to be quite popular.

> "There was something about this place that you just loved. It was family."
> (Dr. Alfreda Geiger, March 9, 1990)

neglected the school while their accounting practice was flourishing, they now devoted themselves single-mindedly to the Institute, developing new curricula in both business and cultural areas and transforming the school from a proprietary business institute into an educational corporation. Yet on the eve of the decade which would witness these significant changes, there was no foreshadowing of what would transpire in a few short years.

Two months after the stock market crashed, it was business as usual at Pace, and more of it than ever before. Enrollment in both day and evening sessions was 3,000, and a sizable list of course offerings for the spring of 1930 was announced. In February 1930, a course in investment finance was added due to public demand. So many students were flocking to Pace that the school had to lease additional space in the Transportation Building. One New York City newspaper explained this development by stat-

To attract full-time day students, the Institute held open houses, luncheons for prospective students and dinners for high school administrators and faculty members. Alfreda Geiger, a faculty member in the Secretarial Studies program, was hired in 1932 to teach Pitman shorthand, the system then taught in the New York City high schools, from which Pace Institute hoped to recruit more students. She described an annual springtime ritual designed to acquaint public school educators with Pace. "On four consecutive Thursdays in May," Homer Pace "invited...guidance counsellors and principals of secondary schools in the metropolitan area, to dinner at the Waldorf."[48] According to Dr. Geiger:

> At about 4:30 p.m. these guests would assemble at 225 Broadway where they were served refreshments, and taken on a tour of the school to view many old Chinese paintings, photographic murals, famous woodcuts, etc. on exhibition in (Homer Pace's) office and in the halls. In fact, the halls...were lined with unusual maps, special prints, and photographs, since Homer Pace had as his hobbies map collecting and photography.

> At 6 p.m. the invited guests were taken to the Waldorf by Fifth Avenue buses which were parked on the Barclay Street side. After dinner, which was served by white-gloved waiters, Mr. Pace would show colored slides of various places of interest visited by him in his travels abroad. They were always most interesting and informative. This was his unique flair for advertising Pace Institute by giving it a "personal" touch. He had great foresight and creativity. This was not the usual commercial advertising, but he established a wonderful rapport between the secondary schools and his institution.[49]

When the Institute wasn't bringing high school educators to Pace, it was sending its own faculty out to the secondary schools. During the 1933-34 school year, Pace faculty members delivered 120 lectures at New York area high schools. Their combined audience totalled 69,889 prospective students! Another recruitment tool was the annual "Press Day" for editors of high school newspapers. Following tours of New York City newspaper offices and printing facilities, the high school students dined at the Institute, met with Pace faculty, heard a talk by a promi-

nent speaker, and viewed exhibits of photography, typography and design mounted by students in Pace's School of Marketing, Advertising, and Selling.

The Institute's popular series of vocational guidance booklets also lured new students to Pace. The publications included "If Not College - Then What?" and "After High School - Then What?" One number in the series became a runaway best seller. Entitled "I Choose My Occupation" and written by Homer S. Pace, the booklet "had a wide acceptance and distribution, particularly among teachers and students in high schools and in preparatory schools."[50] This work covered the principal areas of employment in business and urged high school students to continue their education, preferably on a full-time basis. The various business occupations were covered more briefly in "From High School to Business," but the emphasis on formal study beyond high school remained the same. The reader was told, "Technical preparation for business is as much a matter of course nowadays as is technical preparation for medicine, law, teaching, or engineering. The young man or young woman who starts out in business without such preparation is handicapped from the very start."[51] Reinforcing this point, the booklet continued, "There was a time when all a young man or young woman had to do in order to make a start toward business success was to "get a job," work hard, and rely for advancement on such practical knowledge as might be picked up. It is different now."[52] The booklet went on to assure prospective students and their parents that Pace stood behind its students long after they had graduated. "The Institute gives helpful vocational advice to its students and graduates. It assists students and graduates in finding suitable and developmental work opportunities," readers were told.[53] A separate publication, "The Placement and Vocational Work of Pace Institute," went into more detail on this aspect of the Institute's services.

In addition to the vocational guidance series (which was printed by Plandome Press, a company owned by Homer S. Pace and renowned for the quality of the work

Homer Pace observing a class, about 1940

performed for outside clients) Homer's public lectures, radio talks, and popular articles helped attract students. The image Homer projected, in both his talks and writings, was futuristic. Envisioning an America and a world beyond the Great Depression, he urged people to prepare for tomorrow. In an article picked up by almost every major daily newspaper in New York City and many smaller papers in the metropolitan area, Homer declared:

> Keeping current is a major problem of the business organization. There is no market for the corset or the automobile of yesteryear. The vanishing trolley car is stream-lined to stem an adverse tide, and the department store remakes its equipment and facilities to conform to modern trends in decoration.
>
> And so it is with an educational institution with respect to its curricula, its methods, and its plant. It must interpret current life - prepare for the problems of today and tomorrow.[54]

Homer's determination to offer students an education which was up-to-date not only helped enrollment, but also equipped students with the prerequisites for success. Even *Forbes* magazine recognized this. Although inaccurate in citing the name of the school, in 1937 Forbes characterized the "Pace & Pace Business Institute" as "very effective."[55]

Charles Dyson, a student at the Institute from 1927 through 1930 and a future Chairman of the Board of Trustees, testified to the effectiveness of the school's educa-

tional methods, saying, "everybody was serious. That was one thing. And the teachers were very good. They were people who came out of business...Good instructors. Good at sticking to the text and bringing in their practical experience with the theoretical. They did that very well."[56]

Another future trustee, Wayne Marks, who studied at Pace Institute in the early 1920s, had vivid recollections of the heavy workload as well as the excellent faculty. He recalled "working all day and half the night on Saturdays and Sundays on the accounting homework."[57]

The faculty also worked very hard. Dr. Alfreda Geiger recalls having five separate preparations — Pitman shorthand, typewriting, accounting, secretarial procedures, and mathematics — for the eighteen hours a week which constituted her schedule in the fall of 1932 when she joined the Institute faculty. Her full-time schedule was split between day and evening classes, and Homer S. Pace sometimes paid unannounced visits to the classroom. "He would just stand in back of the room...observe the teaching method, then leave. However, if one did not live up to his expectations and standards, there would be a future replacement. As a result, we had a very dedicated, conscientious faculty."[58]

Besides teaching, full-time faculty members were involved in co-curricular and extra-curricular activities. Alfreda Geiger recalled her role as advisor to the senior prom committee and chaperon at the annual event held at the Waldorf-Astoria Hotel. Extra-curricular activities in the inter-war period also included tea dances, ping pong, a camera club, a debating society, student theatricals, a glee club and sports. Pace had basketball, baseball and tennis teams which regularly played against other schools. Education always took precedence over extra-curricular activities, however.

For Pace Institute to remain effective from an educational standpoint in the 1930s and beyond, it had to comply with all New York State regulations governing the preparation of candidates for the C.P.A. examination. This meant revising the curriculum and securing accreditation

Library at 225 Broadway - 1941

of the accounting program. In 1933 all of this proved more time-consuming and difficult than anyone could have guessed when Pace Institute proposed the establishment of the New York Professional School of Accountancy and applied for registration under Section 1498a of the C.P.A. laws. To help its cause with the State Education Department, the school urged satisfied graduates to write to Albany. One person whose thoughts appeared on the letterhead of the international accounting firm of Arthur Young & Company declared:

> When I graduated from Princeton University in 1914 I knew nothing about accountancy. The only training in accountancy that I received in school was...at Pace Institute. From my knowledge of that training and from the opportunities that I have had to study the accounting curricula of colleges throughout the country in connection with the work I did as Chairman of the Bureau for Placements of the American Institute of Accountants...I believe that the instruction offered at Pace Institute is as satisfactory as that offered anywhere else in the country.[59]

The State Education Department evidently was not so sure. Despite the testimonials it received, the department was not persuaded to register the Pace program and recognize its school of accountancy. Indeed, the state recommended that Pace affiliate with an institution authorized to grant college degrees in New York State. This possibility was explored but dropped. Instead, Pace chose to apply

for a provisional charter as a corporation approved by the state to provide instruction on both the secondary and higher education levels. This meant phasing out the educational activities of the partnership of Pace & Pace, which had operated the school since 1906. Under the provisional charter granted on May 17, 1935, Pace Institute would have trustees elected by the shareholders. The shareholders were members of the Pace family and the first trustees were the incorporators, Homer S. Pace, Frederick M. Schaeberle, Charles T. Bryan, and Homer's sons, Robert S. Pace and C. Richard Pace.

A week after Pace received its provisional charter, representatives of Pace Institute and four other New York State business institutes met in Albany, "for the purpose of arriving at an agreement in respect to the petition for the establishment of the classification of collegiate schools of business."[60] This action was prompted by the strengthening of the requirements governing the educational preparation of candidates for the New York State C.P.A. examination. The state would shortly require cultural or liberal arts courses as well as technical courses.

Pace Institute quickly introduced cultural courses, but nevertheless, Institute officials were apprehensive that their graduates might be barred from the examination because Pace was not a full-fledged college. One solution to this problem was for the State Education Department to classify business institutes maintaining high standards as collegiate schools of business. Dr. Harlan Horner, the Assistant Commissioner for Higher Education, preferred another solution. He stated, in May 1935: "More and more I wish Pace Institute might become a degree-conferring institution in this field of its endeavor and thus avoid even the appearance of a step backward in a field in which she has rendered such excellent service."[61]

In his reply to Dr. Horner, Homer S. Pace said, "We have considered very carefully your suggestion with respect to obtaining status under a provisional charter as an institution of higher education for which degrees would be conferred during the life of the provisional charter in

C. Richard, Charles, Homer and Robert Pace
Formation of Pace Institute - 1933

the name of the University of the State of New York. We are inclined to take this step if a practicable plan can be worked out."[62] Soon after the exchange of letters between Homer Pace and Dr. Horner, Irwin Conroe, an Associate in Higher Education with the State Education Department, journeyed to Manhattan for an in-depth look at Pace Institute. He found much to commend and a number of things to criticize. After reviewing a copy of Conroe's report, Homer wrote to Dr. Horner. "We are glad to note the matters in respect to which Mr. Conroe's report gives us favorable mention," said Homer, adding:

> In respect to the matters which he considers unsatisfactory, we had already taken steps to adjust the existing conditions in respect to some of them - for example, the provision of a more adequate faculty room for the use of instructors, the provision of a more adequate social room for men students, and further development of the library.
>
> In respect to certain of the other matters adversely commented on, I am afraid that we did not succeed in laying an accurate picture before Mr. Conroe and believe that a further investigation...would cause him to modify his report in some of its aspects. I have in mind most particularly the portions commenting on instructor-student contacts, instructors' interest in students, faculty responsibility, and salary scale.[63]

It was clear that the state was not prepared to recognize Pace as a full-fledged college. Homer S. Pace could accept that but what he could not countenance was the state's hesitation in approving "the application for recognition of the accountancy course now offered by Pace Institute in preparation for the examinations for the certificate of certified public accountant."[64] The state's procrastination had already been costly. Homer pointed this out to Dr. Horner, in October 1935, stating:

> You are familiar with the conditions under which we are working. We had hoped to have a favorable decision well before the beginning of the school year....In the meantime, we enrolled a considerable number of students in this course on the statement of the facts as they existed at the time of registration. Many others who had planned to register at Pace Institute went elsewhere against their wishes because of the lack of official confirmation. The students who enrolled and their parents are asking us, almost from day to day, as to the status of the application and whether a registered student can proceed with the assurance that the recognition will be granted. We also have daily inquiries from practicing accountants, from alumni, and from high-school officials and teachers.[65]

This was one letter Homer may have wished he had never written because the state officially registered "the courses in the School of Accountancy in the Pace Institute" at the very time he was drafting his letter.[66] Dr. Horner informed him of this in a strongly worded letter which declared, "I am a little sorry that you felt obliged to inject into your letter the tone I find in it. I had supposed it was clearly understood that we should not take final action upon your application for registration until sometime this fall. These are not matters that we act upon hastily or prematurely."[67] Clearly Homer had to smooth some ruffled feathers and he managed to do so by telling Dr. Horner, "I am sorry indeed if the tone of my letter...conveyed to you in the slightest degree any contrary idea on my part. I realize that this application is only one detail relating to one profession while you have the educational supervision of

PACE INSTITUTE NEW YORK
GRADUATING CLASS OF 1934
AND FACULTY
SCHOOL OF SECRETARIAL PRACTICE
SCHOOL OF SHORTHAND REPORTING

several professions in your care, and that our application had to take its regular course. Only yesterday I wrote a letter to a young man in Havana who had inquired as to the status of our application, explaining that considerable time was necessarily involved in the consideration of an application of this kind."[68]

Now that accreditation was in hand and an apology had been made to Dr. Horner, Pace Institute could proceed with the formal announcement of the registration of its accounting program. In November 1935 the following statement went out to alumni, students and the press:

> Announcement is made of the registration by the State Education Department...of the four-year day school curriculum and the six-year evening curriculum of the School of Accountancy Practice of Pace Institute.
>
> The registration will entitle the graduates of these courses to such experience credit as may be autho-

rized by the regulations of the Commissioner of Education....

> The registration will also cover the recognition of these courses as qualifying students who complete them...for admission to the C.P.A. examinations subsequent to January l, 1938, as provided by Section 1498a of the Education Law.[69]

Pace Institute was back on track and moving full speed ahead.

BROADENING THE CURRICULUM

In the 1930s Pace built upon the strong foundation laid earlier and branched out, not geographically, but in terms of curriculum. In addition to a separate accounting school, Pace Institute established a School of Secretarial Practice. For a former stenographer like Homer, this addition was a natural one. He had always retained a lively interest in the field which had provided him with an entree to the business world years before. New and improved methods plus the achievements of expert practitioners were bound to draw his attention. This explains the invitation extended to John R. Gregg, "originator of the Gregg shorthand system, one of the foremost shorthand systems," to address the faculty and students of the Institute's School of Secretarial Practice at a January 1930 dinner held at the Machinery Club.[70] Gregg's appearance generated considerable publicity for the Institute's new school.

The shorthand proficiency tests sponsored by Pace later that year yielded a similar result. The Institute made the tests available at no cost to stenographers and secretaries. In announcing this service, one New York newspaper pointed out that this was "believed to be a unique development in the educational field."[71] Since most secretaries and stenographers possessed "no credentials testifying to their ability," Pace Institute was providing them with something which would increase their marketability while, at the same time, interesting them in the school's varied offerings in business.[72] The hope was that at least some of those seeking the free credential would enroll at Pace to study forms of stenography which they had not already mastered, such as court reporting.

The Institute's courses in this area were justifiably famous because of the quality of instruction and the high standards to which students were held. In 1932 the Institute staged a full-scale mock trial as part of a final examination in a legal and court reporting course. A newspaper account of this unusual occurrence noted:

> The scene was that of a courtroom with judge, witnesses and attorneys as members of the cast.
>
> The trial was planned to test the mental potentialities of these students as well as their dexterity in shorthand writing, the ability to distinguish the different voices and to record them in such a way that the transcript would show plainly who the various speakers were and what each said. Court testimony was taken at rates from 200 to 280 words a minute for a thirty-minute period.[73]

In 1936 the State Education Department was suffi-

ciently impressed by the Institute's shorthand and secretarial courses to register officially the two-year course of study in the day school division of the School of Secretarial Practice and the three-year course of study in the evening division. Before taking this step, however, the state insisted upon the inclusion of cultural subjects in the secretarial practice curriculum. Since such courses were also required for students planning to sit for the C.P.A. examination, Pace broadened its offerings to include English literature, the history of civilization, international relations, American government, economic and social geography, psychology, and personality development. In a 1935 press release captioned, "Courses Broadened at Pace by Addition of Cultural Subjects," it was noted that "substantial additions in space, in library facilities and books, and in faculty have been made necessary by the enlarged scope of the work at the Institute."[74]

The cultural courses proved viable in the day program in Secretarial Practice but it was a different story in the evening. Many of the students who enrolled for part-time study avoided the cultural courses, thus prompting Homer Pace to point out to the State Education Department in 1941 that "the students are largely earning small salaries, and their reasons are due partly to their inability to pay the tuition cost of a full program."[75] But there was more to it than that. Homer theorized that evening students avoided the cultural courses "partly because of their inability to realize the importance of work in English, psychology, and other cultural subjects."[76] He proceeded to inform the state that "the result of offering the diploma course has undoubtedly been to reduce largely the number of students."[77] To rectify this situation the Institute was planning to offer a two-year evening course "restricted to shorthand and typewriting subjects." In notifying the State Education Department of the school's intention, Homer said: "We shall not be able, of course, to have this course accredited as a diploma course, but we wish to have you informed as to what we are offering."[78]

At the same time that it was revising the evening program in Secretarial Practice, Pace Institute was making changes in the programs of the School of Marketing, Advertising and Selling. Back in 1936, when the day and evening secretarial programs were registered by the state, a two-year course of study in advertising and marketing in the day and a three-year course in the evening had been approved. A two-year day program and a three-year evening program in selling and marketing had been registered at the same time. In 1941 Homer Pace informed the State Education Department that it was increasingly difficult to interest students in the three-year programs and that the Institute was planning to "offer two-year evening school programs, restricted to technical subjects."[79] Despite this change, Pace was not entirely abandoning its broadened curriculum for, as Homer hastened to add: "We are still offering, in diploma courses of study that are continued, practically all of the cultural subjects heretofore given. We no doubt shall find quite often that an evening school student in marketing or shorthand will desire to carry cultural subjects such as English, psychology, economics and the like. We shall use every effort, in such instances, to build up the program of technical subjects by the addition of cultural ones."[80]

Homer Pace's assertion notwithstanding, it was the technical courses that attracted students to the Institute, and whenever a need for such offerings arose, the school responded. In 1937 approval was sought from the New York State Superintendent of Insurance for a course in Insurance Practice and Brokerage. Two years later, when the state increased the requirements for licensure, the 90-hour Pace course was deemed sufficient.

Another technical area in which Pace excelled in the 1930s was photography. Long an avocation of Homer Pace, who delighted in taking pictures, especially during his trips to Europe and the Far East, photography became part of the Institute's curriculum in 1938. An exquisite brochure entitled "Professional Photography" was published that year. It began with the observation that "photography offers an attractive occupational opportunity for both men and women."[81] Prospective students were told, "in art, in science, and in commerce, there is an increasing demand for the photographic recording of that which is about us — of things that we see and, in many instances, of things that we do not see except as the camera, or the microscope and the camera combined, make them visible to the eye."[82] Those who read further were treated to an interesting discourse on the history of photography and an analysis of different types of photography ranging from portraiture to aerial photography. At the end of the brochure were descriptions of the 20 photography courses comprising the Institute's two-year certificate program.

To promote its photography program, Pace Institute hosted annual photographic contests for high school students in the tristate area in the late thirties. Multiple cash prizes were awarded. In 1939 fourteen monetary awards ranging from $5 for honorable mention to $50 for first prize were distributed. Winning photographs were displayed at the Institute and the students who took those pictures assembled at the school to receive their prizes and participate in a critical discussion of the photographs.

The success which characterized the Institute's photography program was not duplicated in another area of the curriculum which the Institute attempted to develop in the 1930s. Although Pace informed the official in charge of the New York State Teachers' Education and Certification Division in 1937 that "for many years we have had in mind the possibility of extending our work to include teachers training courses," the state offered little encouragement.[83] A year went by before Dr. Herman Cooper, the Assistant Commissioner in charge of this area, visited the Institute. Besides examining the curriculum, Dr. Cooper met with Pace officials, who emerged from the discussions with the distinct impression "that Dr. Cooper would be very antagonistic toward any application which Pace Institute might make for official registration as a school of education."[84] Lillian Smith, one of the Pace administrators who sat in on the meeting with Dr. Cooper, explained his opposition in terms of the widespread belief that there were already enough institutions in New York City offering education courses. But there was more to it than that, as Dean Smith pointed out: "Dr. Cooper said in answer to our question in respect to the training of teachers...that all of the teacher training acceptable to the Department for licensing purposes was given in degree-granting institutions having schools of education. He was very emphatic in respect to the matter."[85] Dean Smith's perception was that "Dr. Cooper has no use for business institutes and stated so very frankly."[86] According to Smith, "Dr. Cooper does not recognize the work of business institutes as the equivalent of the work of junior colleges."[87] Lillian Smith continued, "It is my feeling, although he did not actually say this, that he was not inclined to consider any of the courses at Pace Institute except the Accountancy Practice courses as being in the field of higher education."[88] Once again, the powerful New York State Education Department was sending a clear signal to Pace Institute.

Even when the Institute was not seeking anything from the state, officials in Albany were closely monitoring the school's activities. In 1938, for example, Homer Pace received a letter from the office of the investigator for the professions in the professional licensing division of the State Education Department. The letter informed President Pace that a Massachusetts man had informed the licensing division that a salesman from Pace Institute "had told him that each applicant for a C.P.A. degree must be a college graduate, except those who learn their accounting at Pace...."[89] Disturbed by the "incorrect information" disseminated by the alleged Pace salesman, the state urged Homer Pace to contact the licensing division.[90] In his reply to the state's accusatory letter, Homer said, "Pace Institute has no salesmen either in New York or elsewhere. In fact, all of the contact it has with prospective students is when they call at the Institute, with the exception that now and again, upon invitation, we send a representative of the school to a vocational conference held by a high school."[91] As for the salesman who approached the Massachusetts man, Homer theorized that he may have been "a represen-

tative of a local school." But, said Homer, "there is no connection...between Pace Institute and this school...."[92]

A year earlier Homer Pace and Pace Institute had been the successful plaintiffs against Nicholas E. Pace or Nicholas E. Pacello and Catherine F. Pace who had used the name Pace Institute in advertisements for their private business school. The defendants were enjoined from so doing in the future but, in the meantime, confusion plagued some prospective students about which school was the real Pace Institute. This was surely one instance where imitation was not the most sincere form of flattery but, in a convoluted way, it was perhaps testimony, albeit aggravating to be sure, of the success of the Institute co-founded by Homer S. Pace.

A NEW DECADE BEGINS — THE 1940S

Lawsuits, appropriation of Homer Pace's own name and that of his school, and scrutiny by the State Education Department were all part of doing business. So, too, was the seemingly constant need to clarify misconceptions about the kind of school Pace actually was. This issue was something which proved to be quite challenging in the early 1940s, due to the State Education Department's omission of business institutes from a list of registered schools circulated to secondary institutions. Homer S. Pace and the State Education Department went back and forth on this for two years until the state conceded that its list had created an erroneous impression.

While all of this was taking place, Homer Pace and his closest associates were seriously contemplating putting the Institute on a non-stock basis and applying to the State Education Department for permission to grant degrees. They ultimately decided to place the School of Accountancy on a non-stock basis but not the rest of the Institute. This did not meet with the state's approval, so Pace Institute signified its desire to continue operating on a stock basis while petitioning the state for an absolute charter. In a letter, written on May 4, 1942, to the State Education

Pace Institute

1942 Faculty and Administrators

Department Homer said, "In view of the fact that our minds have not come together on a plan for establishing the School of Accountancy Practice on a non-stock basis as originally contemplated, the best thing to do from our viewpoint is to maintain the present set-up, and to petition the Regents for an absolute charter. If, in their judgment, they deem it best for us to go ahead on the basis of a renewal of the provisional charter, then of course we shall accept their decision."[93] The Institute did not have to wait long for the Regents' decision. On May 18, word was received from Albany that "the Board of Regents, at its meeting held in New York City, May 15, 1942, formally voted to amend the charter of Pace Institute in accordance with the petition of the trustees...and to replace such provisional charter...by an absolute charter."[94] The major difference between the provisional and absolute charter was that the latter eliminated the Institute's authority to provide instruction on the secondary level.

Less than a week later, Homer St. Clair Pace, who had been suffering from hypertension, was stricken with a cerebral hemorrhage while working in his office at the Institute. He was taken to Beekman Downtown Hospital where he died the next day. His brother Charles Ashford Pace, co-founder of Pace Institute, had passed away on December 12, 1940. Charles's demise was viewed as a great loss to the Institute although he had not been "actively associated" with the school for almost a decade and indeed had resigned from the firm of Pace & Pace in 1933, at which time he assigned all property rights in the firm to Homer in return for an annuity. Since Homer's death was more sudden than his brother's, his passing stunned his associates at the Institute.

Homer was the quintessential Pace Institute man, one who could not be easily replaced. The board of trustees, therefore, resolved, "that out of respect to Mr. Homer St. Clair Pace, the office of president shall be kept vacant for the remainder of the fiscal year and until his successor shall be appointed."[95] Other tributes took the form of obituaries in newspapers and business periodicals throughout the country. A number of these articles revealed a side of Homer which had been rarely glimpsed. "Outside of his business interests, Mr. Pace had many hobbies, among them the collection of antiques," declared *The New York Sun*.[96] The *Brooklyn Eagle* noted, "Mr. Pace was author of many books on accounting and related subjects. In recent years he had traveled extensively through the Orient and other parts of the world. He was a charter member of the Gourmet Society, and numbered among his friends were many of the best known chefs in New York."[97]

Homer St. Clair Pace was 63 years of age when he was interred in a New Lexington, Ohio, cemetery. Marking the gravesite is an unpretentious stone bearing the following inscription:

HOMER ST. CLAIR PACE
TEACHER
1879-1942 [98]

When the master teacher and educational entrepreneur was buried, the school he had co-founded was in its thirty-sixth year of continuous operation. That school was Homer's legacy, not to his family, consisting of his widow Mabel, sons Robert and Charles Richard, and daughter Helen, but to the tens of thousands of students who would be educated there in the future. In accordance with Homer's wishes, the Pace family would surrender all claims to the Institute and would guide it through a rebirth as Pace College, a non-profit institution.

Homer Pace working at home in Brooklyn Heights

Students & Faculty

There are more than 100 fields of study at Pace, in business, the arts and sciences, computer science and information systems, education, nursing, and law.

3

Chapter   From 1942 to 1959

A TIME OF READJUSTMENT

For three months following the death of Homer S. Pace, Pace Institute was
without a president. Since it was both wartime and summertime, the school
was able to function well enough during this period, but the leadership vac-
uum had to be filled before the start of the fall term. Therefore, at its meeting of August 27, 1942, the Board of Trustees resolved "that Robert S. Pace
be appointed, and hereby is appointed, president of Pace Institute for the
remainder of the fiscal year and until his successor shall be elected."[1]

Within a few months of his appointment as President, Robert Pace
became a member of the United States armed forces. The Institute was once
again leaderless, but not for long. Frederick Schaeberle carried on in President Pace's absence, guiding the school through a difficult time of transition.
Despite some serious problems, most of which were war-related, the Institute continued to enjoy an excellent reputation. In 1943, the American
Association of Commercial Colleges characterized Pace as "probably the
most renowned school of its type in the world."[2] There was even praise
from the Ivy League. "It is accepted here at Princeton that your training program is superior to those offered at the Wharton School, Temple University
and Rutgers University," wrote a Princeton faculty member.[3]

During this period Pace Institute became a member of the Association of
Business Institutes of the State of New York. Dean Alice Ottun was named
Pace's official liaison with the association. Miss Ottun was also in charge of
enrollment, never an easy job, and one which was particularly difficult at
this time because of the government's ever changing manpower needs.
When Uncle Sam called, even the most dedicated future C.P.A. had to relin-
quish his seat at the Institute to head for basic training. Draftees, however,

*Fountain Outside
Dow Hall,
Briarcliff*

> "When I came, Pace was in rented floors in the Transportation Building. The chief executive officer was the dean, Miss Alice Ottun, who really was a presence there from eight in the morning until probably ten at night, sitting in her office in the corner with the door open, watching people go in and out. She was a good-looking woman and had a lot of charm and was a true executive. Women executives were rare in those days. And a very competent woman."
>
> (Dr. Bernard Brennan, Pace Oral History, December 8, 1983)

Robert S. Pace

could return to school upon completion of military service and any unused tuition remaining from the semester in which they withdrew could be utilized. This policy was eminently sensible in view of the number of students forced to withdraw in 1942 and 1943.

With fewer students, the Institute needed less space. Happily, the U.S. government was in the market for downtown office space and Pace was able to sublet 10,000 square feet to the Department of Justice. The number of students continued to decline, however, so much so that Pace Institute seriously considered curtailing new enrollments in the Accountancy Practice program for the duration of the war. Admitting new students to a program which they might not be able to complete because of cancellation of advanced courses due to low registration would have been unethical. Continuing the program, on the other hand, implied financial hardship for the institution. After seeking advice from the State Education Department, the trustees decided to maintain the Accountancy Practice program despite the additional financial burden of offering advanced instruction to limited numbers of students.

Faced with declining enrollments, the Board of Trustees, as early as 1942, discussed the possibility of 10 percent salary reductions for faculty. Department heads and officers experienced a diminution in income for the duration of the war. Other economies included curtailed

library hours. Beginning in 1943, the library opened at 1:00 p.m. These economies helped, but in addition to trimming the budget, the trustees looked for ways to augment income. They considered the possibility of introducing correspondence courses, but decided against it. Summer courses, as part of an accelerated program, seemed to be a better idea. So, too, was a new real estate course, which received widespread coverage in New York area newspapers, including *La Prensa*. The newspapers also featured the Institute's evening math courses for service-bound men and women. Lasting eight weeks, these intensive offerings in college algebra and trigonometry satisfied the one-year math requirement of the military.

The publicity accorded the Institute's new offerings did not detract from its programs in Accounting and Secretarial Practice. Indeed, the administration made a concerted effort to demonstrate the viability of these programs as preparation for both wartime and post-war careers.

Edward J. Koestler, a well-known accounting faculty

member and director of the school's textbook publishing business, became the Institute's spokesman for accountancy. In talks, interviews, and articles, Koestler pointed out that ambitious young men and women selecting a field of endeavor were wise to ask whether the occupation served a basic need, whether it was a growing field and whether the remuneration was satisfactory. On all three counts, accountancy was a fine choice for bright, diligent young people, especially women, according to Koestler.

Speaking at a career conference for female students of Ridgewood High School, Koestler declared that a combination of college and business training was the key to a successful career. For students who wanted to enter the job market soon after graduating from high school, Koestler advised a year's secretarial training, which he felt would not only increase the individual's efficiency but would also aid the war effort.

In 1943, when the draft was depleting the supply of male civilian workers, Koestler conducted a survey of the needs of business. Not surprisingly, his scientific sampling of paid newspaper advertisements indicated that women employees were sought for four different categories of employment: office positions; technical-industrial jobs, primarily in factories; sales; and miscellaneous non-office positions.

Koestler's survey revealed that the greatest demand for female workers was in business. Fully 67 percent of the ads for female workers were placed by firms seeking office personnel and nearly three-quarters of those jobs were for stenographers, bookkeepers and accountants. Koestler had spotted a trend and Pace Institute capitalized on it by introducing a short evening course in accounting designed for women. Thoroughly captivated by this idea, metropolitan dailies ran detailed articles about the new program. Typical of these pieces was one published by the *New York Journal-American* beneath a banner headline proclaiming: "Evening Program at Pace to Train Girl Accountants."[4]

The women's rights movement was two decades away, and to male journalists women were still girls, but at Pace

> "...the career of Robert Pace can be summarized as one of linkage between the past, present, and future — in recognizing the claims of the past he fulfilled his father's legacy, in focusing on results and achievement he is a model for the present, and his integrity serves as a conscience for the future."
>
> (Dr. John E. Flaherty, Pace Oral History, February 17, 1984)

Institute they seem to have been taken more seriously. In announcing the new program, Frederick M. Schaeberle consistently referred to its potential students as "women" rather than "girls." According to Schaeberle: "Bookkeeping offers excellent opportunities to the woman who is attracted to the technical and confidential work of accounting."[5] Referring to the limitless employment opportunities afforded women who possessed a background in accounting, Schaeberle mentioned positions in non-profit institutions and government, as well as business firms. Noting that women were not well-represented in bookkeeping and accounting positions because of the tendency of schools during the interwar period to direct female students towards secretarial studies, Schaeberle expressed the hope that this situation would change before long. Writing in *Accredited News*, he said, "Thirty-five years ago, there were probably as many women taking bookkeeping courses as there were taking short-hand courses. Conditions have changed to such an extent that the number of women bookkeeping students is relatively small."[6]

Commenting on the female student's potential for this field, Schaeberle wrote, "There are no inherent difficulties, either as to natural aptitude or employer prejudice, to deter a woman from bookkeeping or accounting work. It is entirely within the ordinary course of events for a woman who has made proper technical preparation and who has developed her executive ability by the right kind of business experience, to advance far beyond the bookkeeping stage and to become a controller or other chief accounting officer."[7]

Comparing male and female students, Schaeberle noted, "Women, on the whole, have as much natural aptitude for accounting work as men. In any group of a hundred high-school graduates, made up entirely of girls, there will be as many who have a natural aptitude for accounting and mathematical subjects as in a group of boys of equal number."[8]

Employers evidently concurred because more than 175 of them sent from one to twenty-nine of their female employees to Pace Institute for the new program. Between February and May of 1943, six sections of a sixteen-week evening course for women were organized. Each was fully enrolled before the first class meeting. The program was so popular that a seventh section was scheduled to begin in mid-May.

Two years after it was introduced, the accounting course for women was still luring new students to the Institute. After taking the introductory course, which cost $47, if tuition was paid in full at the time of registration, or $49.10 if the student opted for the multi-payment plan, some women continued their studies. The Institute publicized the benefits of further study for women, noting, "Beginning accounting positions such as those for which preparation is made by this short course offer many opportunities for advancement to more responsible positions. The work has been so laid out that the ambitious student may after completing this course, carry on her studies into the field of advanced accountancy without overlapping or duplication of studies."[9]

A number of women who studied at Pace Institute fared very well in terms of employment during the war years and the immediate post-war period. Mrs. Frederick Bull, a Pace graduate, was appointed assistant secretary of the Manufacturers Trust Company in 1948. The significance of the appointment was underscored by the new officer's hometown newspaper, which proudly declared in a headline, "Mrs. Bull First Woman to Hold N.Y. Bank Post."[10]

Another graduate of Pace Institute, Alice Lovejoy, was an Army pilot during the war. Miss Lovejoy forfeited a position at the National Broadcasting Company to join the WASPS, or Women's Airforce Service Pilots. Already an accomplished pilot before entering the military, Alice Lovejoy received special training in instrument navigation and then became a flight leader ferrying planes to take-off points.

Another woman who had studied at Pace remained on the ground but managed to make her own contribution to the war effort by serving as secretary to the president of Sperry Gyroscope. One of 400 women interviewed by the company's personnel manager, Virginia Maxwell was chosen for the multi-faceted position which included, according to Newsday, reminding the boss "when to take his medicine."[11] The newspaper, which published a lengthy article about the accomplished Miss Maxwell, noted that she assisted in arranging dinner parties and even helped "to marry off" her employer's sons "in fine style."[12] She also did the tax returns for her boss's entire family and kept "their checking accounts, insurance, real estate and investment records."[13] One of her other duties was to stay with her employer's wife at the family's Glen Cove estate when he was out of town. Although liberated women of the late twentieth century would find some aspects of Miss Maxwell's job unacceptable, the fact remains that the former Pace student was an extremely competent administrator who handled myriad details for her high-powered boss.

Women's rights advocates might also have misgivings about Kathleen Hoagland, an accountant turned novelist. One newspaper began a rather lengthy article about this former Pace student by enumerating the housewifely chores Mrs. Hoagland was deferring, such as dish washing, making a pudding, and hanging curtains, by taking time out to chat with a reporter. Presumably Mrs. Hoagland got around to these tasks because, by her own admission, housework was a diversion. When she wasn't whipping up gourmet meals for her husband and six-year-old daughter, Kathleen Hoagland was writing several

"Essentially the corporate culture that Robert Pace inherited and advanced was simply the means for implementing the traditional mission of Pace since its inception. This educational purpose included such features as: creating the atmosphere for students to learn how to learn, converting information into professional results, urging students to take responsibility for their own development, stimulating the importance of commitment in the teaching process, recognizing that the student was the client and the purpose of all institutional activities, and fostering an atmosphere of staff and faculty collegiality by making Pace a decent place to work."

(Dr. John E. Flaherty, Pace Oral History, February 17, 1984)

thousand eminently publishable words a day. At the time Mrs. Hoagland was interviewed, her first novel, *Fiddler in the Sky*, had just been published by Harper and Bros., and was already receiving favorable reviews from newspapers across the nation.

The success of Pace Institute's female students notwithstanding, the school had to do more than attract talented women in order to remain solvent during the lean years of World War II. Although the accounting course for women brought in badly needed tuition, other ways had to be found to help balance the budget. Some additional revenue was obtained from administering the Army and Navy qualifying tests for the United States government. The examinations had a dual purpose: to determine which young men, between the ages of 17 and 21, were suitable for college training, and to assist the military in assigning those candidates deemed ineligible for higher education to other types of training.

In July 1943 Pace Institute, in concert with the New York City Veterans Administration, explored the possibility of becoming a rehabilitation training center for disabled war veterans. Pace subsequently received a contract under which the Veterans Administration assigned disabled veterans to the Institute. As soon as the war ended, the

administration announced the establishment of a special counseling program for male and female veterans interested in beginning or resuming studies. Tuition was also increased following a ruling that government price ceilings were not applicable to services.

From an administrative standpoint, Robert S. Pace's resumption of the presidency in September 1945, following his return from service, was an important development. No sooner was he back in his office at 225 Broadway than a refinement and strengthening of the curriculum began. This was dictated not merely by the return to peacetime conditions, but by a New York State Education Department decision to revise the qualitative requirements for approved courses of study designed to prepare students for the C.P.A. exam. Irwin J. Conroe, the Assistant Commissioner for Professional Education, noted in a letter to Robert Pace: "We would like it clearly understood that we have no interest in dictating to the schools or colleges what they shall include in their professional course of study in accounting or what they shall exclude...."[14] But he quickly added: "...we draw attention to the fact that our approval of such course of study depends upon the conformity of such institution to a recognized pattern of subjects, both professional and liberal."[15]

In his reply to Dr. Conroe, Robert Pace said, "Entrance requirements have been tightened and CPA students must generally maintain a 'B' average (89% or better) to proceed with their work. A sizable part of our Accounting and Law texts were revised and brought up-to-date last summer and the revisions will continue down through all the semesters as fast as the printer can turn out the work. All of these factors, plus an unusual seriousness and desire upon the part of the students to concentrate on their studies, should eventually make themselves evident in the results of the State Licensing Examinations."[16]

Besides increasing the academic requirements for CPA candidates, Pace Institute placed considerable emphasis on developing its student leadership qualities. Even in highly technical courses, a concerted effort was made to

Commencement - Class of 1949 - Waldorf-Astoria, New York City

underscore the managerial approach and, beginning in 1948, a special trustees' award, consisting of a gold medal, was presented at commencement "to the member of the graduating class who has shown the most outstanding qualities of leadership."[17]

PACE BECOMES A COLLEGE

The trustees who were making this leadership award were themselves models of leadership, especially in light of their decision to transform the school from a proprietary business institute into a full-fledged college. This was in keeping with the wish expressed by the late Homer S. Pace. Following Homer Pace's death, his widow and children (Robert, Richard, and Helen) relinquished all claims to the assets of Pace Institute. In 1944 the trustees discussed the

possibility of changing over to a non-stock corporation. The matter was reconsidered in 1946 and on December 3 of that year the trustees resolved "that the President be and he hereby is authorized to address an appropriate petition to the Board of Regents of the University of the State of New York, requesting that the charter of Pace Institute be amended and its outstanding capital stock retired in accordance with the foregoing resolutions."[18]

At the time this request was made, the Institute's academic programs enjoyed the approval of the State Education Department. The C.P.A. program had been registered, which meant that graduates could be admitted to the state licensing examination. Pace was the only for-profit school and non-degree granting institution in New York State which had this registration. The time had arrived, though, for Pace Institute to join the ranks of degree-granting schools. This entailed submission, in 1948, of a formal petition to the New York State Education Department, waiver of past and future rights to earnings by the shareholders of the corporation, a minimum of $500,000 in financial resources (something which the Institute was able to achieve by 1948, as a result of increased tuition from veterans and other new students) and cancellation of the contract between Pace Institute and its publishing subsidiary, the Business Text-Book Publishers, Inc.

The entire process took two years, but finally, on December 20, 1948, Pace received word that "the Board of Regents, at its meeting on December 17th, formally voted to amend the charter of Pace Institute by authorizing the corporation to confer the degree of bachelor of business administration (B.B.A.) and by changing the name of the corporation to Pace College."[19] The special announcement sent by Robert Pace to alumni a few days later noted that "the basic structure of the major courses of study in effect at Pace College will remain the same."[20] For the immediate future, the four-year Accountancy Practice course and the certificate programs in Secretarial Practice and Shorthand would not be altered, but the Marketing, Advertising and Selling course would be lengthened to four years.

In the months that followed receipt of the official notifi-

> "We've been blessed with a long period of stability here — stability of management where people know the customs, the methods of carrying things out and the internal morality. It appears just as certain and stable as the sun rising and setting. That's been going on a long time. So what Ed had to do was to engineer a transition from a proprietary institution to a self-governing operation. And he did it, under the greatest of strains. But this is one of Ed's great skills, the ability to turn problems into opportunities. Ed has knowledge of how this institution works. He started off at Fordham, being registrar, but when he came over here, he had to know every job around here....to know this place inside out."
>
> (Richard Matthews, Pace Oral History, May 12, 1983)

cation, the college held a charter presentation dinner, adopted yellow and royal blue as the official school colors, acquired a seal and emblem, and held a mid-year commencement in March at the Waldorf-Astoria. The practice of holding commencements had resumed in 1947. That year wartime graduates plus students completing requirements in the immediate post-war period received diplomas. The March 1949 commencement was especially significant because it was the first graduation since Pace achieved college status and, with more than 500 students receiving diplomas, was the largest commencement in the school's history.

The optimism which prevailed at the March commencement was dampened a bit in May, 1949, when the State Education Department provisionally registered, for one year, the courses of studies leading to the B.B.A. at Pace. This caused considerable confusion for alumni and students, and engendered consternation among the trustees because the accounting program had been continuously registered since 1935 and the registration had become absolute in 1942. "The fact is...," wrote Robert S. Pace to the State Education Department, "very few if any institutions have been preparing students for the New York State C.P.A. exams as long as Pace College. After 45 years of successful work in this field, it is difficult to understand a provisional registration for C.P.A. preparation."[21]

President Pace's words fell upon deaf ears. The state was unyielding. Yet, the college, which awarded its first B.B.A. degrees in 1949, kept trying. In May, 1951, Robert S. Pace had Dr. Edward J. Mortola, who had joined Pace Institute as Assistant Dean in 1947, telephone the State Education Department about the potentially damaging listing of Pace College as provisionally registered under Schools of Accountancy and Business Administration in an official handbook widely used by high school guidance counselors and others. When the state official with whom Dr. Mortola spoke insisted upon listing Pace provisionally in the next edition of the handbook, Robert Pace had no choice but to inform the trustees that "the matter should be followed up promptly for further information, clarification, and friendly and equitable adjudication, if possible."[22]

Although the college had a legitimate grievance, Robert Pace was informed a month later that the State Education Department had "provisionally registered for a period of three years...the day and evening curriculums offered by Pace College...leading to the degree of Bachelor of Business Administration with the major in marketing, advertising and selling, and the major in accountancy and business administration."[23] This was better than the one-year provisional registration granted earlier, but the point is that it was still "provisional," and even this concession was not forthcoming until the State Education Department conducted a thorough investigation of Pace. Part of the state requirements consisted of a visit in 1949 by an evaluation team dispatched by the Assistant Commissioner for Professional Education, Irwin A. Conroe.

The experts from Albany found the quality of teaching quite acceptable, despite the excessive hours some faculty members were spending in the classroom. Indeed, the state investigators uncovered one instructor who was teaching a total of 30 hours per week, divided between the day and evening sessions. The team also found fault with the college's administrative structure. "Department heads at the present time are only figureheads," said Conroe in a letter to Robert Pace, adding that they had "no voice in the appointment of faculty members who may serve under them, and no voice in the matter of dismissal of unqualified teachers in their respective disciplines."[24] The college's failure to award tenure and to assign faculty to traditional professorial ranks also evoked criticism, as did the paucity of Ph.Ds. Concerning the latter, Dr. Conroe recommended hiring people with advanced degrees to teach liberal arts courses. "The curricula of Pace need bolstering up and rounding out in the humanities," declared Conroe.[25]

But, most of all, the "autocratic regime of centralized authority" had to be modified.[26] "Clearly the institution needs to study well and painstakingly its administrative

setup," warned Conroe, who then tried to soften the blow by concluding, "Despite these rather severe criticisms, it must be pointed out that we are mindful of the fact that Pace cannot be expected over night to change from a highly specialized institution in the field of accountancy to a well-rounded college in all that the name implies. We do expect, however, that during the period of provisional registration Pace will make the necessary improvements in the various areas outlined above, to warrant more than provisional registration."[27]

Reaction to the Conroe report was swift and decisive. The board of trustees and the administration carefully digested the state's recommendations and within three weeks President Pace informed Dr. Conroe, in writing, that "active plans are already under way with respect to all the suggestions that you have made."[28] Robert Pace continued, "All of us here at the College appreciate the care with which you have made your suggestions and I have the assurance of all of my associates that they not only agree with most of the criticisms, but that they will cooperate in every way."[29] After assuring Dr. Conroe that he would contact him in the near future about steps "taken to remedy matters," Robert Pace added that Alice Ottun, who had long been associated with Pace Institute and who had remained at the school through the hectic post-war period of increased veteran enrollment, had submitted her resignation as Dean on May 25, 1949.[30] The task of implementing Dr. Conroe's recommendations, therefore, fell to Dr. Edward J. Mortola, acting Dean. A new era was about to begin at Pace College.

In the days and weeks ahead, Dr. Mortola worked closely with President Pace to comply with the directives of the New York State Education Department. One of their priorities was strengthening the liberal arts and securing approval to grant the B.A. Towards that end, Dr. Adrian Rondileau, Dean at the Associated Colleges of Upper New York, was appointed Dean of Liberal Arts at Pace in February 1950. In an interview with *The New York World-Telegram*, Dean Rondileau, who possessed expertise in

SIMON LOEB

Simon Loeb, a member of the Pace University Board of Trustees from 1951 until 1962, was founder and senior partner of the accounting firm of Loeb and Troper. A prominent member of his profession, Mr. Loeb was a member of the New York State Board of Certified Public Accountant Examiners, the New York State C.P.A. Committee on Grievances and the Board of Governors of the Accountants Club of America. Mr. Loeb also served as vice president of the Accountants Club and president of the New York State Society of Certified Public Accountants.

An alumnus of New York University, class of 1908, Mr. Loeb taught auditing at City College and served on Pace University's advisory board of accountancy. Mr. Loeb's alma mater awarded him a presidential citation in 1962. In 1975, thirteen years before his death at the age of 91, Mr. Loeb received an honorary doctorate of Commercial Science from Pace.

both public and private higher education, was very bullish on the private sector. Contending that a private college can be "efficient, and critical of itself," Pace's newest administrator elaborated on the comparison between private and public institutions, declaring that in the latter there can be "a lack of control of economy of effort."[31] He went further, stating that the private college had to be "the pace-setter in what it teaches and how it teaches."[32] On March 15, 1950, less than a month after appointing a Dean of Liberal Arts, the trustees resolved to petition the Regents to amend Pace's charter "to give the College authority to confer the degree of Bachelor of Arts (B.A.) and the degree of Bachelor of Laws (LL.B.)"[33]

In April, Albany dispatched Dr. Carroll V. Newsom, Assistant Commissioner for Higher Education, to assess Pace's readiness to offer the new degrees. Prior to his visit, Dr. Newsom said, in a letter to Provost Mortola, "we shall want to explore very carefully your entire situation. A well rounded offering in the area of the liberal arts must include many types of courses that you have not offered in the past. Also, there is the matter of library facilities, laboratory facilities, and so forth. Undoubtedly, you have given much consideration to all of these matters."[34]

Dr. Mortola's reply to Dr. Newsom included an enumeration of the steps Pace College had taken to strengthen the liberal arts. Pointing to the fact that over half of the college's offerings had been in the liberal arts in the past few years, Dr. Mortola continued, "Our new liberal arts curriculum has been organized on the basis of a core of general education which is considered essential for the broad development of the individual, integrated with programs of specialized courses which might permit a student to develop a meaningful major chosen from a variety of fields of study."[35]

Most assuredly, the administration was thinking in terms of a very comprehensive institution. Further proof of this was President Robert Pace's assertion that "the master plan of Pace College provides for a College of Liberal Arts, a School of Business, and a School of Law."[36] The President stated further: "The old concept of various schools of business will be discontinued."[37]

The notion of a Pace College School of Law was a bit of a surprise to the State Education Department. Upon being notified of this, the college hastened to assure the State that much serious thought had preceded the decision to apply for permission to grant the LL.B. as well as the B.A. According to Dr. Mortola, "the decision of the College concerning the inception of a Law School is actually the result of planning which began in the days of Pace Institute and was solidified when we became a College."[38] Citing a recent court decision which "made the relationship between accounting and law even more obvious," Dr.

Mortola said that "we will meet the needs of our community by this extension of our offering...."[39]

The State Education Department was not persuaded. Following an inspection visit in the spring of 1950, Assistant Commissioner Newsom informed Robert Pace that "the request for both the law school and the opportunity to move into the liberal arts field will impress the Regents as being quite an undertaking."[40] Newsom warned: "...there is considerable likelihood that the petition may be turned down."[41] He therefore suggested postponing the establishment of a law school. As for the request to grant the B.A., Dr. Newsom felt that Pace's case would be stronger once the college moved into a building of its own.

This certainly was not what the trustees wanted to hear, but they acquiesced by resolving to withdraw the petition to confer the B.A. and the LL.B. If ever there was a case of one step backward and two steps forward, this was it. Within days of the trustees' action, Provost Mortola was in Albany conferring with Dr. Newsom. The meeting was quite cordial, Dr. Mortola reporting afterwards, "On several different occasions during our conversation he made a point of making complimentary remarks concerning Pace College. He stated that he considers that we have a fine program and that we are in a position, ever to 'show up' some of our larger neighbors in the city if we make the most of the areas in which we are working."[42]

In addition to discussing the liberal arts program at Pace, Drs. Mortola and Newsom spoke about the gnawing problem of provisional registration for the Accounting program. The Assistant Commissioner assured Dr. Mortola that the word "provisional" did not have to be used in the Pace College Bulletin because, in essence, the term was one used by the Department of Education "and need not be publicly reported."[43] Better still was the assurance from Dr. Newsom that he would "take steps to adjust the 'provisional registration' as soon as possible."[44]

Reporting to President Pace on his meeting with Dr. Newsom, Dr. Mortola said that the Assistant Commissioner had found a lot to like at Pace: for example, the hiring of respected faculty in liberal arts disciplines, such as artist Peter Fingesten; the school's use of IBM machines for registration; its record-keeping system; and its statement on non-discrimination. Dr. Mortola was also able to tell President Pace that his meeting in Albany had concluded with an assurance from Dr. Newsom that he would work with Dr. Mortola on a revised petition for the Bachelor of Arts.

Newsom kept his word. He and Dr. Mortola corresponded over the next few months, and in October, soon after Dr. Newsom had been promoted to Associate Commissioner for Higher Education, Dr. Mortola informed him that "our Liberal Arts program is under way in the day school, shakily as far as numbers are concerned but with strength in purpose and outlook."[45] The Provost added: "The infant still needs much nourishing and we shall take advantage of your original offer to call upon you for guidance in developing our new offspring."[46]

Actually, the infant was doing just fine. By January 1951 the State Education Department provisionally registered the first two years of the program following an on-site inspection by two officials from Albany. Speaking for both himself and his colleague, one of these visitors told Robert Pace that they "had very favorable impressions in general of your liberal arts program as it is developing."[47] He continued, "The college's approach to curriculum building through the active participation of the faculty seems to me eminently sound, and I am aware of the fact that the liberal arts program as now planned will be subject to further growth through this process. Wider offerings will eventually be necessary if you are to have a four-year program with majors in the liberal arts field but for present needs the first two years of the program are well organized and adequate, although I realize that they, too, will be revised. Your stress upon the development of general education courses and upon the use of visual aids is highly commendable."[48]

Pace College left nothing to chance in pursuing state approval of the B.A. Provost Mortola journeyed to Albany in the late spring of 1952 to confer with Dr. Newsom. The

Assistant Commissioner for Higher Education, Ewald B. Nyquist, was invited by Dr. Newsom to sit in on the meeting. In a letter to the chairman of the board of trustees of Pace College, Dr. Mortola described what had taken place in Albany. He said, "I had lunch with Dr. Newsom and Mr. Nyquist where we picked up our discussion concerning the Liberal Arts program at Pace. They concurred that we should not attempt to expand into too many areas of specialization and, as Dr. Newsom stated, all institutions should not attempt to do all things. Incidentally, Dr. Newsom pointed out that, in general, we would be dealing with Mr. Nyquist in most of these matters inasmuch as his position as Assistant Commissioner for Higher Education gave him responsibility over all of our program except the professional areas."[49]

Dr. Mortola emerged from that meeting with a date for "Mr. Nyquist and Miss Kelly, the Registration Officer for the Department," to visit Pace "for the purpose of an inspection which would in turn lead to a recommendation for amendment of our charter to include authority to grant the A.B. degree."[50] The inspection took place in October, and it revealed deficiencies in foreign languages and the sciences. The college was urged to offer additional courses in these areas. Within a few weeks, Dr. Mortola assured the State Education Department that "we are working now on plans to make a foreign language a requirement for every Liberal Arts student and for inclusion of a standard science course..."[51] At the same time, he pointed out that four Pace students would complete all requirements for a B.A. by the end of the spring semester. "We should, therefore, be grateful if you would move ahead with whatever steps are necessary to pave the way for our application for an amendment to the charter so that we may receive authorization to grant the A.B. degree," stated Dr. Mortola, who concluded his letter to Ewald Nyquist by saying, "May I thank you again for your helpfulness and for your frank and thoughtful criticisms. We at Pace are all dedicated towards working for the achievement of the highest possible status and prestige of the College. We are particularly grateful to you and to Dr. Newsom for your guidance and helpfulness during these years of growth and development."[52] In December the board of trustees submitted a petition to the State Education Department requesting permission to grant the B.A. Two months later President Pace received the following telegram:

> Petition on A B granted
> Ewald B. Nyquist[53]

In April the Bulletin to the Schools issued by the University of the State of New York contained the following brief but significant announcement: "The Regents amended the charter of Pace College, New York City, to authorize it to grant the degree of bachelor of arts. It was previously authorized to grant the degree of bachelor of business administration."[54] Two months later, at the June 1953 commencement exercises at the Waldorf-Astoria, four students received B.A. degrees.

EXPANSION WITH A CAPITAL E

A factor in the Regents decision to authorize Pace to grant the B.A. was the school's physical expansion. That there would be adequate classroom, laboratory and office space for the new liberal arts program, as well as existing programs, was never in doubt. In the immediate post-war period, as the school expanded, President Robert S. Pace frequently reminded the trustees of the urgent need for more space. The trustees responded in 1949 by authorizing the purchase of 290 Broadway, but the sale did not take place because the architects and engineer engaged by the college to inspect the building uncovered structural problems. The board then proceeded to explore the possibility of purchasing some lower Manhattan real estate from Columbia University and erecting a new building. After Columbia rejected the Pace bid for the property bounded by Barclay Street, Greenwich Street, Park Place and West Broadway, the trustees decided to purchase 41 Park Row.

41 Park Row, New York
Architect's drawing

Built in 1858 for *The New York Times*, the building had been expanded over the years, from five to sixteen floors. By purchasing 41 Park Row, the college acquired 110,000 square feet of usable floor space, compared with the 61,000 square feet it occupied at the time of purchase. According to Charles T. Bryan, chairman of the board of trustees, speaking to an overflow crowd at the 1951 Pace commencement in the grand ballroom of the Waldorf-Astoria, acquisition of the former newspaper building "would permit the college to add a number of desirable features that are not now practicable."[55] Among the improvements envisioned by the trustees were an auditorium, cafeteria, sizable library, science laboratories and gymnasium. Mr. Bryan added: "Space will be available for increased student activities. Space will be available for alumni affairs to serve the more

than 70,000 former students."[56]

Alumni were especially enthusiastic about the new building. The *Pace Alumni Magazine* reported in the fall of 1951 that the renovations were already underway and that 50 classrooms, rather than the 35 occupied by the college in its rented quarters, would be available. Plans for the library, which was to occupy two entire floors, included shelf space for 50,000 books and one seat for every three students. As for recreational facilities, the magazine declared, "Facilities in the sub-basement will include regulation size bowling alleys, a large swimming pool, a full-size handball court, and a gymnasium. Extending from the sub-basement into the basement, a balcony with seating space for spectators will overlook the swimming pool. A similar balcony is also planned for the gymnasium. The bookstore, a sixty-five-foot shooting range, shower rooms and locker rooms are also among the facilities planned for the basement."[57]

The plans for the recreational facilities turned out to be a bit too ambitious, but the renovations needed for strictly academic pursuits were completed. To finance all of this, the trustees authorized a development campaign and appointed the college treasurer, Frederick M. Schaeberle, as Director of Fund Raising.

While Mr. Schaeberle raised the necessary money, work progressed at 41 Park Row. As the approximately 100 commercial tenants moved out, the renovators set about their work in different parts of the building. Changes in the overall plan were also considered. For example, the trustees discussed the possibility of creating living space for the President in the new building. Given the fact that President Pace spent between twelve and fourteen hours per day at the college and was obliged, at times, to do official entertaining, the idea had merit but no action was taken.

Once the last commercial tenant, the Old Times Cafe, vacated its space on the ground floor of 41 Park Row, the renovations went full speed ahead. By April 1953 the college was holding classes in the building. A temporary certificate of occupancy had been issued by New York City

pending the completion of all planned renovations and
some fire safety improvements.

The well-being of everyone at the college had always
been President Pace's top priority. Before 41 Park Row was
ready for occupancy, the President organized daily fire
safety patrols of 225 Broadway and regular inspections at
41 Park Row to prevent fires during reconstruction of that
building. In 1959, following a devastating fire in a Chicago
school, Pace College examined its fire safety program.
Although an unannounced inspection by the New York
City Fire Department uncovered no violations, the college
augmented its fire prevention program by installing sprin-
klers and automatic detection devices.

Making 41 Park Row safe and attractive certainly
enhanced the college's academic environment, but even
before the final touches, which included a plaque dedicated in 1959, were put on the historic *Times* building, it

41 Park Row and Environs Circa 1960

was evident that Pace needed additional space. In the
spring of 1959, 4000 students and 150 faculty members
were fully utilizing all sixteen floors of the new building.
Despite a public assertion that a day student population of
l,200 would be optimum, the trustees were unwilling to
cap the institution's growth at a time when they felt that
"the opportunities for a downtown university in this City
of New York are almost limitless."[58] They therefore set
about finding new space for expansion.

Discouraged by the high price of land in lower
Manhattan, which at the time cost approximately $45 per
square foot, the trustees heeded President Pace's suggestion
"to muscle in on a Title I Housing Project."[59] This was the
genesis of the Civic Center building. With characteristic
speed when it came to real estate matters, the trustees authorized the architectural firm of Skidmore, Owings & Mer-
rill to undertake a preliminary study for a new Pace campus
and college officials began negotiating with the City of New
York. While it would be years before the Pace Civic Center
building would be erected, the wheels had been set in
motion and once again, Pace College was on the move.

Frederick Schaeberle and Robert Pace

BEYOND THE B.A.

Besides struggling with the institution's very real space needs, in the mid and late 1950s the trustees were understandably concerned about the curriculum. Attaining full collegiate status and securing the right to grant the B.B.A. and B.A. were milestones, to be sure, but what the general public fails to realize about higher education, whether private or public, is that a college or university is in a sense always on trial. Program registrations must be renewed, accreditation maintained and standards upheld. It is truly a never-ending process, one which causes administrators to lie awake nights pondering the query most frequently addressed to them: "What have you done for me lately?" Indeed, in a complex institution, where program registration, accreditation of the professional schools and overall accreditation by both the state and a regional association take place at different times, administrators, and also faculty, feel that they are constantly on the line. This was certainly the case in the mid-1950s when Pace's Liberal Arts curriculum was awaiting renewal.

In keeping with past practices, the State Education Department dispatched a team to investigate the situation at the college. In general, the experts from upstate were impressed. Speaking of the new facility at 41 Park Row, one of them said: "Your new building lends itself very nicely to the needs of the College and it is indeed a considerable improvement over the former location."[60] As for the Liberal Arts curriculum, the team from the state enumerated certain improvements they deemed desirable, such as "a testing program particularly in the area of outcomes," enhancement of the library collection "especially in the fields of mathematics and science," better grade distribution and "the revision of the statement of purposes and objectives of the College."[61] The registration of the Liberal Arts curriculum was, nevertheless, promptly renewed for a period of two years. "The registration is limited to this period," a team member pointed out, "primarily due to the relative newness of this curriculum, and also because

certain phases of the entire College program are in transitional stage...."[62]

In 1956 the registration of the Liberal Arts curriculum was again renewed, as was that of the Business curriculum. A year later the college received permission from the State Education Department to award the degrees of Associate in Arts and Associate in Applied Science. An evening program in Liberal Arts began in 1958 and a Division of General Studies was established in 1959.

The college also moved ahead in the area of teacher education. Reacting to the national shortage of professional educators in 1956, Dr. Mortola wrote, "Coupled with a carefully developed program of professional education courses, our business and liberal arts courses can produce a group of teachers who will bear a different mark and who will bring a fresh and distinctive outlook to the high school classroom."[63] He also noted, "In a period of virtual emergency on a national basis, Pace can perform a worthy and necessary function in helping to provide teachers who have breadth in their general preparation, marketable competence in their specialization, and an understanding of the principles of learning, the behavior of the adolescent, and the methods of instruction which pertain to their special field."[64]

Although the college was eager to begin training future teachers, the State Education Department put the idea on hold for two years following an extensive evaluation of all of the institution's programs in May 1956. The report noted that "the quality of work that has been thus far carried on in English and in the social studies would provide adequate background for teaching these subjects in secondary schools."[65] A follow-up letter from Associate Commissioner Nyquist declared: "Pace College should be encouraged to develop teacher education programs in academic subjects and in business education."[66] But Mr. Nyquist added that the committee felt it would be two years before Pace could offer degrees in Education.

The Associate Commissioner's letter contained more bad news. "The readiness at this time of Pace College to

undertake responsibilities and commitments at the graduate level is highly questionable," declared Mr. Nyquist.[67]
This pronouncement was in response to a trustees' petition
to the Regents for authorization to confer the M.B.A.
Within two years, however, Pace College resubmitted its
petition and was then granted permission to award the
M.B.A.

In 1960 the college began offering a combined B.B.A.—
M.B.A. program. A year earlier, an independent study program for undergraduates was approved and an In-Service
Institute for high school biology teachers was conducted
under a National Science Foundation grant. A 1959 vote
by the Board of Regents to amend the charter of Pace College permitted the school to confer the honorary degrees of
Doctor of Laws (LL.D.) and Doctor of Humane Letters
(L.H.D.). Since 1954, Pace College had been able to confer
the honorary degrees of Doctor of Commercial Science
(D.C.S.) and Doctor of Civil Laws (D.C.L.). Somewhat
different from honorary degrees were the special diplomas
approved by the trustees for former students who had
completed most but not all of the requirements, and had
distinguished themselves in their careers.

By the time Pace College began granting graduate
degrees, the institution had been accredited by the Middle
States Association of Colleges and Secondary Schools. The
quest for accreditation had begun in June 1954 when the
trustees resolved to apply to Middle States "to make an
inspection for the purpose of approving Pace College at the
earliest possible date."[68] At a lengthy board meeting in
September, the trustees discussed a variety of educational
matters, including a tenure plan for faculty. This plan was
the first in Pace's history. The trustees also discussed phasing out the deans of business and liberal arts and upgrad-
ing "some of our present assistants," such as Dr. Jack
Schiff, Chairman of Marketing, and Dr. Joseph Sinzer of
the Department of Social Sciences, and aggressively pursuing Middle States accreditation.[69] Provost Mortola dwelled
on the preparatory work required for a Middle States visit
and underscored the necessity of obtaining accreditation,

*"During Pace's first accreditation review in 1956 by
sister institutions, a member of the team, the Dean of
Liberal Arts at Princeton, said he was impressed that
Pace had nine chief executive officers in the Fortune 500
list, which was more than Princeton, not to mention the
scores of financial vice presidents and partners in the
leading accounting firms."*

(Dr. John E. Flaherty, Robert Pace Memorial)

in part because "our graduates are not being accepted by
some universities for advanced standing or for graduate
studies because Pace College is not fully accredited."[70] It
would be 1957 before a Middle States team evaluated Pace
and, in the meantime, the college undertook a rigorous
self-evaluation guided by consultant C. Richard Pace (no
relation), Associate Professor of Higher Education at Syracuse University.

Of this effort, the Middle States evaluation report noted: "The administrative leaders of the College are sincere
and energetic men who want to see Pace College an honor-
ed member of the education community. Their evaluation
report was scrupulously honest."[71] The report went on to
say: "Conversations with the administrators indicate that
their published statement of policy and objectives is conservative rather than pretentious; that their real ambitions
for the College are higher than those they have given to the
public."[72] Those ambitions did not include enormous
expansion of the student body, however. At least this was
the perception of the Middle States team or visiting committee, chaired by Claude E. Puffer, Vice Chancellor of the
University of Buffalo. The committee's final report stated,
"Some five to ten years ago, Pace College made some very
fundamental decisions concerning its future. In accordance
with this policy, the College is now working to transform
itself into a high-quality, non-residential institution of limited size; to eliminate all traces of its previous proprietary
traditions....Its location and program are most favorable
for a limited size, quality institution. The College officers

and faculty are devoted to this principle. They do not plan to compete with neighboring institutions in size."[73] After reviewing the evaluation report submitted by the visiting committee and considering the Self-Evaluation Question-naire prepared by the college, the Commission on Institu-tions of Higher Education voted, in the spring of 1957, to accredit Pace College. Another milestone had been reached on the long journey from institute to university.

Along the way to Middle States accreditation, the col-lege had undertaken certain reforms aimed at making life easier for its students. For example, in 1952 the block sys-tem of registration was altered to permit students to make their own schedules. A Student Loan Fund was also estab-lished that year. Two years earlier the trustees had autho-rized an endowment campaign.

Another method of bringing in money was to affiliate with outside groups. In 1951 the trustees discussed a possi-ble affiliation with the Dale Carnegie Institute of Effective Speaking and Human Relations. During the 1952-53 aca-demic year, the college offered courses in typing and stenography in conjunction with fourteen business firms which paid the tuition of employees attending Pace.

In 1953 the trustees considered an affiliation with the Ruskin Research Foundation for Bio-Chemical and Medi-cal Research, based in New Rochelle, New York. Simon L. Ruskin, M.D., wrote to Charles T. Bryan, chairman of the Pace board of trustees: "Pursuant to our conversation, I should be delighted to cooperate with your Board ... towards the organization of a medical school...." but the trustees decided not to proceed with this matter.[74] In 1954 the trustees considered the possibility of affiliating with New York Law School. President Pace and Provost Mor-tola "investigated the corporate set-up at Columbia Uni-versity and its affiliated schools and colleges, and had found that the affiliated schools were separate corporate entities."[75] But after learning that "Columbia had some voice in the appointment of the presidents of the affiliated colleges," the chairman of the Pace Board of Trustees con-cluded that "a similar arrangement between Pace College

SAMUEL MILLER

A native New Yorker born in 1892, Samuel Miller was a 1913 graduate of City College. Three years later, he received a law degree from New York Law School and joined the firm of Campbell & Scribner. By 1920 Dr. Miller was a partner in the firm of Scribner & Miller. Although he specialized in criminal law initially, he went on to attain fame as an expert in real estate law and manager of personal estates.

In the 1930's, Dr. Miller was an organizer of the Clinton Trust Company. He subsequently became a Director of this bank and then Chairman of the Board of Directors prior to Clinton's merger with Chase Manhattan. Following the merger of the two institutions, Dr. Miller became a member of Chase Manhattan's Advisory Board.

From 1953 until 1970 Samuel Miller served on the Board of Trustees of Pace University. Less than a year after his election to the board he became its Chairman, a position he held until 1970. As Board Chairman Dr. Miller oversaw a $16,000,000 fund raising campaign and guided Pace through an exciting and challenging period in which the college evolved into a comprehensive university with campuses in New York City and Westchester County and new buildings in both locations.

In recognition of his numerous contributions to Pace, one of the academic buildings on the Pleasantville campus was named Miller Hall upon its completion in 1969. Two programs of special interest to Dr. Miller were located on that campus: the Pace Little School, which was equipped by Dr. Miller, and the School of Nursing, to which he made sizable contributions. In 1966, on the occasion of the groundbreaking for the Civic Center campus, Samuel Miller was awarded an honorary Doctor of Laws degree. Samuel Miller, who was described by his fellow Pace trustee Dr. Mortola as "the gentlest and strongest of men" who "led... with vision, persuasion and good humor," died in 1973.

and New York Law School would not be suitable."[76]

Although the trustees of Pace College were unwilling to enter into any arrangements which would limit the institution's autonomy, they were not unaffected by events which transpired beyond the walls of the college. Both the Korean War and the larger Cold War had an impact on Pace. It was during the Korean conflict that the trustees authorized the establishment of ROTC at Pace. A Civil Defense program was established in 1951. Courses for Army personnel on Governor's Island were also offered during the 1950s. At the same time that it was reaching out to new constituencies, either by dispatching Pace faculty to the Army base on Governor's Island or by encouraging military personnel to journey to Pace's lower Manhattan campus, the college was thinking of utilizing technology to deliver educational services to even larger audiences. For this reason the trustees voted to support "the plan of the Board of Regents for the construction of a network of educational television stations throughout the state as an integral part of the state educational system."[77] According to the board, "the integration of television into the educational system of the state as an important new facility for the improvement of the educational and cultural development of the states is essential in these times...."[78] The full potential of educational television would not be realized even forty years after Pace endorsed the Regents' plan, but the enthusiasm with which the board embraced the state's proposal for an educational television network is a reflection of the board's vision and its commitment to expanding the college's role as a force in higher education in the State of New York.

THE SEMICENTENNIAL OF PACE COLLEGE

The visionary quality of the Pace board was especially apparent during the year-long celebration of the Semicentennial of Pace College. Fully aware of the importance of the fiftieth anniversary of a rapidly developing institution,

the trustees began preparing for the celebration more than a year in advance.

In addition to an intense effort by a planning committee of faculty and administrators, an attempt was made to heighten public awareness of the anniversary and the institution marking it. Towards that end President Robert S. Pace addressed business and financial leaders at the Downtown Athletic Club in December 1955. In his brief overview of the school's history, he stated: "First, for emphasis, I will say what Pace College is not, and never has been. It is not a business school."[79] President Pace pointed out that unlike traditional business schools, class work at Pace, from the very beginning in 1906, "was on the university lecture method, with four-month semesters and two semesters a year."[80] The depth and breadth of the education provided by Pace had enabled many of its graduates to excel in business, according to President Pace, who noted that several hundred Pace alumni were officers of major corporations. The success of Pace graduates would be only one theme of the anniversary, however.

At the start of the Semicentennial year, 1956, President Robert S. Pace and board chairman Samuel Miller formally announced the anniversary theme originated by Dr. Jack Schiff, Chairman of the Marketing Department, "Responsible Participation in an Economy of Free Men."[81] The elaborate printed brochure containing information about conferences and other events planned for the Semicentennial year, which began with the June 1956 commencement exercises and concluded with those of June 1957, underscored certain aspects of the history of the college, stating, "A healthy American economy has been — and continues to be — a matter of special concern to Pace College, since its objective has been to prepare young men and women to take places of leadership in that economy. Hence the Semicentennial theme...has significance for Pace College and the community at large."[82] Elsewhere in the announcement publication, another important point was made, namely that "inherent in the Semicentennial theme is the premise that economic freedom, like political freedom, is not a status but a process. It must be watched and worked at to be earned and kept."[83]

The Semicentennial theme was underscored at a Founder's Day convocation held on October 6, 1956. That morning 400 leaders from government, business and education gathered in the Council Chambers of the New York City Hall, a stone's throw from Pace, to discuss "Man and Management - the Endless Challenge." With Professor Richard M. Matthews, Chairman of Pace's Department of Accounting, Finance and Management, presiding, the morning symposium consisted of several substantive addresses. Dr. John V. Walsh, Professor of Social Sciences at Pace, spoke about "The Problem of Continuity and Control in Political Society," while Dr. Edward H. Litchfield, Chancellor of the University of Pittsburgh, discussed "Continuity and Control in the Modern Corporation."[84] Management consultant, author, and professor of management at New York University's Graduate School of Business Administration, Dr. Peter F. Drucker selected for his topic, "The Commitment of Management."[85] The principal theme of the Semicentennial, "Responsible Participation in an Economy of Free Men," was the subject of Senator Margaret Chase Smith's luncheon address.

Speaking to the more than 600 invited guests seated in various locations throughout the 41 Park Row building, which Pace students dubbed their "skyscraper campus," the Senator analyzed the balance between security and freedom declaring:

> The preservation of individual freedom requires a reasonable minimum of social security, so that the shirkers can compare what is attainable to thrifty workers with what a benevolent government provides for those who take only the advantages, and shirk all the disadvantages of daily earning their way.
>
> No government can devise a system of security that will completely eliminate the struggle in life. The test-proven way of successfully meeting the struggle of life is self-development. The best thing that our government can give to you and me is not a state-controlled security or special advantage, but rather

Honorary degree recipient - Senator Margaret Chase Smith

Honorary degree recipient - Emanuel Saxe

Honorary degree recipient - Theodore S. Repplier

Honorary degree recipient - Peter Drucker

Honorary degree recipients -
E. Litchfield, C. Noyes, T. Repplier, M.C. Smith

Semicentennial formal procession

91

Semicentennial Convocation, City Hall
Council Chambers - R. Matthews, standing; left to right -
J. Walsh, E. Litchfield, P. Drucker

the opportunity for self-development.

You and I cannot escape the fact that the ultimate responsibility for freedom is personal. Our freedoms today are not so much in danger because people are consciously trying to take them away from us, as they are in danger, because we forget to use them. Freedom may be an intangible but like most everything else, it can die because of lack of use. Freedom unexercised may be freedom forfeited.[86]

Senator Smith was awarded an honorary degree at the convocation which followed the luncheon. Other honorary degree recipients were Charles F. Noyes, Chairman of the Board of the Charles F. Noyes Company, Inc., Dr. Emanuel Saxe, Dean of City College's School of Public and Business Administration, Drs. Drucker and Litchfield, and Dr. Theodore S. Repplier, President of the Advertising Council. Dr. Repplier delivered the keynote address at the convocation held at St. Paul's Chapel. The convocation was preceded by a formal procession from the college, through City Hall Park, to St. Paul's. Representatives from 134 colleges and universities throughout the United States donned academic attire for a procession which was as historic as it was colorful. Prior to 1956 the most recent event of this type in lower Manhattan had taken place in 1775!

Once inside the chapel, the distinguished guests heard Dr. Repplier speak about increasing the social responsibility of business in his keynote address, entitled, "As a Nation Thinketh."[87] Dr. Repplier observed that ideas, rather than weapons, would decide the outcome of the Cold War. He spoke about a new form of capitalism, "People's Capitalism," with "increasing social justice for all," which he characterized as "the moral answer to the communists...."[88] According to Dr. Repplier, "It is a variety of capitalism previously unknown, in which the people themselves both power the means of production and share in the rewards."[89] Describing the American economy in 1956 as "neither laissez-faire capitalism nor the harsh, exploitative capitalism of 19th century colonialism," Dr. Repplier said: "It is something so new that many Americans do not know they have it."[90]

When all was said and done on October 6, 1956, the aspect of the celebration which may have touched some members of the Pace community more than anything else was the greeting sent by New York Senator Herbert H. Lehman to the editor of a special anniversary issue of *The Pace Press.* The Senator summed up the aspirations of many at Pace by declaring: "May your next fifty years be as successful as the past fifty have been."[91]

As Pace College entered its second half century, it would cast two searching glances at its past, one at the 1957 commencement, which was the culmination of the Semicentennial celebration, and the other at a gala golden anniversary banquet at the Waldorf-Astoria Hotel on April 27, 1957. Attendance at the banquet almost equaled the college's total population of full-time day students at the time, 650. Fortunately for the staff of the Waldorf, the number did not come close to that of the school's evening population, which totalled 3,300. In any event, as the guests enjoyed a sumptuous repast consisting of prime ribs of blue ribbon beef with all the trimmings, they heard President Robert S. Pace's remarks about the institution's proud history and Vice President and Provost Dr. Edward J. Mortola's comments about recent developments at the

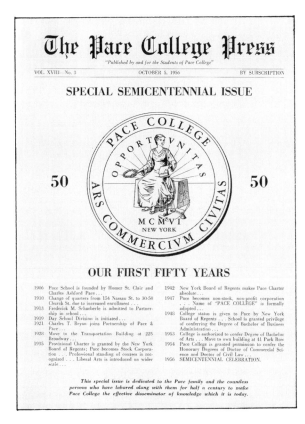

The Pace College Press
"Published by and for the Students of Pace College"

VOL. XVIII—No. 3   OCTOBER 5, 1956   BY SUBSCRIPTION

SPECIAL SEMICENTENNIAL ISSUE

50   **50**

PACE COLLEGE · OPPORTVNITAS · ARS COMMERCIVM CIVITAS · MCMVI NEW YORK

OUR FIRST FIFTY YEARS

1906 Pace School is founded by Homer St. Clair and Charles Ashford Pace...
1910 Change of quarters from 154 Nassau St. to 30-50 Church St. due to increased enrollment...
1913 Frederick M. Schaeberle is admitted to Partnership in school...
1919 Day School Division is initiated...
1921 Charles T. Bryan joins Partnership of Pace & Pace...
1928 Move to the Transportation Building at 225 Broadway...
1935 Provisional Charter is granted by the New York Board of Regents; Pace becomes Stock Corporation... Professional standing of courses is recognized... Liberal Arts is introduced on wider scale...

1942 New York Board of Regents makes Pace Charter absolute...
1947 Pace becomes non-stock, non-profit corporation ... Name of "PACE COLLEGE" is formally adopted...
1948 College status is given to Pace by New York Board of Regents ... School is granted privilege of conferring the Degree of Bachelor of Business Administration...
1953 College is authorized to confer Degree of Bachelor of Arts ... Move to own building at 41 Park Row
1954 Pace College is granted permission to confer the Honorary Degrees of Doctor of Commercial Science and Doctor of Civil Law...
1956 SEMICENTENNIAL CELEBRATION.

This special issue is dedicated to the Pace family and the countless persons who have labored along with them for half a century to make Pace College the effective disseminator of knowledge which it is today.

college and future plans. Keynote speaker Dwayne Orton, editor of IBM's *Think* magazine, analyzed the interdependence of business and education, a familiar theme at Pace and one which would resurface repeatedly as the college moved ahead in its second half-century.

Reminiscent of similar gatherings years earlier, the gala banquet at the Waldorf was a fitting way to wind down the Semicentennial year and to rekindle enthusiasm for the tasks which lay ahead. Pace was on the verge of a quantum leap forward. The momentum for a big jump was surely evident on the night of April 27, 1957. So, too, was the realization that the next decade would be every bit as challenging as the previous fifty years.

FACULTY, STAFF, AND STUDENTS

One of the challenges facing the college as it expanded in the years following the Semicentennial was maintaining the kind of quality which had characterized Pace education in earlier years. With the abandonment of Pace published

texts and the new emphasis on academic freedom, quality control became more difficult. A partial solution to this problem was the establishment of a Faculty Council committee on college teaching methods and examinations in the early 1950s. The committee's "Report on Effective Teaching" in 1952 posed an all-important question, namely: "What makes the great teacher?"[92] The committee's response was:

> Ability to stimulate intellectual curiosity
> Broad and accurate knowledge of subject matter,
> Sympathetic understanding of students,
> Wide range of scholarship,
> Carefully planned daily classwork.[93]

Describing great teachers as "artists in human relations," the report elaborated on methods individual educators could use to enhance their effectiveness in the classroom. Towards that end, Dr. Joseph Sinzer, who had come to Pace in 1950 as Chairman of the Department of Social Sciences and was named Dean of Faculty in 1955, conducted teaching institutes for both new faculty and those who had been at the college for some time. To accommodate both day and evening faculty, the institutes were scheduled from 4:00 to 8:00 p.m. on a Friday. The first part of the program was devoted to classroom management, educational philosophy and teaching techniques and aids. Following a half-hour break for coffee, sandwiches and ice cream, the session resumed with an analysis of public speaking for educators and the organization and preparation of lectures, seminars and discussions.

Explaining his own love of the teaching profession, Dr. Sinzer declared, in an article entitled "Why I Teach," published in the *Pace Alumni Magazine*, "Human communication is so difficult, the true communication of mind with mind so rare, and the challenge of them both so great that the moment the chord of response is struck in my students' consciousness — I experience a lasting happiness."[94]

When it came to communicating with the administration, the faculty sometimes used the American Association of University Professors as an intermediary. A Pace College chapter of the A.A.U.P. was formed in 1951, two years after the establishment of a Faculty Council. The latter was an especially active group whose members were concerned with diverse aspects of college life. The report of the Faculty Council chairman for 1950-51 noted the establishment of committees on faculty members' out-of-class responsibilities, institutional routine and effective teaching techniques. The report also noted: "We may...measure the activities and progress of the Faculty Council by saying that during the past year we have approved sixty-three promotions in faculty rank; discussed forty-two specific items...."[95] During the 1952-53 academic year, criteria for tenure recommended by the Faculty Council were accepted by the board of trustees. Understandably, the Faculty Council was concerned about promotion and tenure,

> "The faculty was small. We had one big faculty room; we didn't have private offices. We were all pushed into the same room, and we developed some very fine friendships. I've got some good friends from out of that room. And there was a good deal of camaraderie. We taught morning and evening, so we lived practically at Pace five days a week. We had a very heavy schedule."
>
> (Dr. Bernard Brennan, Pace Oral History, December 8, 1983)

but they were also interested in the question of compensation, which they felt should be tied to faculty effectiveness. In 1953 the Faculty Council resolved that "salary increments for faculty members be granted on the basis of merit and recommendation exclusively."[96]

The Council also discussed the question of sabbaticals for faculty. With its usual thoroughness, the Council appointed a special committee to research the matter. The committee investigated this type of leave at other institutions and reported that elsewhere sabbaticals were granted for "research, writing, travel, health, and in one case graduate study."[97] Elaborating a bit on the health rationale for a sabbatical, the report noted that leaves were for "either

prevention of breakdowns or recuperation from illness...."[98] The committee recommended that Pace establish a sabbatical policy and that leaves of a half year at full pay and a full year at half pay be granted for "research, writing, (but the recipient shall not be required to use the sabbatical period for the purpose of preparing a dissertation except at his own request), health or travel."[99] The board of trustees of Pace College endorsed the idea of sabbaticals, but in establishing a formal policy they resolved "that sabbatical leaves will be granted only for clearly defined and well-advanced scholarly projects in the areas of research, writing, and publication."[100] Further evidence of the trustees' commitment to scholarship was an appropriation, in 1959, for a newly established Committee on Scholarly Research.

Although scholarly productivity was being emphasized, good teaching was hardly forgotten. In 1959 a donation by an alumnus who preferred anonymity permitted the establishment of the B and J award for excellence in teaching. Over the years the monetary aspect of the award, initially $250, was eliminated, but the recognition itself, known later as the Kenan Award for Outstanding Teaching, retained its original significance.

Since Pace remained primarily a teaching institution, it is not surprising that the board of trustees agreed to allow superior faculty members to remain in the classroom, for a reduced number of hours, past the normal retirement age, by establishing the position of professor emeritus in residence in 1959. Another concession to the faculty was the elimination of the requirement that they pick up and return attendance rosters every day. Presumably, this gave the faculty a bit of extra time, which they could choose to spend in the William A. White Memorial Lounge in the basement of 41 Park Row.

Dedicated to a popular law professor and furnished through a contribution from Pace alumnus Joseph I. Lubin, the lounge was paneled with Tudor oak from the Billingbear House in Berkshire, England. The historic ambience created by the installation of paneling from a house erected in 1480 and restored in 1567 may have had something to do with the rules adopted for the faculty lounge. To create a peaceful environment for the full and part-time faculty using the lounge, telephones, radio and television were not allowed in the subterranean room.

In the 1950s it was advisable for faculty to grab every moment of solitude available to them because much was expected of them outside as well as inside the classroom. They were supposed to participate in co-curricular and extra-curricular events and when attendance lagged, the administration reminded them of their out-of-class responsibilities. For example, in 1950 President Robert S. Pace used the first page of the weekly in-house publication, *Strictly Confidential*, to enumerate upcoming activities ranging from a bowling match to a holiday dance dubbed the Reindeer Trot. The list of events preceded the following message:

BELIEVE IT OR NOT

The reason we are publishing the above list of events is to encourage your attendance and participation....your President felt distinctly lonesome last Saturday night at the Pace College-Yeshiva University basketball game.[101]

Besides being encouraged to attend events, faculty members were urged to become advisors to student organizations. In 1953 *Strictly Confidential* proclaimed: "You can enjoy your hobby and faculty-advise student groups in four student activities NOW: Orchestra, Camera Club, Wall Street Club and Fencing."[102] It seems that everyone from budding photographers to the Manipulators, as the day student members of the Wall Street Club were known, needed some help from the faculty. This was very much in keeping with the administration's belief that student development did not cease at the end of a class or a course but ideally continued outside the classroom. The objective of all of this faculty-student interaction was to prepare the student to compete and excel in the future, or, as President Pace phrased it during an assembly: "We're trying not to raise kennel dogs but Pace Setters!"[103]

A loyal ally in this noble effort, Frederick M. Schaeberle was one of several key administrators to leave the college in the 1950s. Ending a forty-three year association with the institution, Mr. Schaeberle, a good friend to "the thousands of students whose problems he...helped to solve as they came to him for help and advice," stepped down as Treasurer of Pace College in 1954.[104] An administrative reorganization, planned even before Mr. Schaeberle announced his intention to retire, led in 1954 to the departure of Dr. Julius Yourman, Dean of Accountancy Practice and Business, and Dr. Adrian Rondileau, Dean of Liberal Arts. The positions vacated by the two deans had been created in 1950 to assist the Provost, but this arrangement proved unsatisfactory from an administrative standpoint. The post of Dean of Faculty was subsequently created. Dr.

> "The regular schedule included both day classes and evening classes, and it was a five-day week. No days without classes. We got to know our students quite well. We saw a lot of our students, and we saw a lot of our colleagues. We saw a lot of the administration people and the staff people."
>
> (Dr. Bernard Brennan, Pace Oral History, December 8, 1983)

Joseph Sinzer was appointed to fill the new position. He was then named Dean of Academic Affairs, and in 1966, Academic Vice President.

In 1955 an unplanned change occurred with the death of corporate Secretary C. Richard Pace. Associated with the school since 1931, Mr. Pace had made significant contributions to the institution in the areas of publications, graphics and production. Prior to his death, C. Richard Pace had been a member of the Administrative Council, a body established in the 1950s to deal with mainly non-academic issues. The Council concerned itself with such varied matters as Asian influenza inoculations for the Pace community, lobby improvements at 41 Park Row, bonus vacation time for staff members whose time cards reflected perfect attendance and punctuality, and even coffee breaks and smoking.

Long before the health hazards of smoking were apparent, the Administrative Council endorsed a policy prohibiting smoking "in the classrooms, elevators, library and stock rooms. In addition, staff members in public view and serving the students may not smoke while on duty."[105] Reiteration of the school's official policy on smoking was necessitated by what the Council determined was "a general laxity on the part of staff, faculty, and students in compliance with College regulations regarding proper attire and smoking...."[106] Department heads were urged by the Administrative Council "to make certain that members of their staff set an appropriate example in these matters."[107]

The question of proper attire arose repeatedly in the 1950s because of the diametrically opposed perceptions of many day students, who longed for a more relaxed college environment similar to that of other institutions, and the administration, which was determined to maintain a business-like atmosphere in the classrooms. Following a 1951 assembly at which "several students were actually dressed in sweaters and windbreaker-type jackets," Dr. Mortola had the following reminder published in *Strictly Confidential*: "Pace students should be required at all times to give evidence of courtesy, good speech, and proper attire. The dress regulations are certainly not unreasonable. If all of us...will work constantly to see that they are enforced, in the long run our students will profit greatly."[108] Students who did not comply with the regulations, which required a jacket and tie for men during the regular academic year and a conservative shirt and tie in summer, were "to be barred from class and referred to the Deans."[109]

In the evening division the same rules applied. "However, faculty members should use good judgment in enforcing the rules" for, as Dr. Mortola pointed out: "Some evening students come from jobs in working clothes which may not be conventional business attire."[110] Exceptions were also made for students who had earned athletic sweaters.

C. Richard Pace

Women students were expected to dress the way they would for a business office and long before "dress for success" workshops, Professor Alfreda Geiger of the Secretarial Studies program enlisted the aid of one of the world's leading cosmetics companies to do a session on "good grooming for office and interviews."[111] Participants were informed that "suitable wear for the office is a tailored suit or dress, heels, hat and gloves."[112] Reinforcing this conservative approach to dressing, the outside expert informed her female audience that certain colors such as royal blue, chartreuse, lipstick red and orange, should not be worn, but "tiny checks and glen plaid suits are excellent for business wear."[113] Heavy make-up and long hair were out, but "the short and simple hair-do is the preferable style for the office."[114]

In time the administration would compromise on the business of student attire, just as they would comply with a student request made in the mid-1950s that faculty members names be listed in the class schedule. By the time these changes were effected, they were perceived not as capitulations but merely modifications in keeping up with nation-wide trends. They were also a reflection of the growing importance of student government which had begun in earnest in 1949, when underclassmen were permitted to elect class officers, just as the seniors had been doing for some time.

Besides presenting student concerns to the administration, officers were very involved with social events. In the 1950s social activities at the college revolved around the different fraternity-like houses. The more than half-dozen houses were all members of a House Plan Association which coordinated the efforts of the individual houses. Besides the usual dances, the houses sometimes sponsored special weekends. In 1955 a winter weekend at the Hotel Thayer at West Point drew a crowd of over 100 "Paceites." Skiing, skating, horseback riding, and hiking lured participants out of their rooms, but the highlight of the weekend seems to have been the crowning of both a winter weekend queen and a winter carnival queen. The former was a female with junior class standing, while the latter was a male student attired in a turn-of-the-century bathing suit.

More conventional attire was worn by students taking part in the annual Ben Day ceremonies held in the fifties. To mark the birthday of Benjamin Franklin each January, members of the Pace Marketing Club laid a wreath at the statue of the famous eighteenth century statesman and printer. The spot where the statue stands was then known as Printing House Square, due to the concentration of newspapers and book publishers in that area in a bygone era. The wreath laying was traditionally followed by a luncheon. Other popular student activities of the 1950s included the award-winning Pace Press, the student newspaper first published in 1948; an outstanding debate team which repeatedly scored victories over even Ivy League institutions; bridge; chess; photography; art; jazz; accounting, marketing and international relations clubs; the Pace Masquers and Torchbearers, a theatrical group; the Pace Musketeers fencing team; and the Keglers bowling team, which was regarded as one of the best in the country in the 1950s. Besides bowling and fencing, there were three other varsity sports: basketball, baseball and tennis.

The college's array of co-curricular and extra-curricular activities was an inducement for prospective students, but a stronger lure was the success of Pace graduates, including Warren Wayne White, B.A. magna cum laude, class of 1957, the first Pace graduate to receive a Fulbright fellowship, and T. Coleman Andrews, class of 1921, who was named Commissioner of Internal Revenue in 1953. By 1960 there were so many Pace graduates in *Who's Who in America* that the editor of the publication wrote to Dr. Mortola about the unusual "proportion of men who have made their mark in the business world without benefit of antecedents of wealth, position and influence." He continued: "I think the list emphasizes the peculiar niche that Pace College has made for itself in the educational world."[115]

Another help in attracting new students to Pace was the excellent series of career publications distributed to high school guidance counselors and prospective students. Some of these pamphlets were quite general, such as "Career Planning: An Aid for High School Students," while others were very specific, including "Accountancy: Indispensable Tool of Control." Several of the publications were aimed directly at women. They included: "Your Work as a Secretary," "Careers in Secretarial Administration," "The Way to Success in Office Positions," and "Careers for Women." The last of these, published in 1952, was ahead of its time with its mention of the two-income family and its prediction about women's entree to top corporate positions. The pamphlet, which was aimed at tuition-paying parents as well as their offspring thinking about college, declared:

> Women today have strong incentives for discovering a way to obtain a college education. They want to make their mark in the world, belong to a working group, participate in the significant events of the day.
>
> You may have heard the magical phrase: "The two-income family." This also provides an incentive for young women to prepare for career goals. A phenomenon of our times, the two-income family evidently is here to stay.[116]

Just how far could women go in business? According to the pamphlet, "opportunities are almost unlimited for women as well as for men if they have the necessary background and training."[117] The pamphlet continued: A representative of a firm whose policy is to promote the best qualified personnel recently said: "As women with college training, ambition, and stick-to-itiveness enter the company in increasing numbers they will force a recognition of women's ability to hold top jobs, and they will be given them."[118]

For the 1950s this was overly optimistic, but it was not completely Pollyanna-ish. Instead, it was a reflection of Pace founder Homer S. Pace's belief that excellence will triumph and that good solid preparation was the best guarantee of future success. Another of Homer Pace's beliefs was that the school was a closely knit community whose members benefitted from their interaction with one another, even outside the work place. President Robert S. Pace shared this view and in the 1950s endeavored to maximize opportunities for socialization.

In addition to the annual President's party, which was held in the spring and featured good food, conversation and dancing, the school held all-college boat rides which were open to students as well as faculty and staff. Other activities included a faculty bowling team and a faculty-staff theatrical extravaganza known as Potpourri for which acts had to be auditioned and approved at least a week before the actual performance. Cultural activities included art shows organized by Professor Peter Fingesten both on campus and at such off-campus locations as the Bank for Savings. Intellectual stimulation was provided by the Vanderhoof Lecture Series, named for its sponsor, Helen Vanderhoof Pace, Homer S. Pace's widow. When the series debuted early in 1960, a year which would be most significant in the development of Pace College, Dr. Edward J. Mortola discussed the objectives of the new series declaring, "There is the hope and the expectation that many will see the opportunity for exposure to new fields of intellectual interest, the challenge of ideas, the development of new knowledge....No prescribed program of study, no limited period of time can provide sufficient opportunity for the intellectually alert. Intellectual life is a continuing process requiring continuous stimulation."[119] And so it was that Pace College marched into the 1960s with a new intellectual and cultural awareness.

Westchester Campuses

Pace Westchester dates from the establishment of the 200 acre Pleasantville campus in 1963. Briarcliff, five miles distant, was acquired in 1977. The White Plains campus resulted from a consolidation with The College of White Plains in 1975. It is the site, also, of The School of Law and a short distance to the graduate center.

Pleasantville

Gannet Center, Pleasantville

Costello House, Pleasantville

Buchsbaum House, Pleasantville

Choate House, Pleasantville

Environmental Center, Pleasantville

Willcox Hall, Pleasantville

Townhouse, Residence Halls, Pleasantville

Marks Hall, Pleasantville

Mortola Library, Pleasantville

Lienhard Hall, Pleasantville

Campus Center, Pleasantville

Briarcliff

The Hastings Center, Briarcliff

Residence Hall, Briarcliff

Dow Hall, Briarcliff

White Plains

School of Law, White Plains

Preston Hall, White Plains

Lubin Graduate Center, White Plains

4

ENTER EDWARD J. MORTOLA

In September 1960, as Pace College began its fifty-fourth year, the school's weekly *Newsletter* published the following statement:

WELCOME AND GREETINGS.....

> Familiar things are happening in our College — standing room only in the Admissions Office, the last minute reshuffling of schedules to provide for an expanding student body, the cheerful sight of faculty, staff and students busily working together to register returning students, and plasterers, carpenters, electricians, et cetera, virtually climbing over one another in the frantic effort to complete construction work before the opening of classes. This is that time of year that stimulates and vitalizes — because it is the prelude to another year of constructive effort — and, more important, because it brings back home all of our faculty and staff for renewed effort in the dedicated work that makes us one family with one purpose.

> In my first official greeting to you as your President, I want to welcome you warmly and to tell you how happy I am to be with you all again.

> —Edward J. Mortola, President[1]

Although the formal inauguration of Dr. Edward J. Mortola as Pace's third President was several months away, the new chief executive officer was already on the job. Hardly the new kid on the block, Dr. Mortola had been at Pace for more than a dozen years before being named President. Before coming to Pace, as Assistant Dean, in 1947, he had been Assistant Registrar at Fordham University, where he had received his B.A., M.A. and Ph.D. degrees. After serving as Assistant Dean at Pace for two years, Dr. Mortola was named Dean in 1949, Provost in 1950, and Vice President in

Ground breaking for Civic Center Campus
Dr. E.J. Mortola: U.S. Vice President, Hubert H. Humphrey
and N.Y. City Mayor, John V. Lindsay

1954. During the next six years, he worked hand in hand with faculty and fellow administrators to strengthen and enlarge Pace College. All this hard work paid off.

By the fall of 1960, Dr. Mortola's freshman semester as President, the College "enrolled its largest day class of full-time freshmen since the post-war period of inflated college enrollments."[2] Total full-time student enrollment increased 31 percent from the previous year while part-time enrollment showed a 10 percent gain. In all, there were 1003 full-time and 3614 part-time students. The graduate programs in Business had attracted 234 students and the Liberal Arts were flourishing on the undergraduate level. Indeed, a survey of full-time undergraduates, done in the fall of 1960, revealed that student interest in non-business courses was high.

Pace College certainly seemed to be on its way to becoming a comprehensive institution, not only in terms of enrollment and course offerings, but also in the area of scholarly productivity. By November 1960, there were enough published authors among the faculty to justify a display of books in the west window next to the Park Row entrance of the college. The exhibit, which was planned as part of the Presidential inauguration, was limited to books published since 1955. Authors were urged to lend copies of their works and to consider donating them to the library after the exhibit had been dismantled. Organizing the book display, the post-inaugural reception and dinner and the ceremony itself were top priorities of administrators and staff in the autumn of 1960.

The actual inauguration took place early in 1961. The big day was January 19, 1961, twenty-four hours before John F. Kennedy was sworn in as President of the United States. With Grace Lamacchia as Student Marshal, the formal procession of colorfully gowned faculty, administrators, student leaders, and guests from colleges near and far made its way from 41 Park Row to the Council Chambers in the historic New York City Hall building. There they heard Pace's new president, who only a short time before had been elected Chairman of New York State's Commission of Independent Colleges and Universities, speak about "a dual need on the part of educated man in the 1960s for competence in dealing with detail and system and for coexisting qualities of mind that will permit him to engage in activities which depend upon imagination and creativity."[3] In the course of his address, Dr. Mortola provided his audience with a little historical background:

> When Pace began a half century ago, its major concern was for technique - system - detail - even conformity. The need then was for men and women trained in the tools of business which were related primarily to control - not to a conceptual attack on problem solving. Today, in a new setting, this institution is devoting its energies to building programs in the liberal arts and sciences, insisting that even its business students devote a major part of their productive study to the liberal arts, and seeking graduate students who are the products of programs that are primarily liberal. Our viewpoint now encompasses the parallel needs for training in the systematic and the specific as the foundations of organization and productivity, and for education in

the broadening and exciting liberal studies as the whetstones of the imagination.[4]

At the conclusion of his address, Dr. Mortola revealed his agenda for the Pace College of the future by declaring:

> This then is the task we set for ourselves in our college in the metropolis - to be preoccupied with the life of the mind; to aspire to the development of human potentialities to their fullest, to heights undreamed of yesterday and only faintly recognized today; to dedicate ourselves to encourage in the minds of men and women the qualities which encompass the specific and the unlimited, the conforming and the creative; to use our knowledge and our convictions to open the minds of our students to truth, to lead them to new power through knowledge and to new happiness through understanding of themselves and their complex natures of mind and spirit.[5]

The vision of Edward J. Mortola, which was so evident in his inaugural address, was not something which emerged, fully developed, on that wintry day in 1961 when he was installed as Pace's third President. It had been evolving, developing and maturing over the years. Now and then, it could be glimpsed even outside the institution where Edward J. Mortola was destined to spend the remainder of his extraordinary career in educational administration. A year before his inauguration, for example, in a talk to the Westchester Association of Adult Education Directors, Dr. Mortola peered into the future and declared:

> Adult education wherever and however it may be provided has as its ultimate function the liberalizing of the human mind. The greatest issue with which we must be concerned is that of keeping adult men and women concerned with continuing education. A world changing so rapidly that we can scarcely comprehend the changes — much less adapt to them — requires that people in our democracy will have minds that are open and eager for new knowledge. Adults may be drawn to the classroom by the hope of vocational or social advancement...but whatever we do, we have a responsibility not only to teach what they immediately want to know, but to open

up before them the possibility of continuing personal development in the world of ideas, issues, and conflict....Our aim must be to help them to be complete adults - emotionally, creatively, and intellectually.[6]

Two years into his Presidency, Dr. Mortola expressed similar views to alumni volunteers who were helping with the College's fund raising efforts. To them he said:

> Education has become one of the largest and most critical aspects of our nation's strength. We depend more and more on education to do the job that must be done in terms of advancing our economy and our national security. We have a responsibility to continue to grow and provide the kind of education that means the most for America's development. We can't stop; rather, we must provide today for the next ten years, and then about five years from now we will have to start thinking again about the next ten years after that.

> Education, including Pace College, must ever be sensitive to the needs of society, must be willing to reassess its contribution, and chart new plans for meeting the current and future needs of our youth and our nation.[7]

Under the leadership of Dr. Edward J. Mortola, Pace College was indeed able to chart exciting new plans for the decade of the sixties and beyond. In many ways, Dr. Mortola proved to be a catalyst actualizing the potential of his associates in higher education, both inside and outside Pace, for the purpose of enhancing quality and providing opportunities for countless students. On October 20, 1965, Dr. Mortola's efforts were recognized at a dinner held in his honor at the Plaza Hotel. The Pace College Alumni Association, faculty, administrative staff, and friends of Pace College joined in tribute to President Mortola on that occasion, declaring:

> In honoring Edward J. Mortola we are also recognizing the emergence of Pace College, under his leadership, as an institution of increasing service and prestige in the community.

> Building on the solid foundation laid down by members of the Pace family, Dr. Mortola, as President of the College, has infused alumni, faculty, staff, and

students with his own vitality and spirit to the end that Pace may meet the educational demands thrust upon it by an evolving world. His vision and dynamic leadership have seen the day-student body triple and the total enrollment of the College double in the last eight years.[8]

When the honoree rose to respond to the many sincere words of praise spoken that evening, he pointed out that the achievements of the past few years had been the result of a collaborative effort, "for Pace is, and always will be, the result of innumerable contributions on the part of thousands of students, teachers, administrators, alumni, trustees and friends."[9] He also peered into his crystal ball to predict that Pace College was about to enter a period of adolescence, an exciting but challenging time which would lead eventually "to a maturity of ever greater dignity, prestige, and accomplishment."[10] The institution's adolescence

Mortola Family At Testimonial
Doreen, Elaine, Edward and Doris

would take the form of vast physical expansion, coupled with curricular enhancement.

Through it all, Pace College benefitted from the advice generously dispensed by the business and professional people who served on its advisory boards for both business and the liberal arts. These people, described by trustee Joseph I. Lubin as individuals "who were willing to help

Leader in Management
Thomas A. Murphy, Charles H. Dyson, John F. McGillicuddy,
John D. DeButts

Pace develop," dispensed advice about specific academic programs and assisted in promotion and fund raising.[11] They also lent a helping hand with the gala Leader in Management dinner, an event which ranks second only to the unified commencements held at Madison Square Garden in the 1980s in terms of magnitude. Begun in 1962 as a way of honoring a business leader and, at the same time, heightening the institution's visibility, the Man in Management award was renamed Leader in Management in the 1970s. Recipients of the award, presented at a gala dinner in the grand ballroom of the Waldorf-Astoria, have been chief executives of leading American corporations.

Another tangible link between the College and the corporations was the Executive Research Conference established in 1962. The Conference was an activity of the Pace College Foundation, a non-profit educational corporation authorized by the Board of Regents in 1962. The Foundation's charter application declares:

> The purposes for which such corporation is to be formed are to provide, create, conduct, supervise and administer research activities and facilities, conferences and publications in connection with the programs of Pace College, for the advancement of education generally and for the benefit of groups, individuals, associations, institutions, business, commercial and professional organizations and any and

all others interested in research and educational activities; and to receive and use money and property, real and personal, of all kinds for the purposes of Pace College and the Foundation.[12]

The Executive Research Conference was a membership program open to a limited number of companies interested in having the College research specific business problems, such as the one Pace tackled for the National Biscuit Company: "Effects of a Morning High Protein Snack on the Manipulative and Mental Efficiency of Young Teenage Students."[13] In 1966 the Executive Research Conference was transferred from the Pace College Foundation to the College's Office of Research. Income and expenditures for all research, including outside projects of the type previously administered by the Pace College Foundation, were made part of the institution's regular budget. The Foundation itself was retained as a separate corporation, however.

PACE BRANCHES OUT: THE PLEASANTVILLE CAMPUS

At the very time the College was experimenting with various models for research, it was undertaking a far-reaching program of physical expansion which would result in a Pace presence outside Manhattan for the first time in many decades. The impetus for the expansion was the gift of a

Mr. and Mrs. Wayne Marks

> *"And then somebody — and I think it was Dr. Mortola, probably — said, there is not a four-year accredited coeducational secular school in Westchester. Why don't we open a branch? I don't know if this sounds like Mickey Rooney and Judy Garland, 'Let's Put On a Show,' but it happened. I think probably it came from a chairmen's meeting."*
>
> (Dr. John Flaherty, Pace Oral History, February 17, 1984)

generous alumnus, Wayne Marks, class of 1928. Dr. Marks, Vice Chairman of the General Foods Corporation, and his wife, Helen, donated their sprawling home on Bedford Road in Pleasantville to Pace in 1962. There was only one string attached to the gift: an informal understanding that a gigantic copper beech tree near the house, which today is the focal point of the upper campus, would remain undisturbed. The house itself, though, has enjoyed anything but a tranquil existence over the years.

Originally constructed to house patients being treated for mental and nervous disorders at Dr. George C. S. Choate's Sanitarium, the Marks residence had been a wing of Choate House, a building Pace College would later add to its Westchester holdings. One of Dr. Choate's most famous patients was the crusading newspaper publisher and politician, Horace Greeley. Following his defeat for the Presidency of the United States in 1872, an exhausted Greeley, who had a farm in nearby Chappaqua, checked into Dr. Choate's Sanitarium, where he died a few weeks later. Dr. Choate himself passed away in 1896, but the Sanitarium remained open for another decade.

In 1909 Dr. Choate's widow had the sizable wing her husband had constructed moved to its present location closer to Bedford Road. Her intention was to occupy the house while turning over her original home to her newly married son. The actual job of detaching and moving the wing from the original home, built by shoe manufacturer Samuel Baker in 1867, began on New Year's Day 1909 and lasted until summer. Considerably heavier than the contractor estimated, the house, pulled by teams of horses, inched along. Getting it past the pond, while at the same time avoiding the beautiful old trees that Mrs. Choate did not want disturbed, were major challenges.

When the house was at last on its new foundation, the interior had to be completely redone. It was well worth the effort, though, because Mrs. Choate lived there until her death, at age 95, in 1926. Thereafter the house had three more private owners: banker Dunham B. Scherer, advertising executive Lewis H. Titterton, and Wayne C. Marks.

After Mr. Marks presented his alma mater with this extraordinary gift, the College gave serious consideration to offering a two-year program in Westchester. The hope was that, upon completion of all lower division courses, students would transfer to Pace in Manhattan. In November 1962 the State Education Department approved an amendment of the Pace College charter to permit the school to "operate an institutional Branch in Westchester

William F. McAloon

County."[14] There was one slight problem, however. Despite the fact that Dr. Marks's generosity had enabled the College to purchase an additional 4.2-acre parcel contiguous with the Marks estate, the school owned only 11.59 acres. The Town of Mount Pleasant zoning law required 15 acres for the type of construction Pace envisioned for the site. In February 1963 Pace went before the town's zoning board of appeals and obtained the necessary variance to permit construction of two Georgian style brick buildings, one on either side of the Marks mansion.

Two months later, a ground-breaking ceremony took place; a cornerstone ceremony was held just a month after the formal ground-breaking. In addition to honoring Dr. and Mrs. Marks, the cornerstone ceremony recognized the contribution of Dr. Charles H. Dyson, whose generous donation funded the science building then under construction. Throughout the spring and summer of 1963, construction proceeded almost without a hitch. Even the weather cooperated. The project had to be shut down for only one day because of inclement weather.

Mr. and Mrs. Charles H. Dyson

"*When Westchester started, we staffed it with New York people and there was a continuity of culture.*"
(Dr. John Flaherty, March 9, 1990)

In mid-summer Dr. William McAloon, who had been appointed Dean of Pace College Westchester, took up residence on the campus to supervise the construction work and continue the job, begun in the spring, of recruiting 100 day and 125 evening students for September 1963. Enrollment exceeded the goals. The freshman class totalled 143 day students. Evening enrollment was 265. Equally impressive was the fact that the evening students were employed by 100 different companies. In addition to the regular day and evening students, 50 women were attending either day session classes or a special lecture series on archaeology offered in the afternoon.

The campus to which all of these people came on opening day, September 16, 1963, was still an active construction site, but Dyson Hall, with its science laboratories and classrooms, was sufficiently completed, at a cost of $15 per square foot, to permit occupancy. When one considers that the building had been erected in only five months, this is no small achievement. Students attending classes during Pace's freshman semester in Westchester joked about driving over dirt roads on campus in the morning and heading home over blacktop in the early afternoon, but, at the very least, the furious pace of construction was a sure sign that

Mr. and Mrs. Byron Willcox

BYRON C. WILLCOX

The name Willcox has a familiar ring to students on Pace's Pleasantville campus. Willcox Hall, named for trustee and alumnus Byron C. Willcox, who, in recognition of the efforts of Dr. Mortola, presented Pace with a gift of $1,200,000 to cover the entire cost of Willcox Hall, has long been a significant building on this bucolic campus. More importantly, it is a lasting reminder of the multi-faceted man who managed to combine a highly successful career in business with a lifetime avocational interest in art.

In his search for opportunity, this Lisbon, Connecticut, native abandoned the countryside and headed for New York City. Arriving in Manhattan less than a decade after the Pace brothers had opened their school, he enrolled at Pace Institute and completed the course of studies in 1916. Although he went on to earn baccalaureate and doctoral degrees in law, Mr. Willcox always felt it was his Pace training which had given him the competitive edge. A C.P.A. in New York and New Jersey, as well as an attorney, Byron Willcox was associated with two of the country's top accounting firms: Touche, Niven, Bailey and Smart, and Lybrand, Ross Brothers and Montgomery. Thereafter he was Vice President and member of the board of directors of The Grolier Society, Inc., the highly respected publishing firm best known for the Encyclopedia Americana and The Book of Knowledge.

Despite the demands of business, Dr. Willcox found time to serve as a Pace trustee from 1956 until 1964. He was also First Vice President and member of the Board of Directors of the YMCA of Ridgewood, New Jersey and President of the Board of Education of Hasbrouck Heights, New Jersey. Given his genuine interest in young people, it is not surprising that Byron Willcox endowed a scholarship fund to enable economically disadvantaged sophomores from New Jersey and Connecticut to continue their education at Pace. In 1963 his alma mater awarded Byron C. Willcox an honorary doctorate in Commercial Science.

the College was an institution on the move.

So, too, was the incredible turnout at an open house held at Pleasantville in November 1963. Four hundred people attended, but before the school could accept additional students, more classrooms were needed. Therefore, in May 1964, construction of Willcox Hall began. Bryon Willcox, class of 1916 and a trustee of Pace College, had pledged $1,000,000 to his alma mater prior to his death in 1963. His estate made the actual donation, and the building named in honor of Mr. Willcox was finished in 1965. At that time the cafeteria was moved from the Marks mansion to Willcox Hall; the library was moved to Willcox from Dyson, and the remainder of Willcox was used for classrooms, the bookstore, a gymnasium, and offices. Inter-office mail service between the New York and

> *"What I found very exciting was that one could develop personal relationships with students. We had a great deal of leeway. No one ever told me what to teach."*
> (George Shanker, March 26, 1990)

Westchester campuses on Tuesdays, Wednesdays, and Thursdays commenced in late September 1965. Earlier that month, in its progress report to the Middle States accrediting body, Pace was able to proudly report that "the College now has 17 classrooms, 1 physical science laboratory and 1 biology laboratory. In addition, there is adequate space for faculty offices, two student lounges, a Student Activities Office and a large reception room in the original Marks' residence. Parking facilities for 300 cars, a large athletic field and three tennis courts have also been provided."[15] In January 1965 the charter of Pace College had been amended to permit the granting of the B.B.A. degree in Westchester. The overwhelmingly positive response to the institution and the tremendous increase in the number of students wishing to earn the baccalaureate degree in a suburban setting had caused the trustees to

rethink their original plan to grant only associate degrees in Westchester. Not only did they move ahead with a full four-year program, but in the spring of 1965 Saturday classes were introduced in Westchester.

At this time the College also attempted to acquire additional property on the other side of Bedford Road. This 400-acre parcel, known as Graham Hills, extended down as far as the Hawthorne interchange. Although the land was owned by the County and administered by its Department of Parks, Recreation and Conservation, it had been considered as a possible site for a new campus of the State University of New York. When S.U.N.Y. chose Purchase, Dr. Mortola wrote to Westchester County Executive Edwin G. Michaelian, "You will recall that, prior to acquisition by the County, we had begun negotiations to acquire some part of this property. Upon learning of the County's interest, we withdrew in order to avoid causing any embarrassment to County officials who had been so helpful to Pace in its development in Westchester."[16] Dr. Mortola informed the County Executive that Pace College was interested in acquiring 100 acres of the Graham Hills property in order "to expand...to a total day enrollment of 2,000."[17] In May 1965 the Board of Trustees resolved to authorize the College "to make application to acquire at least 100 acres of the Graham Hill site in Westchester County."[18]

Twenty-five years later Pace had still not expanded to the other side of Bedford Road but, in the interim, it acquired additional land contiguous with the original campus. By the summer of 1968 Choate House was being transformed into a dormitory and thought was being given to renovating Smith House for use as an executive conference center. But it had not been all smooth sailing. There had been a legal dispute with the Briarcliff School Board involving property desired by both the school district and Pace College. A compromise was ultimately reached, and in November 1968 Pace was able to reveal its master plan for the Pleasantville campus. Addressing the board of directors of the Westchester County Association, a power-as construction proceeded on the other new additions to the campus, Pace College acquired the Robert Green property in Pleasantville, thereby enlarging the campus by thirteen more acres.

Students arriving for the 1970-71 academic year were greeted by not only a bigger campus, but also a newly inaugurated mini-bus service between Pace Westchester and Pace New York. The bus departed from Pleasantville five days a week at 12:30 p.m., made the reverse trip leaving New York at 2:30, and departed from Pleasantville on its final run of the day at 6:15 p.m. Curiously, the first published schedule indicated that the estimated travel time between Pleasantville and New York in the afternoon was one hour! The approximate time for the evening trip to Manhattan was one hour and fifteen minutes. Presumably, members of the Pace community who ended up sitting in traffic rather than breezing right through as the schedule implied had time to contemplate the incredible growth of the university in the 1960s and early 70s. Anyone who has been around Pace, even for a short while, quickly realizes that the institution is constantly evolving. Both historically and contemporaneously, Pace is a dynamic environment.

Indicative of that dynamism was the dedication of Lienhard Hall in December 1971. Named for Gustav O.

Dr. Samuel Miller laying cornerstone for Miller Hall at Pleasantville

ful and influential organization of businesses and corporations, Dr. Mortola spoke about the new dormitories which would rise on part of the College's 175-acre campus by 1970, plans for a student center, and another classroom building to complement Miller Hall, then under construction. He summarized developments at Pace by saying, "The success which the college has already enjoyed and the warm reception it has received in Westchester gives us confidence that it will succeed. Already the college has an enrollment of 1,700 students. It now has its third building under way and within the next three years four additional buildings will be completed."[19]

One of those buildings, Miller Hall, named after Samuel Miller, Chairman of the Board of Trustees, was in partial use by the fall of 1969. During the spring of 1970,

"...I think it's a fundamental problem that every multi-disciplinary campus has, whether it's Penn State or Ohio State, Michigan State. How do you keep this unity within diversity? And it's very difficult. I think it was through the strong commitment of Dr. Mortola and Dr. Schiff that held us together. I think there are a tremendous number of centrifugal forces happening that are natural there. I'm sure there are a good many people from Pace who couldn't find Westchester on their own, and Westchester would return the compliment. I think that the autonomy is developing. I know it's very hard to keep it together as you grow. I think it's a serious, serious problem that you have. I don't know what the answer is."

(Dr. John Flaherty, Pace Oral History, February 16, 1984)

GUSTAV O. LIENHARD

Although Gustav O. Lienhard had spent his childhood Hastings-on-Hudson, he returned to the city of his birth to study accounting. The school he chose was Pace Institute and after graduating in 1926, he joined the accounting firm of Pace, Gore and McLaren.

In 1932 Dr. Lienhard became an accountant in the comptroller's department of Johnson & Johnson. By 1933 he was Assistant Treasurer of a Johnson & Johnson subsidiary, the Chicopee Manufacturing Corporation. Within a decade, Dr. Lienhard became executive vice president of Chicopee and in 1945 was named president of the company and member of the board of directors of Johnson & Johnson, the parent corporation. In the mid-1950s, this outstanding Pace alumnus became chairman of the board of Chicopee and President and general manager of another Johnson & Johnson subsidiary, the Permacel Tape Corporation. Within a year, Gustav Lienhard was named chairman of Permacel's Board of Directors and a member of the executive committee of the Johnson & Johnson board of directors. In 1963 Dr. Lienhard became chairman of the board of Johnson & Johnson. Two years later, he was elected president of Johnson & Johnson Worldwide. Upon his retirement from this position, in 1971, Dr. Lienhard became president of the Robert Wood Johnson Foundation.

Despite the demands of business, Gustav Lienhard found time for community service which took the form of membership on the boards of the College of Medicine and Dentistry of New Jersey and Robert Wood Johnson University Hospital. Dr. Lienhard also served as president of the hospital.

From 1965 until 1987 Gustav Lienhard was a member of the Pace board of trustees. In recognition of his outstanding contributions to his alma mater, he was awarded an honorary doctorate of Commercial Science in 1960. In 1975 the University's school of nursing was named for him. Gustav Lienhard died in 1987, at the age of 81.

Lienhard, class of 1926, who served as president of the Robert Wood Johnson Foundation and a Pace trustee, the building contained classrooms and laboratories for the School of Nursing. The following December the Student Center was dedicated. Six months earlier, the person who had supervised both the physical and academic expansion of the Pleasantville campus, Dr. William F. McAloon, retired and was succeeded by physicist and former Columbia University administrator Dr. Warren Goodell who, in 1977, was succeeded by Dr. Thomas P. Robinson.

Dr. McAloon bade farewell to Pace at the 1972 commencement exercises on the Pleasantville campus. Since 1968, there had been separate commencements for New York and Westchester. In Pleasantville, the ceremonies took place outdoors, but in June 1972 a heavy downpour sent graduates, faculty, administrators, trustees and guests scurrying for the auditorium. Despite the unplanned interruption, Dr. McAloon was able to deliver a farewell address which contained a plan for Pace's future in Westchester County: "Part of that blueprint should be a dedication to become an institution of higher learning where scholarship is prized. Another part of the blueprint should be the continuing tradition that we have here at Pace to become a place of warm human influences that merge into an experience never to be forgotten by our graduates."[20]

BUILDING FOR THE FUTURE: THE NEW MANHATTAN CAMPUS

During the years that Dr. McAloon was guiding the development of Pace Pleasantville, the New York campus was keeping up with Westchester in terms of growth and change. Convinced that the College had an important role to play in Manhattan, President Mortola envisioned a vital and considerably larger New York campus. In his annual report to the trustees, in November 1960, Dr. Mortola said:

> In the community immediately surrounding Pace, an amazing renaissance is taking place. Under the lead-

ership of such men as David Rockefeller and John Butt of the Lower-Downtown Manhattan Association, a tremendous building program has been stimulated. Not only the great Chase-Manhattan Building, but also Dun & Bradstreet, Western Electric, RCA, many insurance firms, and others too numerous to mention have taken part in the great Lower Manhattan building boom. Housing, too, now plays an increasingly important part in the Downtown community, and with the creation of the Civic Center, the future erection of a new Municipal Office Building, and a new Federal Center, government, too, is adding to the spirit of vital growth that characterizes this area. Pace must find a way to build in this bustling community. New offices mean more people in evening classes, and expansion to meet the increasing demand will be inevitable. This will be especially true within a few years when Pace becomes the only undergraduate evening College in Downtown New York as Fordham University moves its City Hall Division to its new Midtown Campus at Lincoln Square.[21]

That Pace College needed additional room in lower Manhattan was undeniable. Enrollment was at a post-war high and the 41 Park Row building was bursting at the seams. The long-term solution was an impressive new

Civic Center campus cornerstone ceremony
Allan Rabinowitz, President Pace Alumni Association; Thomas McShane, Chairman, Faculty Council; Dr. Edward J. Mortola; Edward Steiniger, Trustee; Samuel Miller, Chairman, Board of Trustees

building but, in the interim, the classroom shortage problem had to be solved. One way out of this dilemma was to lease space at 150 Nassau Street. The College attempted to secure 15,000 square feet of sublet space from an insurance company which, in the early 1960s, occupied several floors of the 150 Nassau Street building, but Pace ended up buying the entire building, renovating part of it for use by the College and leasing the remainder to outside tenants.

By the start of the spring semester in 1965 twenty-three classrooms, a student lounge, and faculty and counseling offices were in use at 150 Nassau Street. The previous year Pace had rented space at 225 Broadway for use by the Graduate School. Renovations at 41 Park Row, in addition to the utilization of space at 140 Nassau Street and 38 Park Row (both of which were purchased in 1972) and 148 Nassau Street, enabled the College to function efficiently through the early 1970s. The crowning jewel of the New York campus, the Civic Center Building, was completed in 1969.

The Civic Center Building was much more than a structure designed to house classrooms, offices and a dormitory. Even before ground was broken for its construction, the building was envisioned as an integral part of a major urban redevelopment project for lower Manhattan. Known as the Brooklyn Bridge Southwest Title I Project, the redevelopment scheme was to have included New York Law School, which withdrew before the project reached the hearings stage. The South Bridge Towers middle income housing complex remained part of the project, however, as did a new Beekman Downtown Hospital. For a time, hospital and college officials considered the possibility of jointly undertaking construction of a parking facility. Pace decided not to go ahead with this, but the College's original plan for the erection of a multi-use building was unveiled in May 1966 when a detailed model of the $12 million campus center, designed by the architectural firm of Eggers & Higgins, was placed on display.

In December 1966 a gala ground-breaking ceremony was held. The principal speaker at the ceremony was

Vice President Hubert H. Humphrey, who didn't seem to mind the fact that the temperature had plummeted from a balmy 60 degrees the day before to 29 degrees with frigid winds. Addressing a crowd of l,000 seated under a green tent on William Street, just across from 154 Nassau Street where the New York Tribune building was being demolished to make way for Pace, Mr. Humphrey said that Pace was "where it ought to be — where the action is."[22] During the actual ceremony, there was considerable action in the vicinity. A wrecking ball and bulldozers were busily demolishing the Tribune building while, at the same time, providing some less than desirable background noise for the ceremony. A block and a half away from the speakers' platform, 35 placard-carrying antiwar protesters were being held back by the New York City police as they demonstrated against the bombing of North Vietnam.

None of this prevented Vice President Humphrey or New York Mayor John V. Lindsay from completing their remarks. When the platform party descended to participate in the actual ground breaking, Lindsay playfully held reporters at bay by threatening to shower them with dirt for having climbed onto chairs, while almost knocking people over, in order to get pictures of the historic event. Quite aside from the fact that Pace's new Civic Center complex would include the first student dormitory built in lower Manhattan since the eighteenth century (when Columbia University, then known as Kings College, was located in the area), the ground breaking was historic because of the nature of the new building which would rise on Nassau Street. A construction industry publication described the structure in glowing terms:

> The horizontal five-story "teaching element" structure will be so constructed as to block city street noises from filtering into classrooms... Corridors along the perimeter of the building will serve as a "sound moat" to exclude the noises of surrounding city streets.
> Stairways and utility rooms will also be located at intervals around the building's perimeter, rather than

"I don't know whether it's fair to say that Pace Institute had a, I don't know what your words were, close personal relationship with the students. My impression was that Pace Institute — my impression — as a proprietary institution took a different attitude toward the students than a typical academic institution would take. I think the attitude was one of concern for the growth and survival of the enterprise. And the enterprise could survive and grow only if the students performed well. So that it seemed to me, this is my own perception, the attitude of Pace Institute was you came to Pace Institute. You were preparing for the accounting profession and you were paying the Institute to prepare you for that profession. And the Institute was going to do the best job it could to prepare you for that profession. But you had to contribute, too. You had to work hard. You had to attend classes. And if you didn't work hard and if you didn't attend classes and hence were not successful on the accounting examination, this would not help the reputation of the Institute. So that the attitude was somewhat "hard nosed." You either performed, did well and succeeded, or else they didn't want you as a student. It seems to me that that attitude was softening to a degree, or modified to a degree, was made to conform more with the attitudes of typical academic institutions or some claim by Dr. Mortola, who has a strong inclination toward good personal relationships. I think fundamentally he feels that the students and the faculty and the staff are part of a family. He says this all of the time and he genuinely feels this way. And so, he has, from the outset, tried to create that kind of a feeling — a familial feeling — within the institution. I think that began to grow with his presence."

(Dr. Jack Schiff, Pace Oral History, June 17, 1983)

placed in the core of the building as is usually done. This will permit later expansion without interruption of use of any part of the building.[23]

Two and a half years later, the new building was a reality. The dedication took place on September 14, 1970; nearly two years earlier, on October 8, 1968, what had been known as Printing House Square, just outside the Civic Center complex, was appropriately renamed Pace Plaza. It had been only 62 years since the young accountant Homer St. Clair Pace had rented an office a stone's throw from here. In a little more than six decades the institution he and his brother founded had become a vital part of the metropolis.

EDUCATIONAL CHALLENGES AND ACHIEVEMENTS

In the early days, the school Homer and Charles Pace had established stressed theory and methodology. The educational process was more important than bricks and mortar. Six decades later Pace College was striking a balance between physical expansion and sound education. The College's goal of becoming a comprehensive institution necessitated the introduction of new courses, majors and entire degree programs, on both the undergraduate and graduate levels. As the 1960s began, emphasis was placed on graduate education. An M.B.A. in Management was introduced in the fall of 1960. Spearheading the program was Professor Richard M. Matthews, Chairman of the Department of Accounting, Finance, and Management, who, together with colleagues in the School of Business plus members of the College's Advisory Boards, spent two years planning the program. Understandably enthusiastic about the new M.B.A., the *Pace Alumni Magazine* declared, "With a long-standing reputation in the field of business education, Pace College is now adding another meaningful phase to its curriculum. Management is considered to be the capstone of a business career. Course work alone is not considered sufficient to prepare for any managerial role, but it will, in addition to vicarious experience in the business community, give the student an opportunity to broaden his intellectual horizons, to gain deeper insight and maturity, and thus enable him to make the sound decisions required of an effective manager."[24]

Besides new programs in Business, the College was enhancing its Liberal Arts Program. In 1962 the Department of Education and Psychology was established. Under the leadership of Dr. Thomas J. McShane as Chairman, one of the department's objectives was to prepare students for teaching certification in the city and state of New York and in New Jersey. In addition to training young people

"We had a chance to do things we never dreamed of. All that energy was suddenly let loose. Now people have to deal with the results of what we created."
(Richard Matthews, March 9, 1990)

who aspired to careers in education, the College offered inservice courses to teachers.

For several years, beginning in 1962, Pace was chosen by the United States Office of Education as the site of a Summer Language Institute for Secondary School Teachers under the leadership of Dr. Rudolph Mondelli, Chairman of the Department of Foreign Languages. Funded under the National Defense Education Act, the Institute brought dozens of educators to Pace to study Applied Linguistics, Methodology, Culture and Civilization and other subjects which would enhance their effectiveness in the classroom. Limited initially to teachers of Spanish, the program was subsequently expanded to include teachers of the French language. Secondary school science teachers and supervisors also benefitted from an In-Service Institute which the National Science Foundation sponsored at Pace for more than a decade.

Another adult group served by the College were women participating in the New Directions program on the Pleasantville campus. Established in 1966 with 23 participants, the program was the brainchild of Robert Hoffstein, the Director of Institutional Research at that time, and had several hundred participants by the early 1970s. The typical New Directions student was a married woman eager to broaden her intellectual horizons with an eye towards a possible career outside the home. Flexible scheduling and thorough counseling by New Directions Dean Dorothy Murphy and her staff enabled the women to balance academic and family responsibilities. Beginning in 1969 the New Directions women were able to enroll their young children in the nursery school recently established in conjunction with the new Elementary Education major. Summarizing the program's success in 1972, the *Pace Alumni News* reported:

> The program has been a most rewarding venture.... It has enabled hundreds of women to fulfill the personal needs of intellectual development while at the same time enriching course discussions through the wealth of experience which they bring to the classroom. Education is a lifetime process, and higher education should never be limited to the young.
>
> Yes, our "New Directions" women are truly liberated - not in the sense of casting aside their present roles, but rather in the sense of adding a new freedom - a freedom to develop intellectually. Through this process each woman adds immeasurably to the lives of others both in the home and in the community.[25]

At the same time that it was providing an opportunity for adult women to begin or resume undergraduate studies, Pace was reaching out to young students of both sexes with its Midday Session, introduced in 1963. Designed for freshmen who were likely to experience academic problems, the program consisted of twelve-week trimesters featuring intensive courses five days each week, with each course having more instructional time than typical undergraduate offerings. Halfway through the Midday Session's first semester, Dr. Mortola reported to the Board of Trustees that 87 students were enrolled in the program and that motivation and morale were "very high."[26]

In addition to the Midday Session, a Management Career Program for Disadvantaged Students, inaugurated in 1968 with the assistance of a grant from the Louis Calder Foundation, provided the opportunity for a college education to youths who would not have ordinarily had the chance to earn a degree. This program offered bright but economically disadvantaged young people a completely subsidized education, on both the undergraduate and graduate levels.

Educationally as well as economically disadvantaged adults were aided by a Pace program begun in 1967 to assist adults in obtaining the High School General Equivalency Diploma. Co-sponsored by the Two Bridges Neigh-

> *"I think the crucial issue was whether we operate with chairpersons as the barons, or we introduce a new level, or I think there had already been introduced, a level of individual —the princes or deans. And we came to the conclusion that we ought to go the latter route. The principle that was established was that there would be schools in the university, and the school would be headed by a dean. The school would have departments. Departments would tend to be local but the dean would be universal. So the dean of the School of Business, the dean of the Arts & Sciences School (I think these are the two important ones at the time) would have responsibility for overseeing the education in their area, no matter where it was given. But you might have two different departments. You might have two departments of English — one in New York and one in Westchester. The problems would be local but the deans would oversee."*
>
> (Jack Schiff, Pace Oral History, June 17, 1983)

borhood Council, Inc. in lower Manhattan, the program was expanded to include reading instruction for elementary school youngsters.

The needs of another special group were met by the John V. Walsh Institute. Named for the late Dr. Walsh, a Pace faculty member who passed away in 1967, the Institute was described, in 1968, as carrying forward Dr. Walsh's "interest in liberating students from the restrictions of credits, fragmented courses, rigid schedules, examinations, the semester system calendar and other practices which have evolved from increasing numbers."[27] Students enrolled in this program attended special seminars, interacted with scholars, and approached higher education from an interdisciplinary standpoint.

In view of the College's physical and curricular expansion, the trustees thought it desirable in 1965 to establish "three schools on the undergraduate level — Arts and Sciences, Business Administration, and Education - each school to be administered by a Dean appointed by the President."[28] The trustees also resolved "that the College develop programs at the Master's level in the Arts and Sciences."[29] On the undergraduate level, Pace was forging ahead in the Sciences in

1966 by introducing a Medical Technology program and a Nursing program in conjunction with White Plains Hospital. In 1971 a full-fledged School of Nurse Education was established, and a nursing program was inaugurated on the New York campus. In 1966 a B.S. program for premedical students was offered for the first time.

On the graduate level, new programs leading to the M.A. and M.B.A. in Business Economics were introduced in 1968, and in 1971 a program in Educational Administration and Supervision leading to a Master of Science in Education made its debut. 1971 was also the year that Pace's Marketing curriculum was rated the best in New York City by marketing executives in Fortune 500 companies. Polled by the New York chapter of the American Marketing Association, these business leaders ranked Pace above other institutions of higher education in the city. The United States Army also called upon Pace to provide on-site educational programs. Beginning in 1972 the College offered a full Associate in Arts degree program at Fort Hamilton in Brooklyn. This was "the first degree extension program offered in its entirety to active military personnel at an army base."[30]

By the early 1970s the array of programs offered by the College was most definitely a manifestation of the institution's academic growth. Besides foreign study featuring summers in Mediterranean countries and science courses in the Caribbean, Pace offered an executive M.B.A. in both New York and Westchester, an A.A.S. in Banking Operations, and a B.B.A. in Banking in conjunction with the American Institute of Banking and special programs for Puerto Rican businessmen. In 1972 a Master in Psychology degree featuring state certification as a school psychologist became part of the curriculum.

All of these new programs were carefully monitored by both the New York State Education Department and the Middle States Association of Colleges and Secondary Schools. In preparation for the visit of a Middle States team in 1967, Pace undertook a rigorous self-examination which included a faculty self-evaluation report. Numerous

faculty members were polled by a committee whose members reached the conclusion that "the feelings of commitment and identification so frequently revealed in the...interviews and questionnaires prove the reality of one of Pace's greatest traditions, a tradition insuring the pre-eminence of human values over all others."[31] Peering into the future, the committee remarked, "A College which prefers the dedicated teacher to the detached scholar, but not at the expense of the disciplined, rigorous demands of the traditional scholar in pursuit of the truth, is what Pace has been and will continue to be as it enters this important new stage in its growth."[32]

The official report of the Middle States team described Pace as "a happy ship," adding, "the rapport between Faculty and Administration is good."[33] The report noted: "People keep talking to one another, in an atmosphere of intense loyalty to their institution. The communication up and down is good."[34] While admitting that "some items we worried about, we found already on the way to a solution," the Middle States team expressed concern about the future development of the New York and Westchester campuses.[35] The team's report concluded, "We think that the growth of Pace College Westchester and Pace College New York will be in different directions....Each will develop according to its potential, its opportunities and its aspirations for the greater good of Pace as a whole. In this manner, every person at Pace will consciously belong to something bigger than he sees each day."[36]

Following the Middle States visit, Divisional Heads of Arts and Sciences and of Business Administration were appointed for Westchester "to assist Dr. McAloon, Dean of Pace College Westchester, during the transition to a greater degree of self-determination."[37] Dr. Jack Schiff, Dean of the Graduate School of Business Administration, was appointed as Provost, and Dr. George Knerr was named Vice President for Student Personnel. These men, together with the President, trustees, and other members of the Pace community, would be called upon to grapple with a host of challenges, including the competition afforded the private sector by the City University of New York's open enrollment policy, which guaranteed a place in either a community college or a four-year public institution to every graduate of a city high school. When the City University accelerated the timetable for the introduction of open enrollment by five years, moving it up to 1970 from 1975, Pace's long-range plan based upon a strategy of "diversity, flexibility and quality," as well as growth, on both the graduate and undergraduate levels had to be revised.[38]

Another challenge emanating from the City University was the possibility of erecting a new campus for Baruch College, the most business oriented of C.U.N.Y.'s four-year colleges, in downtown Manhattan where it would have posed a direct threat to Pace. Happily, Baruch stayed at its home farther north on the island of Manhattan, but, for a time, open enrollment caused the number of students at Pace New York to drop. This diminution in the number of students resulted in the termination of some non-tenured faculty and the transfer of others to Westchester. The drop in enrollment turned out to be less precipitous than originally feared, but the early 1970s was, nevertheless, a sobering time for an institution which had enjoyed remarkable expansion in the previous decade.

A TUMULTUOUS PERIOD: THE LATE SIXTIES AND EARLY SEVENTIES

As Pace marched into the 1970s, it was increasingly apparent that enrollment, curriculum and physical plant were taking second place to student concerns on the College's list of priorities. The unrest sweeping over college campuses nationwide was felt to a lesser extent at Pace, but it was felt just the same. To understand the changes occurring at Pace in the seventies, it is helpful to know something about the quality of student life in the preceding decade.

During the 1960s, most of the social life at Pace revolved around the House Plans. The oldest of the houses, Dyson, formed in 1951, was very prominent for both its service activities and the social events it sponsored.

During the 1962-63 academic year, Dyson House hosted the first faculty cocktail party. This gathering, in Dyson Den, helped solidify the already warm relationship between students and faculty. The annual Coronation Ball held by Dyson House was a highlight of the year. The event was open to all Pace students, as were the social activities sponsored by the other men's houses: Franklin, Hamilton, Kingsmen, Madison, Monroe, Patton, and Tappan. Wilson House, established for New Jersey residents attending Pace, generally held its events on the other side of the Hudson, a practice which effectively limited attendance to those students living in New Jersey. One of the few women's organizations at the College, Parker House, welcomed to its activities (which included the Parker Paddy, a St. Patrick's Day party) not only Pace students but women from other colleges as well.

In the mid-sixties there was talk of nationalizing the house plans, but the administration was opposed to national fraternities and sororities on Pace campuses. In 1966 an ad hoc committee established to examine the problem of the nationalization of house plans reported to Dr. Mortola that it was the consensus of their group "that at the present time, it would be unwise for the College to depart from its traditional policy of opposition to national fraternities."[39] Two years later, however, "Criteria for a House Plan or Local Fraternity for Association with National Fraternities" were adopted by the Board of Trustees.[40]

Affiliation with national fraternities was an indication that Pace students were becoming less insular and more concerned about what was transpiring beyond their own campuses. To a degree, Pace undergraduates were eager to be like students elsewhere. For this reason, there was considerable opposition to the College's rigid dress code. Yet, as late as 1965, the administration was determined to enforce the code, as evidenced by a letter Dr. Mortola sent to the faculty midway through the fall semester. Since there had been numerous instances of noncompliance with the code, Dr. Mortola said:

Robert S. Pace and Edward J. Mortola

That old perennial - student dress- is still with us. I write only to remind you that institutional policies have not changed. We still expect male students to wear jacket and tie to class and to college activities, and women students similarly to wear appropriate attire.

Without making this matter a major concern and certainly without distracting us from our primary function of teaching, I must ask your help in the reasonable enforcement of this policy.[41]

Dr. Mortola concluded his letter by assuring the faculty that while they were free to deal with inappropriately attired students as the problem arose in their own classes, they had the option of seeking "administration support"; in other words, they could direct the student offender to student personnel administrators.[42]

By 1968 the administration had relented, but dropping the tie and coat requirement did not end the concern over student attire. In the spring of 1968 the Pleasantville Faculty Council's Sub-Committee on Student Dress Regulations reported, "While dress at the Westchester campus is not confined to business attire, the student is expected to dress neatly with proper regard to what conforms to good taste. Blue jeans, sweatshirts, and shorts of any kind are not considered proper for the classroom. Women students

are expected to wear dresses or skirts except when extreme weather conditions make other attire more appropriate."[43]

The students would eventually prevail in the matter of attire, and the once banned jeans and shorts would become ubiquitous in the 1970s. In the meantime, though, there were other battles for Pace undergraduates to fight. One of them was aimed at securing a larger voice for undergraduates in the administration of student affairs matters and in the overall "academic and regulatory decision-making" of the College.[44] Student leaders threw down the gauntlet with a full-page proclamation in the *Pace Press* in 1966. In the next two years student representatives were added to such Faculty Council committees as Curriculum Planning, Athletics, Student Affairs, Publications, Admissions and Scholastic Standing, and in 1968 a Committee on Student Interests, with representation from students, faculty, and administration, was organized. To many students, however, this was not enough.

In February 1969, 84 students submitted a formal request for a meeting with the board of trustees. A meeting

"In the sixties...it was when I was chairman...there was a vote up at Westchester, where they voted to strike or not to strike. The students voted to strike. That was in the days when all the students all over the country were doing one thing or another. The Westchester people voted to strike but keep the classes open for anybody who wanted to go to class. I think it was the best educational week that they ever had, because the students who were striking got people to come and speak to them in the auditorium from 11:00 until 2:00. In New York, they voted not to strike. And they had some complaints. I asked them to meet with me on Saturday morning, because that was the only time we could get all these people together. And the people had a number of complaints. They just were going to come in and give us the list of complaints and then run out. But we kept them there. Ed knew all of them. There were probably twenty-five people and Ed knew all of them by name...I said, Let's all announce our names, and each one did this. It was a good meeting. We talked about what they had at issue and resolved it."

(Dr. Charles Dyson, Pace Oral History, May 10, 1983)

was scheduled for March 8, but instead of having a substantive discussion with the trustees, the students who were present demanded that a general meeting be scheduled in the near future. The day before the initial meeting with the trustees, 300 students crowded the lounge at Pace New York to participate in a session held by the Coalition for a Reconstructed Pace College. Individuals and representatives of student organizations aired their grievances and demanded such reforms as unlimited cuts, the establishment of a grade review board, curriculum revision, including the introduction of Black Studies courses taught by African American faculty members, the elimination of censorship of student publications, and the creation of a College Senate which would have representation from all segments of the Pace community.

Students were able to bring their demands directly to the trustees in an enormous meeting held on March 26. Hundreds of students crowded into Schaeberle Hall for a discussion which centered mainly on the students' demand for a Pace Senate. Two days earlier, Dr. Mortola had appointed Dr. Thomas Robinson, the Dean of the School of Arts and Sciences, as special assistant to the President with responsibility for coordinating "efforts to develop a constitution for the proposed College Senate acceptable to students, faculty, administration and alumni."[45] In announcing Dr. Robinson's appointment, Dr. Mortola pointed out that a task force on the College Senate would be created in cooperation with the students and the Faculty Council.

During the next few months, various constituencies worked feverishly on a constitution for the Senate. On July l, the trustees "unanimously agreed that the proposed constitution be mailed...as soon as physically possible to students and faculty and that receipt and tallying of responses should be assigned to the firm of Peat, Marwick, Mitchell & Company, CPAs, in order to protect the privacy of all respondents."[46] Of the students who responded, 80 percent favored the establishment of a Senate. The faculty voted 88 percent in favor of the new body.

Election of Senators took place in the fall of 1969 and the Senate held its first meeting on December 2 of that year. The guest speaker on that occasion was Dr. Joseph W. McGovern, Chancellor of the New York State Board of Regents, who congratulated Pace on being in the forefront of the movement to grant students a voice in institutional governance. "Whatever may be the feelings of those who agree or disagree with the formation of such a body," he said, "it is important to begin and it is important to set your sights high."[47]

The establishment of a College Senate, together with student membership on the Education Committee of the Board of Trustees beginning in 1970, went a long way towards alleviating some of the discontent among undergraduates, but it did not bring an end to all unrest, particularly that associated with the growing disenchantment with the war in Vietnam. In October 1969, as the finishing touches were being put on the new Senate, Pace students marched to Wall Street during a nationwide moratorium to protest the war. Back on the New York campus, a faculty-student discussion of the history and contemporary aspects of the war attracted 150 undergraduates.

In May 1970, hundreds of Pace New York students participated in a mass meeting to oppose the United States invasion of Cambodia and the deaths of four students during a protest at Kent State University. Pace undergraduates in both New York and Westchester expressed their support for a nationwide student strike, and in an attempt to persuade the administration to go along with it, one hundred Pace students took up residence in the corridor outside the President's office. A large banner opposing the invasion of Cambodia and the killings at Kent State was hung from the front of Pace's handsome new Civic Center building in what was intended to be a peaceful protest. The banner infuriated construction workers, who were demonstrating their support of the Nixon administration's military policy.

On Friday, May 8, 1970 members of construction crews from throughout the city gathered in front of

Federal Hall National Memorial on Wall Street, where an anti-war demonstration was taking place. Pace students participating in this peaceful event reported that the workers "proceeded to encircle the anti-war protesters standing on the steps in front of the statue of George Washington."[48] A split second later, there was bedlam. According to eyewitnesses, "Within moments, the workers began an attack with full force, beating students and bystanders with construction tools and clubs while sweeping police aside...the mob was met with only token and passive resistance by police."[49] The workers then proceeded up Broadway to City Hall, where they stormed the building to protest the city's display of the flag at half-mast in memory of the students who died at Kent State. Some of the workers then spotted the Pace College protest banner and 40 to 50 angry construction men raced over to the College. Pace students who had been at City Hall watching the events there were driven ahead of the construction men. The workers caught up with the students at Pace Plaza and immediately began beating students, female as well as male, with pipes, bricks, chains and fists. Students who collapsed on the sidewalk were kicked. Some of the young people succeeded in gaining entrance to the Civic Center building through the one door which was unlocked, whereupon the construction workers followed them inside but were persuaded to leave by faculty members who happened upon the scene.

Once outside, the workers burned the protest banner which had been draped from the front of the building. When a handful of students standing on the roof of the Civic Center building tossed rocks down at the workers, "about ten workers rushed the building and succeeded in gaining entrance."[50] According to the *Pace Press*:

> The rest, seeing that no resistance was being offered, followed them, again driving students before them. They began to break the large panes of glass in the outer wall of the building using pipes, bricks, crowbars and their feet.
>
> Once inside, they crossed the hallway and began smashing the panes of glass in the inner wall enclos-

ing the Admissions offices. Those students encountered in the hallway were set upon with crowbars, bricks and the like. Some were beaten over the head with metal wastebaskets.[51]

A squad of police was needed to clear the building of workers. The brutal attack sent nine Pace students, one of them with a concussion, and one staff member to Beekman Hospital. When it was over, Dr. Mortola said, "On Friday, May 8, the Pace College Community in New York City suffered a dreadful experience which has left all of us saddened and deeply pained. Pace students and staff were viciously attacked in an irrational act by a large group of men identified by those present and in all the public media as construction workers, along with others who had joined them."[52] Peace returned to the embattled College after that fateful day in May 1970, and a year later an environmental issue closer to home absorbed the energy and attention of Pace Westchester students. When construction of a student center at Pleasantville threatened the very existence of an adjacent farm, a committee was formed to save the farm and transform a cottage, erected in 1811, into a nature center. In the spring of 1971 the Farm Committee of Pace Westchester convinced the administration to spare the farm. Thus was born the Environmental Center, which has proven to be a valuable resource for area schools and the general public, as well as members of the Pace community. Craft classes for adults, nature study for youngsters and annual fairs have made the center a very lively place since the early 1970s.

Students were not the only Paceites who were organizing in the sixties and seventies. Faculty members were uniting in an attempt to secure higher salaries and other benefits. Convinced that membership in a national union, the United Federation of College Teachers, would improve their bargaining position, some faculty pressed for a federally supervised election. The National Labor Relations Board oversaw an October 1971 election in which 95 percent of the faculty eligible to cast ballots did so. The union was defeated by a vote of 132 to 73.

SUCCESSFUL QUEST FOR UNIVERSITY STATUS

As the epoch of organization and protest came to an end, Pace College pressed ahead with its efforts to realize a major goal which had thus far eluded it: the attainment of university status. Beginning in the mid-1960s, the trustees and administration had moved in this direction by supporting the introduction of doctoral programs. In February 1965 the Development and Executive Committees of the board of trustees "recommended that a study be made as to the possibility of developing a Ph.D. degree program in the field of business."[53] Two and a half years later, Pace sought permission from the Board of Regents to confer the "Master of Business Administration at Pace College Westchester; Ph.D. in Business Administration at Pace College New York City; and Master of Arts at both New York and Westchester."[54] At the same time, a petition was submitted "for change of name of the College to Pace University."[55]

Five years would pass before Pace was accorded the right to offer a doctoral program leading to the Doctor of Professional Studies or D.P.S. degree. The new degree in business was intended for managers who already possessed a master's degree. These experienced executives were not compelled to interrupt their careers while pursuing a terminal degree at Pace, but within ten years of their admission to the program, they had to complete 55 credits, 12 of which were awarded for the doctoral dissertation. Participation in interdisciplinary seminars, successful completion of oral qualifying examinations, and an oral defense of the dissertation were other requirements of the program.

Securing permission to award a doctoral degree was only one hurdle Pace had to overcome on the long road to attaining university status. Other formidable obstacles took the form of affiliations with outside institutions, something the New York State Education Department viewed as eminently desirable. The first of these affiliations was with the Haskins Laboratories.

Founded in the 1930s by Dr. Caryl P. Haskins, who

Edward J. Mortola and Joseph I. Lubin

later became president of the Carnegie Institution of Washington, D.C., the Haskins Laboratories gained world-wide recognition for research on topics ranging from tropical parasites to psycho-linguistics. By the 1960s there were three research groups at Haskins: Biology, Marine Microbiology, and Linguistics. All three shared a building in midtown Manhattan until they were forced out to permit the creation of additional offices for the nearby United Nations. At that point the groups were spun off as separate entities, with the Marine Microbiology group joining Yale and the Linguistics group affiliating with both Yale and the University of Connecticut. In 1970 the Biology group of the Laboratories became part of Pace College New York.

At the very time that the affiliation between Pace and the Haskins Laboratories was being worked out, the College was seriously considering several other such relationships. Merger negotiations took place with the Mercantile

Library, a prestigious private institution in midtown Manhattan, the College of Insurance, and the Optometric Center of New York, but no affiliations resulted. It was a different story with New York Law School. Founded in 1891 by a group of Columbia University law professors, fully accredited New York Law School numbered among its early faculty members Woodrow Wilson and Chief Justice Charles Evans Hughes. A New York Law alumnus, John M. Harlan, was also appointed to the Supreme Court.

Despite its proud tradition, New York Law was facing a period of uncertainty in the early 1960s, occasioned by the City of New York's acquisition of its building on William Street. Forced to move, the school bought a building at Worth and Church Streets. From the standpoint of convenience, the new location was ideal, for it was within easy walking distance of the courthouses at Foley Square. In economic terms, however, the new building was problematic because it required costly renovations. These expenditures, together with the indebtedness assumed in connection with the acquisition of the structure, led the school's board of trustees to seek financial assistance from the Joseph I. and Evelyn J. Lubin Foundation, Inc. Since Joseph Lubin was a Pace alumnus and a member of the College's board of trustees in 1962 when New York Law approached the Lubin Foundation, it seemed only natural to explore the possibility of an affiliation between Pace and New York Law School.

Negotiations between the two institutions began in 1964. Two years later Pace and New York Law were considering an actual merger. At a meeting of the Pace board of trustees, in the autumn of 1966, Dr. Mortola "underlined the fact that the possible merger with the Law School and the development of a Ph.D. program in the School of Business Administration were two steps of major significance in the College's move toward University status."[56] In the spring of 1967, however, several members of the board of trustees of New York Law expressed reservations about an affiliation with Pace until the outcome of the Middle States evaluation of the College was known. This

JOSEPH I. LUBIN

The grand gentleman for whom Pace's largest schools are named received his Certificate in Accountancy from Pace Institute in 1921. A native New Yorker born on the Lower East Side, Joseph Lubin had attended local public schools in the city before enrolling at Pace. With his Pace training in accounting and a law degree from New York University, Joseph Lubin went on to establish the nationwide accounting firm of Eisner & Lubin.

He also served as chairman of the New York State Board of Certified Public Accountant Examiners and as a director of the New York State Society of Certified Public Accountants. During the Second World War, Dr. Lubin was Special Deputy Chief Investigator of the War Production Board and Chairman of the Appeals Board of the New York County Selective Service. He also served on the board of the National Civil Service League and for a time was treasurer of the League. His corporate board memberships included United Cigar, Whelan Drug Corporation and the Phoenix Securities Corporation.

A great supporter of education, Joseph Lubin was chairman of the Founders Society of the Albert Einstein College of Medicine and a member of the board of trustees of Syracuse University, New York University, and Yeshiva University. From 1961 until his death in 1983 Joseph Lubin was a member of the Pace University board of trustees. In 1955 his alma mater awarded him the honorary degree of Doctor of Commercial Science. Two years before he died, Joseph Lubin presented Pace with the largest single donation ever received from an individual, a land trust fund that over a fifteen-year period would amount to $7.5 million.

prompted Dr. Mortola to write, "It seems to me an unwarranted delay and an unjustified concern on the part of any Trustees of the New York Law School to feel that our plans should await this future action....Pace is in a very strong position. It already has accreditation. Academically, financially, and administratively it is in excellent shape."[57]

These words were not lost on the trustees of New York Law. In November 1967 a letter of intent was signed and the wheels were set in motion for a full-scale affiliation to take effect in September 1968. In the meantime, the Board of Regents and the American Bar Association had to approve the affiliation; Pace trustees had to be appointed to the board of New York Law and law school trustees had to be selected to serve on the Pace board. With 9,500 students, 8,000 of whom were in New York, Pace was clearly the larger of the two institutions. New York Law School had an enrollment of 500 but, despite its relatively small size, the affiliation agreement called for the law school to remain autonomous. An exchange of faculty between the two institutions was envisioned, however, as was movement of qualified Pace undergraduates directly into law school.

A full-scale refurbishing of the New York Law School building was also considered. Towards that end, Pace dispatched an architect to the law school in 1972, but the lukewarm reaction to his suggestions caused the College administrator who accompanied him to inform Dr. Mortola: "... it was a distressing afternoon, and I think we might as well have been talking to the statue of Ben Franklin."[58] The impasse over refurbishing notwithstanding, New York Law School's board of trustees endorsed Pace's petition to the Board of Regents for university status. Board chairman John V. Thornton wrote a strong letter of support on Pace's behalf in February 1973. Soon thereafter both schools were talking about a full-fledged merger and the possibility of establishing a law school in Westchester.

New York Law School desired a merger which would have permitted it to remain "a separate corporate entity."[59] Pace took a decidedly different approach. The College envisioned a "New York Law School of Pace University" and a law school dean who would "report directly to the President of Pace University."[60] Such diametrically

opposed views rendered a merger impossible, and the existing affiliation untenable. The affiliation was therefore terminated on June 30, 1975, by mutual consent of the two institutions. By that time Pace had been a university for two years and was in the process of establishing its own law school.

Although the relationship between Pace and New York Law School was stillborn, the mere existence of the affiliation proved helpful in the College's quest for university status. An affiliation between Pace and New York Medical College paid a similar dividend. In 1967, when the 108-year-old medical school announced that it was planning to leave Manhattan, where its facilities were both old and cramped, Dr. Mortola wrote to Westchester County Executive, Edwin G. Michaelian, "Because there has been considerable discussion about the location of a Medical School in Westchester County, it seems to me that I should write to let you know that I would be willing to explore the possibility of a Medical School on Pace's Westchester campus."[61]

In his reply to Dr. Mortola, the County Executive said: "In all candor, there has been some talk on the part of those responsible for operating the New York Medical College that a future affiliation with the State University would probably be desirable."[62]

Undaunted, Pace pursued an affiliation with New York Medical College while simultaneously exploring the possibility of joining with St. Vincent's Hospital to establish a medical school. Although the latter proposal was dropped, early in 1973 Pace College and the New York Medical College agreed to a transfer of the medical school's Graduate School of Nursing to Pace, with degrees henceforth jointly conferred by Pace and the New York Medical College. The two institutions also agreed to explore the possibility of establishing joint doctoral programs in biochemistry and microbiology, a combined undergraduate-M.D. program for disadvantaged students, a program of paraprofessional education in the health sciences, and programs in mental retardation.

The trustees of Pace College endorsed the affiliation with the New York Medical College because they believed that it would help Pace attain university status. Some of them had misgivings, however, fearing that the affiliation would impose new financial burdens on the College. Gustav Lienhard, for example, wrote, "While I realize that university status will be very beneficial to us in many respects, we certainly must — and I know you are — be deeply concerned with the economic picture, which I don't happen to feel is going to improve too much in the next several years ahead for private schools."[63]

Although the 1973 affiliation with the New York Medical College was seen as a potential financial drain, an agreement concluded two years earlier with the American Academy of Dramatic Arts was viewed more favorably. Under the terms of this accord, Pace was to award the degree of Associate in Arts to "those students who successfully complete the American Academy of Dramatic Arts program and the requisite remainder of the curriculum at Pace for that degree."[64]

The various affiliations made by Pace College in the early 1970s were helpful in obtaining university status. Indeed, without them it is unlikely that the College would have reached its goal in 1973 because only eight years earlier the New York State Education Department had concluded that Pace did "not merit the name university" because it lacked doctoral programs and professional schools, and had "no appreciable liberal arts and sciences graduate enrollment."[65] The state also said that the College "library of some 65,000 volumes is not consonant with the scope of a university."[66] The lack of a sufficient number of doctoral degree holders on the faculty and the paucity of research were also advanced as reasons for not according Pace university status.

In 1969 the state adopted new requirements for university status: three doctoral programs and several professional schools. For a time, it seemed unlikely that Pace would achieve the elusive goal, but the administration and trustees persevered. The minutes of a March 1972 meeting

of the board of trustees state that Dr. Mortola "pointed out that in one unit of the State University over a seven year span, 19 different doctoral degrees have been approved."[67] The minutes state further that "Pace has been seeking authority to grant a doctoral degree for more than five years but has been frustrated by State Education Department bureaucratic maneuvering. It was moved by Dr. Pace...that the petition for changing of designation from Pace College to Pace University submitted on July 28, 1965 be updated and reactivated in the Department of Education and if there should not be a positive response in a reasonable time the College should undertake appropriate legal action."[68] Three months later, T. Edward Hollander, Deputy Commissioner for Higher and Professional Education, wrote that "while Pace comes close to qualifying it does not do so at present."[69] Dr. Hollander also said, "The Department does believe that Pace College would qualify as a university if it should offer (either directly or through an affiliated institution) a medical degree and a law degree, in addition to its present doctorate in professional studies."[70] Dr. Hollander advised Pace to withdraw its petition for university status. The College did so, albeit reluctantly, but continued to negotiate with New York Law and the New York Medical College. In February 1973, just as the affiliation with the medical school was being approved, the Pace board of trustees resubmitted the petition for university status. In the meantime, in September 1972 New York State Commissioner of Education Ewald B. Nyquist wrote to Dr. Mortola, saying, "I am indeed hopeful that Pace College will qualify as quickly as possible for university status....Pace College has come a long way since its origin as an institute offering professional programs. It is hard to identify another institution in the state that has developed so fully while maintaining high standards of academic performance in so short a period of time."[71] Despite his kind words, Commissioner Nyquist reiterated what Deputy Commissioner Hollander had said about the need for affiliations with a medical college and law school. It was only a matter of months before

> "Of the dreamers, Ed was the chief dreamer. He saw probably the future with greater clarity than any of us, although I think Ed's vision was the result of what he had done already. I don't think he set out with any grand design. He saw opportunities. And for Ed, to see opportunity was to act. And his successes generated more opportunities and attracted good people. And Ed had no time, nor has he the desire, to stand over somebody. 'What are you doing?' 'Do this and then tell me.' He gives you a big chunk and away you go and report now and again. So we went both dreaming and creating the future. I don't think we were aware of doing it at all. It was just something we were doing. People would say, 'You know, you're the biggest in this or that'...There were so many things always to do that seemed important. That was what you were doing, not thinking about, gee, look at all the things we're doing! We never once did that because there was so much that should be done. We didn't have time to talk about what we were doing. There was always the feeling that we should be doing more than what we were doing or what we hadn't yet gotten to do."
>
> (Richard Matthews, Pace Oral History, May 17, 1983)

Pace was able to satisfy the State Education Department in this regard, due to the affiliations with New York Medical College and New York Law School, and, at long last, on March 23, 1973, the Board of Regents approved the College's petition. Pace was now a university!

Reporting this development in an article entitled "Pace Graduates to a University," the *New York Times* declared, "Pace College capped its 67-year climb from humble origins as a trade school to the top rung in higher education yesterday when the State Board of Regents designated it a full-fledged university."[72] The *Times* went on to report that Pace President, Dr. Edward J. Mortola, had just unveiled plans for a thirty-story tower opposite City Hall to house many of the university's graduate programs. Designed by the firm of I.M. Pei, the Academic Center tower "would include commercial spaces and public plazas and walkways to unite the campus with the retail and pedestrian areas along Nassau Street."[73] Pace officials were careful to point out that construction of the proposed building was dependent upon the University's fund-raising efforts and that, in any event, "even if the necessary money were raised, construction would not begin for another four or five years."[74]

Nearly twenty years after Pace had been accorded university status, the Academic Center tower had not made it off the drawing board. Countless other projects took priority but, at the very least, the concept of the tower served as a beacon for the state's newest university as it marched confidently into a period of unprecedented expansion in the mid-1970s. For Pace, university status was a commencement rather than a culmination, and the best was yet to come.

EDWARD J. MORTOLA

Describing a legend in his own lifetime is surely the greatest challenge an author can ever have. Had someone undertaken to write a biography of Homer St. Clair Pace in the 1920s, 30s or early 40s, they would have found themselves in the same situation as anyone attempting to write about Dr. Edward J. Mortola in the 1960s, 70s and 80s. Yet a great deal was written, especially about the Mortola management style.

An article in *Change* magazine in 1977, for example, discussed that inimitable style within the context of the challenges facing private colleges and universities. A 1975 feature story in the *New York Sunday News* on the role of university trustees, most notably, Dr. Charles Dyson, then Chairman of the Pace University Board of Trustees, pointed out that while trustees run the institution, "Dyson leaves new programming to Dr. Edward Mortola, Pace's cherubic, gregarious president." The article continued: "Mortola is Dyson's kind of man: practical, enamored of big business, able to line up New York money. And sharp. He can spot trends; he can also, as they say at Pace, 'envision new student segments in the population.' (*New York Sunday News Magazine*, October 12, 1975)

Visionary that he was, Edward J. Mortola could see things before others could begin to imagine them. In other words, the man who became President of Pace in 1960 was a creative academician, the third in a not-so-long line of poets in three-piece suits which the institution has been fortunate enough to have at the helm since 1906. With the exception of Homer St. Clair Pace, Edward Mortola had the longest tenure as President of the school Homer and his brother founded. While he had not known Homer personally, his long and felicitous association with Robert Pace, Homer's son and the institution's second President, began in 1947 and ended only with Robert Pace's death in 1989. This relationship provided the continuity which helped the institution move forward without losing sight of its origins.

It would have made Letizia Pellerano Mortola very proud had she lived to see her son inaugurated as president of a great institution. According to Letizia's youngest child, Edward, who was born in 1917 in the family apartment above his father's New York City restaurant, this mother of five who, like her husband, John Batista Mortola, had emigrated from Ruta, a small town outside Genoa, "went as far as the sixth grade when her father decided that was enough education for a woman. She knew more about college values, about the structure of education," Dr. Mortola told the interviewer for the Pace Oral History Project in 1984, "about the need for learning than any of us. She always had a vision of our going on to education. Education was the ultimate goal of the way she was going to raise her children, and her husband John supplied the caring and support that produced a remarkably cohesive family."

He continued: "She was a truly intelligent woman. She knew the uses of the mind and she wanted to see the mind develop as much as possible. She wanted to make possible for her children what she had been denied." And for her youngest child she had something very definite in mind. "When I was a kid, literally twelve or thirteen years old," Edward J. Mortola said, "my mother said, 'Someday, Eddie, I want you to be president of a college.' Literally. I can remember that clearly."

At the time Edward Mortola was a bright and eager parochial school student. Before long he would attend Regis High School, an endowed institution. This proved to be a turning point for the young scholar. "My life would have taken a very different course if I hadn't been accepted to Regis. Throughout my life, I've always felt that Regis was the most important educational experience I had," said Dr. Mortola in 1984. From Regis it was on to City College for one year and then Fordham University where he earned a B.A. in mathematics in 1938. Three years later Edward Mortola was awarded an M.A. in Administration from Fordham. In the interim he had been Assistant Registrar at Fordham's School of Education and a mathematics instructor at Cooper Union and at Townsend Harris High School.

During World War II he attained the rank of lieutenant commander in the Navy. His wartime duties included teaching at the Midshipmen's School at Columbia University, directing the registration division of the U.S. Armed Forces Institute at Madison, Wisconsin, and serving in the Bureau of Naval Personnel in Washington, D.C. It was also during the war, in 1941, that Dr. Mortola married the brilliant and charming psychologist Doris Slater. In the immediate post-war period Dr. Edward Mortola was awarded a Ph.D. in Educational Administration from Fordham University where he served as Assistant Registrar in the University's City Hall Division. He was also a lecturer in the University's Graduate School of Education and an adjunct faculty member at St. Peter's College in Jersey City and Cooper Union in New York City.

Beginning in 1947, Dr. Mortola held a series of increasingly responsible positions at Pace: Assistant Dean (1947-1949), Dean (1949-1950), Provost (1950-1954) and Vice President (1954-1960). In interviews conducted in 1984 for the Pace Oral History Project, Dr. Mortola explained his first big promotion, from Assistant Dean to Dean of Pace College. "It came about very suddenly," he said, "Unexpectedly. And because of a problem involving the Dean. So that when it happened I had not really been anticipating any change for some time to come. There were one or two other people, I guess, who were considered for the job of Dean. But I went to see Robert Pace and I said, 'I'm sorry this has happened but I'm ready to take over. So if you want me, I'm here.'

Robert Pace did indeed want Edward J. Mortola, so much so that he nominated him to be Pace's third President. Robert Pace had had ample time to observe Dr. Mortola in action and he was fully convinced that his designated successor was the right person to shepherd Pace's plans for a new campus in lower Manhattan's urban renewal district through city, state and federal bureaucracies. That, as anyone familiar with Pace surely knows, was merely the beginning. For the next twenty-seven years, twenty-four as President and then, as Chancellor from 1984 to 1987, as well as Chancellor and Chairman of the Executive Committee of the Board of Trustees from 1987 through 1990, Edward J. Mortola dreamed big dreams and saw most of them come true. By the mid-1980s the college of 4,500 students he had been named to head a quarter century earlier had 28,000 students in six locations in New York City and Westchester. Aside from the more than 500% increase in enrollment, the following statistics are worth noting: 3,200 faculty and staff in eight schools and colleges; 50 buildings; 260 acres of land.

How was all of this accomplished? The answer is Edward J. Mortola's leadership style. In an 1986 interview for the Pace alumni magazine, Dr. Mortola shared his views on this subject saying:

Leadership is identified through results and is dependent on the creation of a capable and dedicated team that shares the mission of the leader and is willing to sacrifice for important objectives to achieve the goals of the institution. Without success in building a team, a leader can have very little effectiveness.

One should quickly put aside the notion that the leader is, or should be, an elitist standing apart from those who follow; leadership is a shared responsibility.

And that it was during the Mortola years. The excellent working relationship Dr. Mortola had with Dr. Jack Schiff was perhaps the best example of shared leadership. Less visible but very significant in the growth and development of the University was the shared responsibility with the trustees, in particular Board chairmen. In addition to his undeniable charm and warmth, one of Edward J. Mortola's greatest assets was his ability to surround himself with people who could assist him in attaining the lofty objectives he had set for Pace. Board Chairman Samuel Miller was one of those individuals. He provided the real estate expertise the University needed. Charles Dyson's strength in the area of mergers and acquisitions was also invaluable, as were the financial and management skills of Board Chairmen Thomas B. Hogan, William G. Sharwell and John C. Haley.

Edward J. Mortola has often said he didn't do it alone and that is true. Yet, without Edward J. Mortola, Pace University, would not be what it is today. He was the catalyst which made it all come together, the magician always capable of pulling still another larger and fluffier rabbit out of the hat. Above all, he was a dreamer, but one who heeded Theodore Roosevelt's advice: "Keep your eyes on the stars but keep your feet on the ground." When asked in 1986 how he wished to be remembered, Dr. Mortola replied: "When I look down the road travelled and the road ahead, I suppose that, most importantly, I would like to be remembered as someone who cared, someone who felt that he had many friends at Pace, someone who spent his life on behalf of this institution and felt that every moment of it was worthwhile."

And worthwhile it was for the institution to which Edward J. Mortola devoted his life. Like Hutchins at Chicago and Elliot at Harvard, the man and the institution are forever linked and this is how it should be; for mathematician Mortola = Pace.

Activities

At Pace University students enjoy a wide range of cultural, academic and athletic activities, clubs and organizations, varsity sports, and study-related travel.

Art

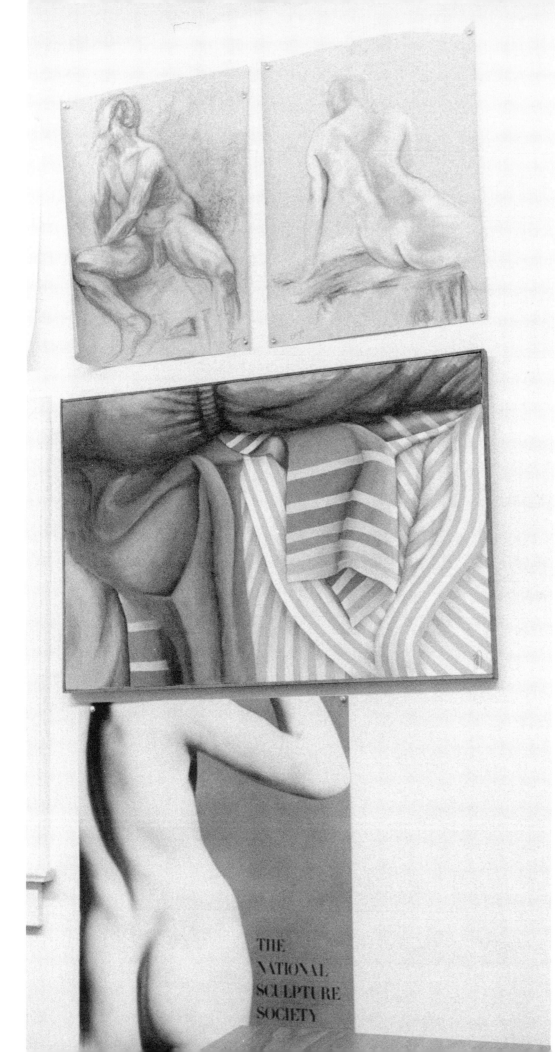

THE
NATIONAL
SCULPTURE
SOCIETY

Sports

Environmental

Chapter 5 From 1975 to 1991

THE UNIVERSITY EXPANDS: CONSOLIDATION WITH THE COLLEGE OF WHITE PLAINS

Nearly seventy years after accountant Homer S. Pace and his attorney brother Charles Ashford Pace had established their proprietary business institute, it seemed only fitting that the trustees and administration of the university which had evolved from the brothers' institute contemplate the possibility of establishing a school of law. But where would the newest school of Pace University be located? The logical place was Westchester County where the University already had a sizable campus. Demographics, corporate relocation and the perceived demand for legal education by residents of Westchester and other suburban counties north of New York City were all factors in the University's decision to go full speed ahead with plans for a new law school in the city of White Plains.

No longer the sleepy provincial town of yore, thanks to an ambitious urban renewal program, White Plains was a modern, efficient city which bustled with the movement of a quarter of a million people during business hours. Corporate, retail and legal business were all thriving in center city and on the fringes of White Plains. More than ever before in its nearly three-hundred-year history, the metropolis which had been designated the county seat in 1759 was pulsating with life.

In the heart of the city, where a courthouse viewed by some as a historic landmark had been demolished to permit construction of a new shopping center, a soaring new courthouse had been built. The very existence of this structure was a powerful argument for establishing a law school nearby. Ideally, the law school would be within walking distance of the courts. The way things worked out, however, the walk was a bit longer than originally contemplated. Instead of building the law school in the urban renewal area of downtown White Plains, the University placed its newest school on the edge of the business district, on North Broadway. Delays in securing the needed property in center city, combined with a unique opportunity to join forces with another educational institution, led to the decision to open a law school on the campus of The College of White Plains, which had become part of the Pace University structure.

Founded in 1923 as a four-year Roman Catholic women's institution, The College of White Plains had been known as Good Counsel College for most of its existence. The school had evolved from Good Counsel Academy, established in 1910 by the Sisters of the Divine Compassion, a religious order founded in 1886. As the college grew from its original seven students, who were appropriately enough called "Pioneers," additional acreage along North Broadway was purchased to supplement the property comprising the two nineteenth-century estates acquired by Mary Caroline Dannat Starr, who had co-founded the religious order with the Right Reverend Monsignor Thomas S. Preston. Known in religious life as Mother Mary Veronica, Mrs. Starr was a convert to Catholicism.

Soon after the order known as the Sisters of the Divine Compassion was established in New York City, the Sisters moved to what was then the rural outskirts of White Plains. There they founded the boarding school to which they devoted their full attention until a few years after World War I, when Good Counsel College opened its doors. The college held its first commencement, for twelve graduates, in 1927. Increased enrollment led to the construction of Preston Hall in 1931. Originally a dormitory, the building, named for Monsignor Preston, became the home of the Pace University School of Law in 1975.[1] How that came about is an intriguing story which deals, in part, with the declining enrollment experienced by many private colleges in the 1970s.

Although Good Counsel College had attempted to attract new students by changing its name in 1971 to The College of White Plains and by becoming coeducational in 1972, the hoped for increase in enrollment did not materialize. Still, at the start of the 1974-75 academic year, the situation was not entirely gloomy. Full-time enrollment had increased by 39 percent over the previous year; a third of the freshman class was male and the budget was balanced. The College's physical plant was underutilized, however, and the enrollment outlook was not optimistic. There was also the troubling matter of the institution's indebtedness to the Department of Housing and Urban Development and to the Archdiocese of New York. At the very time it was grappling with these problems, the College's board of trustees was conducting a search for a successor to Dr. Katherine Restaino, who had announced her decision to resign as President of The College of White Plains in 1975. While a search committee appointed by the board sought a replacement for Dr. Restaino, the trustees pondered the College's future.

By early 1975 some of the trustees were amenable to the idea of joining forces with another institution of higher education. The minutes of a CWP trustees meeting held on March 8, 1975, reveal that Mercy College had approached Dr. Thomas Horton, chairman of the CWP board of trustees, "suggesting conversations concerning a merger with that institution. It was agreed that this course of action would not be pursued...."[2] The minutes of the March 8 meeting also state that "Dr. Edward Mortola of Pace University had approached the trustees regarding a possible merger of the two institutions and the location of the Pace University Law School on The College of White Plains campus."[3] The CWP trustees "agreed that further exploration of this matter should be undertaken by Dr. Horton and Dr. Restaino."[4]

For the next month, however, other possibilities were explored. Under consideration were mergers with Iona and Manhattan, "neither of which expressed interest" and with Fordham University, which did express its interest "if there were a mutual interest on the part of the College of

CHARLES H. DYSON

The brilliantly creative but unassuming man for whom the Dyson College of Arts and Sciences is named was born in New York City in 1909. Twenty-one years later, Dr. Dyson, who had spent his youth in New Jersey, graduated from Pace Institute in the city of his birth. Immediately thereafter he pursued a career in public accounting, becoming a manager at Price Waterhouse & Company. Dr. Dyson left Price Waterhouse during World War II to serve as a consultant to the Secretary of War. He attained the rank of Colonel in the U.S. Army during the war and was awarded the Distinguished Service Medal. In 1944 he was a representative of the U.S. Treasury Department at the International Monetary Conference at Bretton Woods, New Hampshire.

Soon after the war ended, Dr. Dyson joined Textron, Incorporated as Executive Vice President and Director. From 1949 until 1951 he was Vice President and member of the Executive Committee and Director of Burlington Mills Corporation. After leaving Burlington, he established a consulting firm and in 1954 founded the Dyson Corporation, known later as the Dyson-Kissner Corporation, a privately held investment firm. The company began when Dr. Dyson invested in a small electric utility hardware business. Through the years, some 100 other companies were acquired.

Dr. Dyson's expertise in mergers and acquisitions served his alma mater well. Elected president of the Alumni Association in 1953, eleven years later he became a member of the Board of Trustees. As a Board member, Dr. Dyson played an important role in the establishment of the School of Nursing and in the creation of the Civic Center campus in Lower Manhattan. In 1963 Dyson Hall on the Pleasantville campus was dedicated to Dr. Dyson in recognition of his generous support and numerous services to the college. Two years later Pace awarded him an

honorary Doctorate in Commercial Science.

In 1967 Dr. Dyson became Vice Chairman of the Board of Trustees and in 1970 Chairman of the Board. During his tenure as Chairman, Pace achieved university status, the School of Law was established and the merger of The College of White Plains and Pace University occurred. In 1974, two years before he relinquished the chairmanship of the Board of Trustees, the University's College of Arts and Sciences was dedicated to Dr. Dyson.

The announcement that the college would be known henceforth as Dyson College took Dr. Dyson by surprise, leaving him almost speechless, but only for a moment. This unassuming man was, after all, a most effective speaker, and one who was unafraid of speaking out on controversial issues including the war in Vietnam. When he learned that he was the only non-political figure whose name appeared on all three of President Richard Nixon's enemy lists, Dr. Dyson interpreted the development as "an endorsement for good standards." This is precisely what he told a New York *Sunday News* reporter who wrote a feature story about his role as a Pace trustee for the October 12, 1975 issue of the *Sunday News Magazine*.

As for Charles Dyson's extraordinary contributions to Pace, *News* reporter Susan Ferraro characterized the Dyson-Mortola partnership as "a booming success." She went on to say: " At Pace, Mortola is the front man and Dyson the behind-the-scenes power, there 'in the pinch.' That pinch is more like a bite when it comes to fund-raising." Discussing another aspect of the partnership, the News reporter said:

> Dyson's genius for acquisition and control has been what Pace needed most. The school first started to expand in 1967, by turning a local hospital's 'diploma' nursing school into a degree program. Dyson pulled the deal together…'We came in and sat around the table,' Mortola recalls. 'Everyone was hesitant - none of us had ever done this kind of thing before. But within five minutes Charlie turned it around. They were all agreeing, yes, that's how it should be.'

Once again the quiet genius had worked his magic, something which he continues to do for the alma mater which is extremely proud of the man who was once characterized by an administrator of Pace Institute as "the best student we've ever had." Without Charles Dyson, it is difficult to imagine Pace Institute, Pace College and, above all, Pace University.

White Plains."[5] At the same time, talks continued with Pace. Dr. Thomas Horton conferred with Dr. Charles Dyson, chairman of the Pace board of trustees on March 22. Three days later Dr. Horton was present at a Pace trustees meeting. On that occasion the Pace board authorized the continuation of negotiations with CWP for the purpose of effecting a merger.

On April 18, Dr. Mortola attended a CWP trustees meeting. The minutes of the meeting state that Dr. Mortola "joined the Board to answer questions and give his vision of the merger prospects. He mentioned that the concept of merger was an important one for all of higher education at this time, and he stated how he thought such a plan could be worked out to strengthen both institutions."[6] Following Dr. Mortola's departure, the CWP board of trustees authorized the executive committee "to pursue merger negotiations with Pace University."[7]

Over the next few weeks the details of a consolidation agreement were worked out. The agreement called for The College of White Plains "to retain its name and become The College of White Plains of Pace University."[8] The agreement also stipulated that "the consolidated institution ('the new University') would immediately assume full responsibility for all assets and liabilities of The College of White Plains and all existing assets and liabilities of Pace University, as well as full operating financial responsibility for both institutions."[9] CWP's facilities were "to be used for appropriate educational offerings: undergraduate liberal arts program, School of Law, Graduate School and new academic center for ecumenical religious studies."[10]

The details of the agreement notwithstanding, there were serious reservations about the proposed merger among the faculty of both institutions. Reacting to the concerns of Pace Westchester faculty, Dr. Charles Dyson attended a Faculty Council meeting held at Pleasantville on May 2. According to the minutes of that meeting, Dr. Dyson "perceived the consolidation as a great opportunity for the creation of an educational facility in this area....by helping The College of White Plains, we are helping our-

selves, primarily because the White Plains campus provides an excellent location for the Law School."[11] Dr. Jack Schiff was also in attendance at the meeting. According to the minutes, Dr. Schiff "indicated that we are not adding faculty only but also students. The College of White Plains has 400 day students and 11 tenured faculty members, who will become fully integrated members of the Pace University faculty. He added that the establishment of the Center for Ecumenical Religious Study was his idea."[12]

On May 16 the trustees of The College of White Plains met to consider the consolidation agreement. Although fifteen members of the board voted affirmatively on the merger with Pace University, three voted against it, one abstained and one was absent. For the merger to take effect, a three-fourths vote, or 16, was required. Despite the outcome of the vote, the Pace board of trustees was told by Drs. Mortola and Dyson that "The College of White Plains board members who voted affirmatively are far from giving up. Additional meetings have and will be held."[13]

On May 30 the requisite three-fourths vote of the CWP board was obtained, but before the merger could take effect, eight members of the Sisters of the Divine Compassion petitioned the Board of Regents to halt the merger. One of the major allegations made by the eight sisters was that CWP trustee, former Westchester County Executive Edwin G. Michaelian, who was also a trustee emeritus of Pace University and director of the University's Institute for Sub/Urban Governance, was an interested director. The law firm representing The College of White Plains argued that Dr. Michaelian's "relationship to Pace was fully and freely disclosed and was a matter of public record."[14] Moreover, the CWP trustees, "sixteen of whom...voted in support of the consolidation with full knowledge of Michaelian's relationship to Pace, have no intention to avoid the agreement of consolidation. Three-fourths of the college's Trustees have been, and continue to be, convinced that the consolidation is in the best interest of the College."[15] The Board of Regents evidently agreed because on

June 27, the Regents "approved the consolidation of Pace University and The College of White Plains, under the name Pace University, effective July 15, 1975."[16]

Undaunted, the eight Sisters persisted. Their attorney attempted to have the consolidation agreement voided on the grounds that the 19 Pace trustees who voted for the merger did not constitute three-fourths of the full board as provided by the Pace charter. In September 1975 the State Education Department ruled "that the whole number of trustees of Pace University...was 24, and that the affirmative vote of 19 of such members satisfied the requirements of Education Law Section 223...."[17] In essence, the ruling reaffirmed the merger.

In October 1975, the Pace trustees were informed that Dr. Edward Kenny, a Pace Pleasantville faculty member who had been appointed acting head of the White Plains campus, was the unanimous choice of a search committee appointed to recommend a qualified person for the White Plains position. A month later, another bit of unfinished business resulting from the consolidation was taken care of when the Pace board of trustees confirmed University tenure for tenured members of the CWP faculty. At the time the consolidation had been in effect only four months, but CWP was already moving in the direction of integration with the larger institution of which it had become a part.

THE PACE UNIVERSITY SCHOOL OF LAW

Several years prior to the consolidation of The College of White Plains and Pace University, the University began the long planning process which led, in 1975, to the establishment of a School of Law. In the autumn of 1972 University officials discussed the possibility of establishing a law school with attorneys, judges and representatives of county and municipal governments. The following spring, after the Board of Trustees had approved at their March 27 meeting the "presentation of a proposal to establish a law school in Westchester County," Pace President Dr. Edward J. Mortola wrote to key members of the bar in Westchester

to inform them of the University's decision to establish a full-fledged law school instead of an Institute for the Study of Law, a proposal which had been considered earlier and then dropped.[18]

On May 12, 1973, Dr. Mortola and Executive Vice President Dr. Jack Schiff appeared before the Joint Legislative Conference on Legal Education to present a proposal for the establishment of a Pace University School of Law. Soon thereafter, the University's Board of Trustees voted to petition the Board of Regents for an amendment of the Pace charter to permit the establishment of a law school. Although Pace still had an affiliation agreement with the New York Law School, that institution was not a party to the University's petition to the Regents. Dr. Mortola told Michael H. Cardozo of Temple University, former executive director of the Association of American Law Schools, who would act as a consultant to the nascent Pace law school, "You probably know that Pace is presently affiliated with the New York Law School, but that affiliation is not so close or binding that we, at this moment, find it appropriate to submit a petition on behalf of the two institutions. Our Trustees are now engaged in the preparation of a more meaningful merger agreement, and when that is effected we would include the New York Law School more effectively in our planning."[19]

In the meantime, Pace was continuing its efforts to obtain unwavering support for its proposed law school from the legal community. Early in 1974, Dr. Mortola wrote the following to the Honorable Morris Lasker, judge of the United States District Court: "A small, quality law school is being planned, not just another law school. It should be able to make unique and significant contributions to the University at large and to the Westchester community. Its graduates should be welcomed into the profession and into allied fields. With the broadening of law curricula and the continuing diversification of lawyers' tasks, and the pertinence of current legal education, and what promises to be developed, to professions outside the parameters of traditional law practice, the fear of a

JACK SCHIFF

Dr. Jack Schiff, who was Dr. Mortola's right-hand man, confidant and alter ego during the period of Pace's greatest expansion, was a native New Yorker. The son of immigrants, Jack Schiff was convinced that education was the magical key which unlocked the door to success in America. Thus, after graduating from Stuyvesant High School, Dr. Schiff enrolled at City College where he received a baccalaureate degree in 1940. Following four years in the U.S. Army during World War II, he enrolled at New York University, where he earned an M.B.A. in 1947 and a Ph.D. in 1951. While attending graduate school, Dr. Schiff taught full-time at City College and, beginning in the summer of 1950, part-time at Pace.

In 1952 Jack Schiff was appointed Professor of Marketing and Chairman of the Marketing Department at Pace College. As a departmental administrator and faculty member, Dr. Schiff broke new ground by introducing programmed instruction and computer simulations to train managerial and marketing personnel. In keeping with a longstanding Pace belief that the best teachers were practitioners in their chosen fields, Dr. Schiff served as a consultant to such corporations as British Airways, American Oil, GT&E, the Bowery Savings Bank, Lufthansa and General Foods. He was also a prolific author who contributed many articles to business publications and was a contributing editor of the *Handbook of Business Administration* and *Handbook of Modern Marketing*. Author of the first programmed course of instruction in basic selling skills, *Salesmanship Fundamentals*, Dr. Schiff co-authored with his brother, Dr. Michael Schiff, *Strategic Management of the Sales Territory*. Dr. Jack Schiff also wrote and appeared in the film "Selling to the Buyer's Needs," produced by the Bureau of National Affairs.

His reputation as author, consultant, teacher and administrator made Dr. Jack Schiff the logical choice, in 1963, for Dean of the Lubin Graduate School of Business. Seven years later, he was named Executive Vice President of the University. It was in this capacity that he played a major role in the new Pace which was emerging in the decade of the 1970s. Drs. Schiff and Mortola were a formidable team in American higher education.

A key ingredient in the dazzling success of the Mortola-Schiff management team was the fine rapport which existed between these two men. Constantly in touch with each other, most mornings they rode into New York together from New Rochelle and usually spent about forty minutes each day discussing major issues affecting the institution. These conversations set the tone for the day. Following their morning meeting, each man undertook to carry out the specific mission entrusted to him.

In recognition of his outstanding contributions to Pace, Dr. Schiff was named Provost in 1982. Despite the demands of a position which entailed responsibility for every aspect of the University with the exception of communications, facilities and finances, Dr. Schiff continued to find time for his lovely wife Lillian, who over the years was a popular figure at Pace, and his sons and he managed to relate individually to members of the Pace community. Whether it was his delightful jokes, his handwritten birthday greetings sent to every faculty and staff member, or congratulatory notes to people who had been promoted, Dr. Schiff's unique way of communicating endeared him to everyone he encountered. It was indeed fitting, therefore, that the Park Row Faculty Center was dedicated to him.

Jack Schiff's impact on the Pace community is perhaps best expressed by the reaction of Pace people to his untimely death in 1984. Upon learning of Dr. Schiff's death, Executive Vice President J. William Nystrom said: "He was a guy who had a lot of caring for individual people....and he had great range. He was interested in art, music, business — the marketplace. Clarity of thought was one of his great characteristics. He was a man of great restraint." Robert Hoffstein, Assistant Provost for Institutional Research and Planning, said: "He was a very fair man to work for. You weren't working for a boss but a friend."

Dr. Joseph Pastore said: "The first time I met him was on a subway late at night. We had a long talk. I was a Pace MBA student in the early 60s, and he was dean of the Graduate School of Business. He was a fantastic individual, and like a father to me - although he wouldn't want to hear that. But, certainly he was a mentor, a colleague, a friend."

In his eulogy for Dr. Schiff, his longtime friend, Dr. Edward J. Mortola, summed it all up by saying: "Jack Schiff - a man to admire - a leader to emulate - a friend to treasure - a person to love."

crowded profession seems to me no longer justified."[20]

In February 1974, a "large and very encouraging meeting of lawyers, judges, and corporate leaders of Westchester County" was held at the White Plains Hotel "to build up community support" for the proposal.[21] This gathering "was judged to have been a most successful effort."[22] At the same time that the University was soliciting support on the local level, it was making a concerted effort to gain the approval of the State Education Department. Early in 1974 a Pace team, consisting of Dr. Mortola, Dr. George Knerr, Vice President for Facilities Planning, consultant Michael H. Cardozo, and State Supreme Court Justice Frank McCullough journeyed to Albany for a meeting with the Commissioner of Education. Their efforts were successful because on June 26, 1974, the Board of Regents authorized the establishment of a Pace University School of Law.

At this time, the affiliation agreement between Pace and the New York Law School was still in force. At a Pace Trustees' meeting held two months later, Dr. Charles Dyson, Chairman of the Pace Board of Trustees, described the future of the affiliation between New York Law and Pace as "uncertain," adding that "the appropriate committees of the two institutions are expected to meet to review this matter further, including the possibility of termination of the agreement."[23] At the same meeting the trustees grappled with the very real problem of where to place the proposed law school. They talked about renting space at the outset and constructing a $2,000,000 building on the Pleasantville campus, which would house the law school for a few years and then be used for undergraduate classes after the law school moved into buildings elsewhere on the campus specifically designed and constructed for its use. The Executive Committee of the board was authorized to explore these alternatives and to begin acquiring books and periodicals for a law library. In the days which followed, committee members became real estate scouts but one of their discoveries, the former American Airlines reservations center on Route 9 in Briarcliff Manor, was

rejected by the full board in late July.

The following spring, both the site selection and New York Law School problems were resolved. At a meeting of the Executive Committee of the Board of Trustees, held on April 22, 1975, "Dr. Dyson noted that he had forwarded to John Thornton, Chairman of the New York Law School, copy of an agreement to end the affiliation between Pace University and the New York Law School to be effective June 30, 1975."[24] With regard to "the status of the Pace University School of Law," the Executive Committee minutes reflect "that the expected merger with the College of White Plains would conclude the search for the best possible location for the School of Law since it is now scheduled to be built on the campus of the College of White Plains."[25]

Besides finding a location for the new law school, the University had to select a Dean and faculty. The tasks of building a faculty and choosing a law librarian fell to Dr. Charles A. Ehren, Jr., a graduate of the Columbia University School of Law and a professor of law at the University of Denver College of Law. Dr. Ehren was named Dean of the Pace University School of Law on July 10, 1975, five days before the consolidation of The College of White Plains and Pace University formally took effect. During the next few months Dr. Ehren began building a staff and worked on developing a curriculum which included both traditional and innovative approaches to legal education. Among the things envisioned by the new Dean were small group instruction, problem-solving, and clinical experience. Dr. Ehren did not have an opportunity to implement any of these curricular proposals. Policy differences with the Board of Trustees led to a change in leadership at the Law School in the spring of 1976.

With the resignation of Dr. Ehren, Dr. Robert Fleming was named dean. A magna cum laude law graduate of the State University of New York at Buffalo, Dr. Fleming had taught at SUNY Buffalo, St. Louis University and Harvard University before becoming associate dean of the State University of New York at Buffalo. One of Dr. Fleming's first official acts as Dean of the Pace University School of Law was to welcome the 250 students comprising the school's first class. On September 28, 1976, when the law school opened, day session freshmen numbered 150 and evening students 100. They had been chosen from a pool of l,400 applicants. Somewhat older than traditional law students, many of the Pace freshmen were in their thirties and forties. Quite aside from the average age of its students, as the only law school between Columbia University to the south and Albany Law School to the north, the Pace University School of Law attracted considerable attention.

Some of the publicity obtained by the law school during its freshman semester resulted from the groundbreaking for the Joseph and Bessie Gerber Glass Law Center on the university's White Plains campus. In mid-October 1976 in excess of 400 guests flocked to a portion of the campus facing busy North Broadway for a ceremony honoring the late Joseph Glass, a corporate attorney, and his wife Bessie, a major benefactor of Pace University who, some years earlier, had offered Pace her estate in Northern Westchester for a possible center for legal education. In addition to the recognition accorded the Glass family on this occasion, New York Governor Hugh Carey received an honorary degree. He addressed those present, as did Westchester County Executive Alfred DelBello, Henry G. Miller, President of the Westchester Bar Association, and Dean Robert Fleming, who asked for community support for the new law school which had opened its doors just a few months earlier. Declaring his intention to head "a quality law school," the Dean said: "We want you to want us to be very good, indeed; if you expect a lot of us, we will perform."[26]

In many respects, the law school was already performing quite well. A library organized by the school's first law librarian, Charlotte Levy, had been assembled and processed in a rented warehouse in Valhalla. As the law school was about to open its doors, the enormous collection, which would grow to over 170,000 volumes by the late 1980s, was moved to the Tudor Room of Preston Hall,

Law Center Ground Breaking
Bessie Gerber Glass, Charles H. Dyson, Edward J. Mortola,
Governor Hugh L. Carey

which served as the law library until January 1979, when the Glass Law Center was completed. Although there were many loose ends when the law school opened, such as the lack of a placement director and an insufficient supply of housing for law students, the freshmen and their eight full-time faculty members forged ahead.

Despite the inevitable problems associated with any new enterprise, on the whole, the first class did well. A few months after the Pace University School of Law awarded its first degrees, Associate Dean James Fishman was able to report that "70% of the first graduating class of the Law School had passed the Bar exam—an impressive percentage for a first graduating class."[27] Dean Fishman also noted that "the Moot Court Team of Pace Law School had won first place at the New York City Moot Court competition."[28] Moreover, the Pace University School of Law had received provisional accreditation from the American Bar Association in February 1978. Reacting to this good news, Dean Fleming said: "We are particularly pleased to acquire this accreditation because it has been achieved in the shortest time possible allowed by the ABA."[29]

The law school was off to a flying start, but it was, nevertheless, plagued by certain problems. Students and some law school faculty were highly critical of what they perceived to be an inefficient registration system and an unsatisfactory way of scheduling final examinations. Divisions within the faculty and between the faculty and the law school dean in addition to apprehension about full accreditation by the American Bar Association all took their toll. To help the law school deal with these and other important issues, Dr. Mortola appointed Dr. Ewald Nyquist, former Commissioner of Education of the State of New York and Vice President for Academic Development at Pace, as liaison with the School of Law in March 1979. In a memorandum to the Law School Faculty, Dr. Mortola stated that "Dr. Ewald Nyquist has been requested to devote the bulk of his time in assisting the Law School in improving its administrative effectiveness..."[30] The President also noted that "Dr. George Mims, Director of several Pace programs intended to recruit and assist minority students, had been assigned on a full-time basis to help recruit minority students and staff for the School of Law."[31]

At the same time that he was reassuring the faculty that the problems the school was experiencing could be resolved, Dr. Mortola was doing his best to prevent the further erosion of student morale. Responding to a student who had communicated with him in writing, Dr. Mortola said, "A number of faculty, as well as Dean Fleming, Dr. Schiff and I, are hard at work on restoring some of the order and unity that are necessary for the future of the School of Law and also that are important to your own sense of satisfaction and enjoyment in attending the school. I hope that you will persist in your pursuit of your law degree at Pace and hope also that you will have full justification for doing so by the time that we enter into the next academic year."[32]

The efforts made by the faculty and administration to correct problems while simultaneously enhancing the reputation of the Law School received a temporary setback with the publication of an expose-type article in the *New York Law Journal* in May 1979. The article contended that "the most obvious example of divisive elements at the three-year-old institution is the racial discrimination complaint filed in Federal Court in February by Associate Professor Hugh M. Wade, a black, against Dean Robert B. Fleming."[33] Since

the case was pending at the time, Pace officials could not comment on this aspect of the Journal's reporting, but Nicholas A. Robinson, Associate Professor of Law and Chairman of the Pace Law School's Committee on Planning and Review, decried inaccuracies in the article in a letter to the editor of the *New York Law Journal*, in which he stated that it was "evident that your news story did not accurately recite, much less explain the growth problems which this new law school has experienced."[34] He went on to say, "There have been disagreements between the Dean and some members of the faculty. That is a situation common to law schools generally. Expectations in a new law school are high; disappointments may have been taken by some persons more severely than would be the case in a school of longer standing. Personality conflicts can and did become mixed and confused with policy disagreements between the Dean and some faculty and among some faculty. If these sorts of issues are worth journalistic scrutiny, they obviously raise complexities and difficulties which require close and careful examination; the uncritical repetition of information from undisclosed sources does not evidence such examination."[35]

The unfavorable publicity generated by the *New York Law Journal* article notwithstanding, the American Bar Association granted the Pace University School of Law full accreditation on August 6, 1980. Attainment of this important goal helped ease the concerns of faculty and students. Less than a year after accreditation was obtained, Dean Fleming was able to report to the Board of Trustees that the enrollment of the Law School was 749. Of that number, 412 were day students and 337 evening students. Fully 45 percent of the student body was female. Other good news cited by the Dean was the establishment of an alumni association, "with representatives in 13 states."[36] Another milestone was reached in January 1982 when the University's School of Law received final accreditation by the American Association of Law Schools.

In reporting this development to the Board of Trustees, Dr. Mortola also stated that Dr. Robert Fleming was retiring as Dean, but that after a leave of absence, he would return as a faculty member. A search committee was formed to recommend a successor to Dean Fleming and, in the interim, former Westchester County Executive and Judge James Hopkins served as Dean. In 1982 the Honorable Janet Johnson, a judge of the Iowa court, was named Dean of the Pace University School of Law. Dean Johnson served for six years, resigning in July 1989. Her successor was Steven Goldberg, who came to Pace in 1989 from the University of Minnesota School of Law where he had been Associate Dean for Academic Affairs and External Relations.

During Dean Johnson's tenure at Pace, curricular innovations included certificate programs in International Law, International Trade Law, Health Law and Policy and a Master of Laws (LL.M.) program in Environmental Law. In 1984 when the first volume of the Environmental Law Review was published, Pace became one of a handful of schools, including Columbia, Harvard, and Stanford, to produce this type of professional periodical. In 1986 the Pace University School of Law established, with the approval of the American Bar Association, the only semester abroad program affiliated with a British faculty of laws.

BRIARCLIFF AND BENNETT

At the very time the university was witnessing the steady growth of its Law School, it was in the process of acquiring yet another campus, in Briarcliff Manor. Founded in 1903 as Mrs. Dow's School, Briarcliff became a two-year women's college in 1933 and a four-year institution in 1964. By the 1970s, Briarcliff College, like many other single-sex institutions, was experiencing financial problems, and some members of its board of trustees were amenable to the idea of exploring innovative solutions to those difficulties. In November 1973 Dr. Charles Dyson, representing the Pace Board of Trustees, met with John Emery, the chairman of the Briarcliff College Board. According to Dr. Dyson, "the main purpose of the meeting was to open the

THOMAS B. HOGAN

A 1939 graduate of the University of Notre Dame, Thomas B. Hogan had a distinguished career in public accountancy. Licensed to practice in New York, California and a number of other states, Dr. Hogan became a partner in the firm of Haskins & Sells in 1951 and subsequently headed the firm's New York City office.

Named to the Pace Board of Trustees in 1962, Dr. Hogan became board chairman in 1976, a position he held until 1983. During this period, the Joseph and Bessie Gerber Glass Law Center was completed on the White Plains campus, the Law School achieved accreditation, the School of Computer Science and Information Systems was established and Pace added new locations in Briarcliff, Midtown Manhattan and downtown White Plains. On the Pleasantville campus the Edward and Doris Mortola Library was completed while in New York three floors of lecture halls, classrooms and offices were added to the Civic Center building. The west wing of the building, containing the addition, was dedicated to Dr. Hogan and his wife, Grace. Dr. Hogan, who received an honorary doctorate from Pace in Commercial Science in 1969, died in 1989.

suggestion of studies being undertaken by both staffs, working together, to determine whether or not there is any merit to a merger of Briarcliff into Pace College."[37] At that time, Dr. Dyson thought "Briarcliff College could continue as a college in Pace University."[38]

Over the next three years, meetings between Pace and Briarcliff officials took place and by late 1976 it was evident that Briarcliff College had to do something to deal with such problems as declining enrollment, difficulty in meeting operating and payroll expenses, a deficit which was then nearing $1,000,000, and default on loans from both the Department of Housing and Urban Development and the New York State Dormitory Authority. In view of these problems, Pace trustee Thomas B. Hogan concluded: "At first blush, Briarcliff is not the most attractive candidate for a marriage with Pace or anyone else."[39] On balance, however, Briarcliff was attractive in Dr. Hogan's opinion. Explaining his views on a possible union between Pace and Briarcliff, Dr. Hogan said, "First, the school owns about 65 acres of land located only a few miles from our present Westchester campus. On that land there are five reasonably well maintained dormitories equipped to hold 640 students and a dining hall and a science hall which were built in 1965 — facilities we desperately need to meet our presently anticipated requirements."[40]

Since the assets of Briarcliff College were inherently attractive, Dr. Hogan urged that Pace "obtain promptly a detailed study of how we would propose to operate Briarcliff if we merged and what the impact would be in terms of costs and revenues."[41] Finally, Dr. Hogan stated, "As a precondition of the merger, if it occurs, we should establish some definite terms with the Briarcliff trustees, HUD and the Dormitory Authority. These terms would assume that we would have such control over the affairs of Briarcliff that would permit the prompt elimination of any significant cash deficits."[42]

In January 1977 Dr. Mortola reported to the Long-Range Planning Committee of the University's Board of Trustees that an arrangement had been made with Briarcliff College whereby Pace would rent 300 dormitory spaces on the Briarcliff campus for the 1977-78 academic year. Dr. Mortola also informed the committee that "N.Y.U. is pursuing Briarcliff as well."[43] By March it was clear that Briarcliff had only one suitor, Pace University, but even Pace was having some doubts. Concerted opposition on the part of Briarcliff students and faculty to a consolidation with Pace helped set the stage for the dissolution of Briarcliff College, the surrender of its charter to the Board of Regents, and the sale of the College's assets to

Pace in return for the University's assumption of the College's short-term debt and long-term obligations to HUD and the State Dormitory Authority.

Although Briarcliff students and trustees conducted a feverish campaign to raise $1.2 million, the amount needed to keep the school open until June 1977, they succeeded in obtaining only a third of that sum. This left the trustees with only one option, namely to accept "a takeover bid by Pace University."[44] The Briarcliff Board of Trustees voted in late March to transfer the institution's assets to Pace. Commenting on this development in an article entitled "Rest in Pace," *Newsweek* declared: "In return for assuming Briarcliff's considerable debts, Pace now owns the college, lock, stock and dormitories."[45] *Newsweek* was really jumping the gun because before the transfer of assets could take place, the Board of Regents and the New York State Supreme Court had to give their approval. In an effort to block state approval for the deal approved by the Briarcliff trustees, the Briarcliff College faculty sued the College's trustees for breach of contract. Students joined in the suit, contending that both they and the faculty deserved a share of the assets of the institution.

At the same time, some Briarcliff trustees were attempting to work out a merger agreement with Bennett College, a two-year institution in Millbrook, New York. Neither the merger talks nor the law suit were fruitful. Although the Board of Regents was willing to entertain the concept of a merger between Bennett and Briarcliff with the transfer of Briarcliff's programs and faculty to Bennett, its insistence that the merged school remain open for the entire upcoming academic year, with any financial deficits being made up by the trustees, proved to be a stumbling block. In the summer of 1977, following an unsuccessful effort to persuade a sufficient number of Briarcliff students to transfer to the Bennett campus, Briarcliff's trustees petitioned the Board of Regents for an order closing the college.

Within months, Bennett went the way of Briarcliff, but its charter was not dissolved. Instead, some Bennett students enrolled in Pace, and certain Bennett programs, notably Equine Studies, were transferred to Pace in the fall of 1977, with the approval of the New York State Education Department. In 1986 the Board of Regents "adopted a resolution consolidating Pace University and Bennett College under the name Pace University."[46] Back in 1977, when Bennett students first began enrolling in Pace, frantic phone calls from Bennett Equine Studies majors seeking accommodations not only for themselves but for their horses kept Pace administrators on their toes, but the Briarcliff situation proved more troublesome over the years. Within a year of Pace's acquisition of the Briarcliff campus, the Village of Briarcliff Manor imposed restrictions on the use of the property. Pace instituted legal proceedings to no avail, whereupon the trustees gave serious thought to a Briarcliff divestiture. As Pace entered the nineties, however, the Briarcliff campus, once so vociferously opposed by Briarcliff Manor residents, was still an integral part of the University.

OTHER CHALLENGES OF THE 1970s

Establishing new schools of the University and acquiring new campuses made the 1970s a challenging decade. The attainment of each major goal required considerable effort and sometimes the race to the finish line took the form of a zigzag rather than a straight line. Making the race more interesting was the necessity of administering a complex University on a day-to-day basis while still pursuing expansionist objectives. In an institution the size of Pace, almost anything could and did happen, and frequently mundane concerns over blackboard cleanliness, food service and the like were overshadowed by the stuff of which headlines are made. A case in point was the Winsey matter.

In 1970 Valentine Winsey, a full-time member of the Social Sciences faculty at Pace New York, was issued a terminal contract for the 1970-71 academic year. When Dr. Winsey failed to sign the contract, the University interpreted this as a resignation. Several months later, when Dr. Winsey signified a willingness to accept the contract, the University refused. Dr. Winsey then formally charged the

Charles H. Dyson and Michael Schimmel who received honorary degree

University with sex discrimination. Thus began a legal odyssey which attracted nationwide attention because of its implications for women's employment. Dr. Winsey was ultimately reinstated as an Associate Professor at Pace University and received tenure. She returned to full-time teaching at Pace New York in September 1976.

Before the final verdict was in on the Winsey case, some members of the Pace faculty in both New York and Westchester were attempting to generate support for a collective bargaining election. This issue surfaced time and again between 1974 and 1978. In February 1978 the National Labor Relations Board supervised elections held in Westchester and New York to determine whether the American Association of University Professors would become the collective bargaining agent for the Pace faculty. The final vote was 179 against and 103 for.

Although collective bargaining was an issue in the mid-1970s, enrollment was not. In the fall of 1975 enrollment reached 13,936, the highest in the school's history up to that time. Particularly encouraging was the increase in day student enrollment at the New York campus, which had experienced a decline earlier in the decade because of the

Open Enrollment policy of the City University of New York. Also very welcome was the 86 percent increase over 1973 totals in the number of undergraduate evening students at Pleasantville. More students meant an increased need for classrooms, but instead of adding classrooms downtown, Pace accepted the recommendation made by Robert Hoffstein, Director of Institutional Research, to establish a center farther uptown. Thus, in September 1976 Pace began offering courses in midtown Manhattan.

The decision to establish a Midtown Center was based upon a survey which revealed that numerous employees of companies in the midtown area lacked either college or graduate degrees. So successful was the Midtown Center that less than a year after it opened, Pace had to move the operation from its first home, in the Equitable Life Assurance Company's Training Center at 51st Street and the Avenue of the Americas, to another building at Fifth Avenue and 44th Street.

At the very time Pace was opening the doors of its second Midtown Center, the University received nationwide publicity thanks to an article in *Change Magazine*, an educational publication. In the November 1977 issue, Ruth Fischer wrote: "Today Pace is something of a phenomenon in the world of higher education. At a time when many private colleges are barely staving off bankruptcy or, at best, holding their own in a no-growth pattern, Pace is flourishing. Apparently unmindful that the golden age of higher education in this country has ended, Pace has doubled its enrollment in the past decade. In 1976-77 alone...enrollment grew 12 percent, compared with a national growth rate for private institutions of .8 percent. At the most recent count, Pace had about 17,000 full and part-time students."[47] There wasn't much about Pace that Ruth Fischer overlooked. Jumping from past to present she commented on everything from Leaders in Management to the New York campus. Of the latter, she wrote, "The building's showplace is the Michael Schimmel Center, a 700-seat semicircular auditorium...There, the University's director of performing arts...imports dance

companies, music ensembles, drama groups, and speakers. There is a professional resident opera company.... The Schimmel Center is the home of the Four Seasons Theater, a company from Chinatown whose performances feature English subtitles projected on the wooden ledge that runs across the bottom of the 60-foot stage."[48] Commenting on Pace students, Ruth Fischer wrote, "The work ethic among Pace students is entirely compatible with their faith in the system. They believe in private enterprise. They also believe in private education....They hold to the traditional view that one gets what one pays for."[49]

With enrollment passing the 20,000 mark for the first time in the institution's history, optimism abounded. Evidence of this was the appointment in January 1978 of a trustees' committee "to investigate all aspects of a possible merger with the New York Medical College."[50] The cost of such a merger, estimated to be at least $10 million because of the College's financial situation, was deemed excessive, however, and instead of a Pace-New York Medical College union, the Roman Catholic Archdiocese of New York, which at the time operated more than a dozen hospitals in New York, "agreed to assume the responsibility for the fiscal viability of the New York Medical College."[51]

Although Pace's enrollment continued to increase, taking on new burdens was not justifiable in the opinion of the trustees. Indeed, in the late 1970s the University sold some existing properties at 140 Nassau Street and 38 Park Row, and began consolidating operations at the Civic Center campus where three sizable new floors would be constructed in the 1980s.

HOW MIDDLE STATES VIEWED PACE

But bricks and mortar alone do not make a university. People and programs do. In the first fifteen years of its existence as a University, Pace was evaluated by the Middle States Association three times, and on every occasion the visiting team scrutinized academic offerings. The team which visited all of the Pace campuses in 1977 was generally impressed, noting: "The Board of Trustees and the President are risk takers. They are quite willing to enter new fields. Thus, Pace is likely to grow still more and become more intricate."[52] In keeping with its status as a University, Pace was urged to offer majors which were in less demand than the popular Business concentrations. The team's final report stated, "The market principle...is not unreasonable. Pace University could hardly expect to survive in its very competitive environment offering esoteric courses and programs not desired by the community. Yet, this is causing some problems. Liberal arts need support regardless of the market. It is the underpinning of all undergraduate work. Education is an existing commitment, a going program that needs the resources to carry out its assigned mission."[53]

Reacting to a Middle States recommendation that an academic vice president be appointed, Dr. Mortola announced in November 1978 that Dr. Thomas Robinson, Vice President of the Pleasantville/Briarcliff campus, would become Academic Vice President. At the same time, Dr. Miriam Moran, Assistant Vice President for University and Community Relations at the White Plains campus, was named Vice President for University Admissions, and Ed Zanato, Special Assistant to the President for Student Services, was appointed University Dean of Student Personnel.

In 1983 Middle States reaffirmed Pace's accreditation, noting that in the previous five years "it would appear that Pace has made significant progress in a number of areas, particularly related to administrative organization, centralization, institutional development and fund raising."[54] Five years later, following a full-scale evaluation, a Middle States team concluded that "cautions are in order for Pace. But, with prudent planning, decisive action, and strong leadership, Pace in the future — like Pace in the past — will defy the odds and do remarkably well."[55] The report also noted that in the previous five years Pace had "faced major new challenges. It has done so while maintaining standards, balancing its budget, and retaining its verve."[56]

PACE AT SEVENTY-FIVE

Just how much verve Pace had became evident during the University's gala seventy-fifth anniversary in 1981. That fall enrollment reached 26,000, a new record, and in the eight graduate and undergraduate schools of the University, more than 100 major academic fields were represented. In celebration of what Pace had achieved during its first 75 years of existence, all sorts of events were planned, ranging from the kickoff event, the Leaders In Management dinner, held in March to honor John F. McGillicuddy, chairman and president of Manufacturers Hanover Corporation, to an anniversary dance for alumni in May, to an innovative exhibition entitled, "A New York Album." The idea for this exhibit of family photos submitted by the students, staff and faculty of the University was conceived by Dr. Jean Fagan Yellin, Professor of English and exhibit curator. The enlarged photographs, some nearly eight feet tall, documented "the historic promise of New York and of education as the gateway to a better life."[57] Extraordinarily popular from the moment it opened at Pace New York in May 1981, the exhibit traveled to Westchester later in the year.

Another feature of the seventy-fifth anniversary was the gala commencements. Speakers at the separate commencement exercises held at Lincoln Center, Pleasantville, and White Plains included such notables as Alan Greenspan, former chairman of the Council of Economic Advisors, and actress Colleen Dewhurst. In all, 3,500 students, comprising the largest graduating class in Pace's history, received degrees ranging from associates to doctorates. In the fall of 1981 all of New York joined in celebrating Pace's anniversary, thanks to Mayor Edward I. Koch who proclaimed the week of October 6 "Pace University Diamond Jubilee Week."[58] On October 6, a Founders' Day ceremony featuring remarks by Pace administrators and a reading from the works of Homer S. Pace was held outside the Civic Center Building. Founders' Day ceremonies were also held at Pleasantville and White Plains. In Westchester

the week of October 5 was proclaimed "Pace University
Week" by County Executive Alfred DelBello, who praised
the University for its "innovative and diversified educational programming," and for having made "a major
impact on the academic, government, business and social
communities in Westchester since 1963."[59]

ACADEMIC PROGRESS

Core Curriculum

On the eve of its seventy-fifth anniversary Pace began a
thorough critical examination of its core curriculum.
Beginning in the spring of 1980 when the President's Commission on the Core Curriculum was established until
1984 when the new core was implemented, a dedicated
group of faculty and administrators, under the extremely
capable leadership of Dr. Joseph M. Pastore, Jr., spent
countless hours examining the University's curriculum,
debating various proposals, and coming up with a series of
recommendations. The Commission started with a key
question: "To what extent has the expanded knowledge
base experienced by the University in the past 20 years
been reflected in its curriculum?"[60] The Commission then
proceeded to identify eight major objectives for general
education at the University. These included the development of critical thinking, verbal and quantitative skills,
appreciation of the human heritage, aesthetics, and "of the
world as a composite of many countries and varying cul-
tures," plus understanding of science and technology and
of the social and behavioral sciences.[61] The new core
implemented in 1983 had credit requirements designed to
achieve these objectives.

When the core had been in place for five years, a committee of faculty and administrators undertook a thorough
reexamination of the basic education provided all recipients
of Pace baccalaureate degrees since the implementation of
the new core. This reexamination, which was ongoing in
1989, was occurring simultaneously with the review of the
various aspects of assessment by another university-wide

JOSEPH M. PASTORE, JR.

A native of Harrison, New York, where he was born in
1941, Dr. Joseph M. Pastore, Jr. received a bachelor's degree
in Business Administration from St. Bonaventure University
in 1963. Two years later he earned an M.B.A. at Pace and in
1969 he was awarded the Ph.D. in Management Science
from St. Louis University.

Dr. Pastore's career in academia began in 1965 when he
became an instructor at St. Bonaventure University. Within
four years he had progressed to the rank of Associate
Professor before being named Dean of the School of
Business Administration in 1969. In 1973 Dr. Pastore became
Vice President for Academic Planning and Provost of St.
Bonaventure University. In 1976 Dr. Pastore came to Pace
University as Dean and Professor of Management in the
Lubin School of Business Administration. Four years later
he became Vice President for Academic Affairs and in 1985
he was appointed Provost.

In addition to his administrative responsibilities at Pace,
Dr. Pastore is a labor arbitrator with the American
Arbitration Association and the Federal Mediation and
Conciliation Service. In this capacity Dr. Pastore has written
many arbitration opinions. His published works in the field
of business have included numerous monographs and
articles. He has also been an editorial advisor to McGraw-
Hill and the Harwood publishing company. Over the years,
Dr. Pastore has also served as a consultant to such
corporations as Dresser-Clark, Inc., Monsanto, Sylvania
Electric Products, Inc., Technicon Corp. and Prudential-
Bache and to public school districts in Massachusetts and
New York as well as to the New York State Education
Department.

committee. The Committee on Assessment was chaired by
Dr. J. William Nystrom, who had been appointed Executive
Vice President of University Projects in 1987, after having

served as executive assistant to the President and Vice President for Administration since 1978. One important goal of the latter group was to explore ways of measuring the outcomes of not only the core curriculum but the entire experience, non-academic as well as academic, which a Pace student has at the University. Thus on the eve of the 1990s, the University was more concerned than ever about the totality of the Pace experience and its implications for the future well-being of graduates.

Dyson College

The school of the university which was most involved with the core curriculum was the Dyson College of Arts and Sciences. A decade before the new core curriculum was implemented, the School of Arts and Sciences was renamed Dyson College in honor of Pace alumnus and trustee Charles Dyson. In recommending to an executive session of the Board of Trustees that the name of the school be changed, Pace President Dr. Edward J. Mortola "discussed the traditional practice in universities which use the term College for the Arts and Sciences and School for graduate and professional areas."[62] Dr. Mortola went on to point out that "the basis of this distinction lies in the fundamental nature of the Arts and Sciences as being the foundation of all academic and professional programs."[63] When Dr. Mortola finished speaking, "it was thereupon moved, seconded and unanimously agreed that the title The Charles H. Dyson College of Arts and Sciences should be established."[64]

Reacting to the trustees' decision, Dr. Dyson, a partner in the Dyson-Kissner Corporation, a privately owned investment company, said that he regarded the trustees' action as "a distinct honor," adding: "In today's world, the Arts and Sciences are at the core of all programs of study, and are becoming more important in every aspect of our living."[65] Dr. Mortola observed, "In naming the School of Arts and Sciences for Dr. Dyson, the trustees have acknowledged the tremendous support that he has extended to Pace in his years of association with it. To

count the ways he has provided that support is to cover the gamut from bricks and mortar and scholarships for deserving students to an extraordinary willingness to be available to administration, faculty and students."[66]

In the years since it was renamed, Dyson College has been a dynamic force within the university. During the tenure of Dr. Joseph E. Houle, who served as Dean of the School of Arts and Sciences and Dyson College from 1971 through 1990, its innovative programs have attracted widespread attention even outside Pace. A case in point is the Psy.D. degree approved in 1979. The first of its kind in New York State, the four-year program was implemented during Dr. Thomas McShane's tenure as Chairman of the Department of Psychology, and was designed for people seeking certification in school and community psychology. In addition to positions in education, graduate students in the Psy.D. program were being prepared for positions in hospitals, rehabilitation centers, government and private practice. To ensure that they would be well-prepared for the positions awaiting them, a two-year internship was built into the program.

An internship was also a vital component of the new Master in Public Administration degree, which was also introduced in 1979. Designed specifically to aid government employees in increasing their effectiveness, the program subsequently admitted to both its governmental and health care administration tracks students who aspired to careers in those areas, including Pace undergraduates who qualified for a combined B.A. in Political Science and M.P.A. At the outset, however, the largest constituency of the M.P.A. program were management and supervisory staff personnel from the Westchester County Department of Social Services. Nearly 200 County employees participated in a management training program under a $900,000 grant from the New York State Office of Manpower Development.

Another highly innovative graduate program was the Master of Science in Publishing, introduced in 1985. Offered at the University's Midtown Center, strategically located in the midst of the publishing area, the new program was initially proposed by Professor Irving Settel of the Marketing Department. It was designed "to help fill the publishing industry's need for professionally trained personnel," according to Professor Sherman Raskin, Chairman of the English Department at Pace New York and Director of the publishing program. Two years after the program had been established, he noted, "Our program educates our students in all pertinent aspects of the publishing business: finance, production, sales and marketing, the legal intricacies of acquisitions and subsidiary rights, editing and more."[67] Successful in attracting full-time employees of book publishing firms and magazines, the program was well received in the industry. Publishers were sufficiently enthusiastic to subsidize employees' tuition, and the Reader's Digest Foundation donated $50,000 to the University to be used for scholarships. The Times Mirror Company provided $150,000 for the same purpose.

In addition to the M.S. in Publishing, another welcome addition to the curriculum was the New York City Humanities Program. Begun in 1980 with grants from the National Endowment for the Humanities and the American Express Foundation, the program was developed by Dr. Jean Fagan Yellin, Distinguished Professor of English at Pace New York, and Dr. Marilyn T. Williams, Professor of History at the New York campus. In addition to interdisciplinary courses dealing with the city, the program, which constitutes a full-fledged academic minor, features a one-semester internship at a museum, historical society, or other cultural institution in the five boroughs. Open to students on the suburban campuses as well as to those at Pace New York, the program has served to enlighten participants about the city's incredible diversity.

Other innovative programs of the Dyson College of Arts and Sciences are the minors in Women's Studies, Film Studies, and American Humanics. Designed to provide training for careers in youth agencies such as the Y's, the American Humanics program, which is offered at a num-

ber of other colleges and universities in the United States, is sponsored by the YMCA, YWCA, Boy Scouts of America, Girl Scouts of America, and other youth agencies. As with many other programs offered by Dyson College, American Humanics includes an internship component which must be completed by students seeking a minor in Youth Agency Administration.

Besides being a time for curricular innovation, the decades of the seventies and eighties constituted a period of expansion for Dyson College in so far as various centers and institutes were concerned. In 1982, for example, a Speech Communication Center was established. Three years later Academic Skills Centers were operating on the suburban and New York City campuses to help students with remediation in verbal and quantitative areas. Promising but underprepared students received assistance in reaching their goals through the Challenge to Achievement Program, and young people recovering from drug addiction were able to take Pace courses at Daytop Village's upstate New York center. Qualified high school students were given an opportunity to accelerate by taking Pace courses in their senior year as part of the Bridge Program, and high school students flocked to Pace annually for special programs which included Journalism Day on the White Plains campus.

High school students and various other audiences received abundant intellectual stimulation from the programs sponsored by the Straus Thinking and Learning Center. Established in 1984 and named for Pace benefactors Dr. and Mrs. Robert K. Straus, the Center, headed by Dr. Rachel Lauer, offers graduate courses and staff development programs in critical thinking. Pace Westchester faculty trained by Dr. Lauer began teaching such courses as Literature, History, and Philosophy from a Critical Thinking perspective in 1988. The Straus Thinking and Learning Center has also conducted workshops for Honors Program participants on the various campuses of the University, special programs for high school students, and conferences on Peace Studies.

Another Dyson College institute established in the 1980s is the Kwan Fong Institute of East Asian Studies, created in 1985. Sponsored by entrepreneur and philanthropist Maria Lee and East Asian scholar Yang-Leung Lin-Fong, the Institute sponsors lectures by authorities in the field of East Asian Studies, art exhibits and other cultural events. A guide in both English and Chinese for Asian students contemplating higher education in the United States was published by the Institute in 1986.

In addition to the programs offered by the various institutes of Dyson College, including the Center for Applied Ethics, the Women's Studies Center, and the Institute and Museum of Philosophy (which operated the world's first Museum of Philosophy at Pace in the early eighties), the University's College of Arts and Sciences has been able to expose Pace students to an exciting array of curricular and co-curricular experiences, due to grants received in the 1970s and 80s. In the mid-seventies, the Ford Foundation's Venture Fund enabled Pace to offer inter-disciplinary courses entitled "Conversations at Pace" to adult students on weekends. A decade later, a Pfizer grant led to the enhancement of Global Studies at Pace. In the interim, Mellon and Exxon grants, as well as a National Endowment for the Humanities Challenge Grant, permitted Dyson College to bring world-renowned scholars to Pace and to enhance various curricular areas.

As part of its efforts to provide intense intellectual stimulation for its students, alumni, and faculty, Dyson College not only pursued grants but also, in 1982, established the Dyson Society of Fellows. Through an ongoing program consisting of weekend conferences on wide-ranging issues, special lectures, and the presentation of scholarly papers authored by Fellows and by candidates for induction into the Society, the Dyson Society of Fellows became a powerful force on all campuses of the University in the 1980s.

In addition to seeking membership in the Dyson Society of Fellows, exceptionally qualified students are also afforded an opportunity to participate in honors programs in both New York and Westchester. In the mid-1980s, The

"If anything, I think the institution will become perhaps more selective than it has been in the past. I think there will be a controlled addition of new programs. I don't think we're going to rush into things, by any stretch of the imagination. I don't think we're going to jump into suggestions that appear out of nowhere...that we start a school in this, that, or the other thing — optometry, or veterinary medicine, or podiatry, et cetera. Maybe this is a part of the wisdom of the age. In other words, you become as you mature...you recognize the things that you're capable of. I think it is demonstrated by the computer science program. We're not just starting computer science. We've had computer science on the scene here, first as electronic digital computer programming, but then going through information science. That's been around here for fifteen or twenty years. But now we are formally structuring the school specifically designed to incorporate all of it under one umbrella and give a direction to it. I think this is a sign of mature growth. I don't think we're going to rush into things haphazardly by way of building things that aren't able to demonstrate, right from the very beginning, that they're going to be a meaningful portion of what this school is doing."

(George Knerr, Pace Oral History, November 15, 1983)

College of White Plains chapter of the national honor society Alpha Chi was judged the best in the nation. Dyson honor students have also excelled in the American Chemical Society's research competition, and University undergraduates have repeatedly won top prizes in the Model United Nations competition and in international debate tournaments. With numerous Dyson students opting for graduate or professional school following completion of their studies at Pace, it is not surprising that prestigious grants, including a Danforth Fellowship, have been awarded to graduates of the College of Arts and Sciences.

The kind of intellectual environment which results in graduate fellowships was cultivated in Dyson College in the 1970s and 80s during Dean Houle's tenure, and continued under Dr. Charles Masiello, Associate Dean of the College, who was named Dean of Dyson College in 1990. Students and faculty alike were stimulated by the lectures and seminars of William Barrett, philosopher and author, who served as a visiting Professor of Humanities throughout the eighties, and Burton Leiser, legal scholar and philosopher, who held the Edward J. Mortola Professorship from 1983 through 1988. Annual faculty conferences consisting of keynote addresses by outside authorities and workshops conducted by Dyson College faculty also enhanced the intellectual environment, as did conferences held under the auspices of the School of Computer Science and Information Systems.

School of Computer Science and Information Systems

Closely allied with Dyson College of Arts and Sciences, computer science programs were offered by both Dyson and the Lubin Schools of Business. When the programs were consolidated in a full-fledged School of Computer Science and Information Systems in 1983, the School was administered by Dean Joseph Houle of Dyson College until a Dean was selected for the new school. In October 1983 Dr. Susan Merritt, Chairperson of the Department of Computer Science at Pace's Westchester campuses and an internationally recognized expert in the field, was chosen Dean. Dr. Merritt immediately set out to build a faculty and earn accreditation in the shortest possible time for the new school's undergraduate programs in Computer Science and Management Information Systems and the master's programs in Computer Science and Information Systems.

In 1986 Pace's undergraduate Computer Science Program became one of only 22 programs in the United States to be accredited by the Computer Science Accreditation Commission of The Computing Sciences Accreditation Board. That same year, the New York State Education Department granted approval for the degree of Master of Science in Information Systems for New York and Westchester. In 1988 the State approved a Master's program in Telecommunications. Besides securing approval for innovative new programs, the School of Computer Science and Information Systems obtained a number of grants during its first few years of existence. For several consecutive

years the School received Graduate and Professional Opportunity grants from the United States Department of Education. A National Science Foundation grant in "Computer Graphics and Computer Vision" was also obtained.

The Lubin Schools of Business

At the very time the newest school of the University was scoring notable successes, Pace's oldest division, Lubin, was equipping itself for the future. In 1980 the Lubin School of Business Administration and the Graduate School of Business were consolidated. Three years later, the combined undergraduate and graduate enrollment of the Lubin Schools was 12,988, the largest of any private college or university in the United States and the fourth largest of all institutions of higher education in the country, exceeded by only three large public universities, the University of Texas at Austin, Arizona State University and Baruch College of the City University of New York.

Guiding the tremendous growth of the Lubin Schools during this period was Dr. Tony Bonaparte, who was named Dean in 1980 to replace Dr. Joseph Pastore, who became Vice President for Academic Affairs. Prior to being named Dean of the Lubin Schools of Business, Dr. Bonaparte had served as Dean of the Graduate School for five years. In 1982 Dean Bonaparte became Vice Provost for Corporate and International Relations while retaining his position as Dean of the Lubin Schools of Business. A year later Lubin was one of a half dozen schools chosen by the United States Department of Education to create comprehensive undergraduate programs in international business studies. Following the resignation of Dr. Bonaparte, in the fall of 1985, Dr. Verne S. Atwater served as Acting Dean of the Lubin Schools until July 1986, when Dr. George Parks, formerly Dean of the Rich School of Business Administration and Professor of Management at Emory University in Atlanta, became Dean of the Lubin Schools of Business. Dr. Parks served as Dean until his death in 1990. Dr. Parks was succeeded by Dr. Arthur Centonze.

Among the programs administered by Dr. Parks was

Mr. and Mrs. Joseph Lubin

the M.S. in Management. Initially authorized by the New York State Board of Regents in 1974, the most striking feature of this degree was the Executive Management program. Only six schools in the United States offered such programs at the time. Another highly innovative program was the joint degree in Management Science with Polytechnic Institute of New York. This was introduced in 1975, just one year after another program designed to meet specific needs, the Graduate Management Program for Women, made its debut. Supported by an Andrew W. Mellon Foundation grant totalling almost $300,000, the two-year program helped exceptionally qualified female Liberal Arts graduates prepare for an increasing number of managerial careers in business. Every student accepted for the program received a partial scholarship and following the first year of full-time study, students were placed in corporate internships. Upon successful completion of the second year of the program, participants were awarded a master's degree.

For Pace undergraduates majoring in business, a new option in 1976 was the Retailing program, which combined classroom instruction with actual positions in the field. The program was conceived and implemented by Pace trustee William Humphrey, who had been chief exec-

utive officer of Abercrombie and Fitch and Executive Vice President of Lord and Taylor. By the mid-1970s qualified undergraduates were also able to take advantage of B.A./M.B.A. and B.S./M.B.A. programs, which shortened the time required to obtain both the baccalaureate and master's degrees. For graduate students wishing to accelerate, the M.B.A. day program, introduced in 1977, was a welcome option. Full-time employees of AT&T, IBM, and the Bank of Credit and Commerce International were also afforded an opportunity to study at Pace. An Executive M.B.A. program designed for AT&T began in 1984, as did an International Management Development Program for the Bank of Credit and Commerce. An IBM/Pace Graduate Business Management Program held its first sessions, on the Briarcliff campus, in 1986.

Other innovative programs of the Lubin Schools of Business were the Master's degree in Economics, introduced in 1983 and designed to train economists for the marketplace; a 1984 pilot program in Computers in Accounting Education; a Business Communication program, which began in 1985; a Hotel Management program, launched in 1986; and a program in Certified Financial Planning which debuted in 1988. The Doctor of Professional Studies program, the first of its kind when introduced in 1972, was still enabling upper-level executives to combine full-time work with part-time study.

Besides the array of degree and certificate programs offered by the Lubin Schools of Business, a number of centers and institutes affiliated with Lubin were doing pioneering work in the 1970s and 80s. They included the Small Business Development Center, the Center for Applied Research, established in the mid-seventies, the Institute for Brazilian-American Business Studies, the Institute for International Banking and the Center for International Business, each of which was founded in the early eighties, the Small Business Development Center, and the Canada-U.S. Business Studies Institute, both created in the mid-eighties. An outgrowth of the Canada-U.S. Business Studies Institute was an exchange program, in research, teaching and executive training, between Pace and the Ecole des Hautes Etudes Commerciales in Montreal. The Corsi Institute for Labor/Management Relations, established in 1967 to honor New York State Industrial Commissioner Edward Corsi, was placed under the auspices of the Lubin School in 1983.

In addition to their various institutes and centers, the Lubin Schools afforded their constituents abundant intellectual stimulation through the Breakfast with the Chief program, which brought top business people to Pace for interactive early morning sessions with business students; the well-attended Tax Seminars, which annually lured professional accountants to Pace; the Peter Drucker Management Development Program; the incorporation of Robotics into the undergraduate Management program; AISEC, a student managed international Business organization; honor societies in Business; and the Lubin Lecture Series, which brought top business people to Pace campuses for both formal presentations and informal interaction with students, faculty and alumni.

Distinguished visiting professors and executives in residence also constituted invaluable on-campus resources, as did the individuals named to academic chairs in the Lubin Schools of Business. In 1983 Dr. Stephen Eyre, Senior Vice President and Corporate Secretary of Citibank and Citicorp, was appointed to the Citicorp Chair in Finance. The following year William K. Grollman was named to the Schaeberle Professorship in Accounting. In 1985 a New York Stock Exchange Chair in Economics was established and Dr. William C. Freund, Chief Economist of the New York Stock Exchange, was appointed to the chair. While distinguished new faculty were coming to Pace, a number of professors who had been with the University for some time were given an opportunity to teach in Pace-affiliated programs in such far-flung places as Sao Paulo, Brazil, Lyon, France, the United Kingdom, India, Switzerland, Nigeria, Morocco and the People's Republic of China.

At the same time it was expanding overseas, Pace was seeking accreditation for its business programs from the American Assembly of Collegiate Schools of Business, an association organized in 1919. AACSB had been accrediting business programs since 1961. After meeting with representatives of AACSB in 1981, Pace Vice President Dr. Ewald Nyquist analyzed the pros and cons of accreditation. While admitting that AACSB's criteria were highly quantitative, Dr. Nyquist, nevertheless, recommended that Pace "immediately undertake the necessary steps to seek accreditation."[68]

In October 1982, Dr. Joseph Pastore, Vice President for Academic Affairs, submitted a lengthy report to the Educational Policies Committee of the Board of Trustees on AACSB accreditation. Dr. Pastore noted that "until 1982, AACSB standards were viewed as highly quantitative, process-oriented, and inflexible."[69] However, "recent changes in AACSB standards show AACSB as more open to qualitative, product-oriented assessments."[70] Dr. Pastore then proceeded to analyze the pluses and minuses of accreditation before concluding that "it is reasonable to argue that the incremental cost relating directly to our seeking AACSB accreditation is nominal considering the benefits."[71] He also noted that "while accreditation may not help, the absence of it may hurt."[72] In this regard he observed that a number of colleges and universities in the New York area already possessed AACSB accreditation and that "our competition, more and more, is citing their AACSB accreditation at student recruitment fairs and in public advertising."[73] Dr. Pastore also expressed concern that graduate schools might discriminate against applicants from schools lacking AACSB accreditation and that foundations would react negatively to grant applications submitted by non-AACSB accredited business schools.

Perhaps the most compelling reason for Pace to seek AACSB accreditation, however, was that lack of accreditation might negatively impact the University's internationally recognized accounting program. According to Dr. Pastore:

> AACSB accreditation of our business program is a condition for accrediting our accounting program.

The latter should carry accreditation (and will probably be easier for us to achieve, given business accreditation). Consider the worst (and hopefully least likely): What if States begin to require that certification as a C.P.A. be conditioned upon study in an accredited program?[74]

Pace Institute had been faced with a similar problem in the 1930s. At that time Homer Pace did what was required to guarantee the viability of the school's excellent accounting program. In the 1980s, nothing less would do. The Educational Policies Committee of the Board of Trustees, therefore, resolved to seek AACSB accreditation in 1982. By the end of 1986 Pace had complied with most of the AACSB requirements, but was deemed deficient in the area of research and publications. Over the course of the next few years, the Lubin Schools addressed this problem and continued to actively pursue AACSB accreditation.

Just as the absence of AACSB accreditation was perceived as negatively impacting the Lubin Schools, so, too, was an article published in the November 19, 1984, issue of *Forbes* magazine. Entitled "The M.B.A. Mills," the article painted an erroneous portrait of exhausted, unqualified students pursuing Master's degrees at Pace at night. *Forbes* charged that Pace's admissions standards were low; yet, in 1984, Pace's admissions index was 160 points higher than the minimum index recommended by AACSB. On the matter of AACSB accreditation, the article referred to "unaccredited Pace," conveying the impression that the voluntary AACSB accreditation the University was seeking was more significant than Middle States and other forms of accreditation which the institution had possessed for years.

The *Forbes* piece also conjured up the image of ridiculously overcrowded classes simply because the reporter who wrote the article happened to observe one of the few truly large classes in a university where only one percent of the classes exceeded 60 students and the average class size was 25. Adding insult to injury, the article insisted that the ratio of part-time to full-time faculty was 2:1, whereas 60 percent of the courses in the university were taught by full-time faculty members and 70 percent of the faculty of the Lubin Schools were full-time.

Perhaps the best refutation of the *Forbes* piece was the success of Pace graduates. For six years prior to the publication of the error-filled article, a Pace graduate earned the highest score from New York State on the national C.P.A. examination. In 1980 the highest score in the entire United States was earned by Pace graduate Sally Hoffman. That year 57,000 people sat for the grueling 19.5 hour examination which was administered over a three-day period. Paceite Sally Hoffman's scores on each of the four parts of the exam ranged from 92 to 99. The Rye, New York, mother of three, who had earned a degree in Sociology at the University of Toronto in the 1960s, before enrolling a decade later in the graduate business program on Pace's Pleasantville campus, claimed that "her training at Pace was absolutely instrumental to her achievement on the exam."[75] Exceptionally qualified Pace graduates such as Sally Hoffman have historically enjoyed splendid career opportunities.

Proof positive of this was a 1984 Executive/College Survey by Standard & Poor's which ranked the University "in the top 12%, or 58th nationwide in the number of alumni from a single institution holding leading management positions in business."[76] In the same survey Pace ranked 8th in New York State. The 1985 Executive/College Survey ranked Pace in the highest 11.4 percent, or sixty-second nationwide and eighth in New York State. A 1986 survey by AACSB found that Pace's Lubin Schools were the largest private business schools in the United States and the second largest, after Baruch College of the City University of New York, of all institutions, public as well as private. In 1988 a *U.S. News and World Report* survey placed Pace's Graduate School of Business among the top four eastern regional schools of business.

School of Education

In contrast with the huge Lubin Schools, Pace's School of Education, founded in 1966, is one of the smaller components of the University but in the 1970s and 80s, it more than held its own within the larger institution. Indeed, the School of Education was gaining statewide recognition for being one of only twelve education schools selected by the New York State Education Department, in the early seventies, to participate in a pilot program for evaluating the effectiveness of competency based teacher training as opposed to formal course work. At the very time it was forging ahead with innovative approaches to teacher training, the Pace University School of Education was offering a well-received graduate program in Educational Administration. Launched with 39 students in the spring of 1971, the program had 350 graduates four years later. A decade later, in 1984, an interdisciplinary program leading to a Bachelor of Science degree in Early Childhood Development was introduced on the New York campus.

By the time the program in Early Childhood Development became part of the Pace curriculum, the School of Education had passed through a time of transition when thought was given to phasing out this division of the University. In a candid report on the School of Education, Pace Vice President Ewald Nyquist, who also served as New York State Commissioner of Education before joining Pace, stated that "selected programs can be pruned and others preserved and relocated for administrative purposes in other sectors of the University, thus eliminating the need for a functional School of Education."[77] Dr. Nyquist also said: "Abolishing the School would not come as a surprise nor generate the same pain and distress usually associated with a painful idea not previously broached."[78] Dr. Nyquist, nevertheless, concluded that "the School of Education at Pace University should be continued" because, in his opinion, "it has a valid base upon which, with renewed purpose and support, can be built a strengthened organization with increased services, better quality, more efficient and economical administration, and a larger student body."[79]

The Board of Trustees accepted Dr. Nyquist's recommendation, and in 1982 the School of Education was reor-

ganized. Office Information Systems was placed in the Lubin Schools of Business and the Secretarial Studies program was moved to University College. Teacher training programs were consolidated on the White Plains campus. In 1983 Dr. David Avdul was named Dean of the School of Education, to succeed Dean Frederick Bunt who returned to teaching as a member of the Computer Science faculty. Assisting Dean Avdul in reshaping the Education program were Dr. Rita Silverman, Chair of Elementary and Secondary Education, and Dr. Sandra Flank, who succeeded Dr. Silverman as chair in 1988.

For the remainder of the 1980s, the School of Education enhanced the quality of its programs while, at the same time, reaching out to ethnic minorities, whether the Japanese and Spanish residents of Westchester, served by the programs in the English Language Center, or recent Chinese immigrants enrolled in P.S. 131 on the Lower East Side of Manhattan. P.S. 131 and a public secondary school, Lower East Side Prep, were participants in Pace's innovative Stay in School Partnership Program (SSPP), which was funded by the New York State Education Department.

To assist minority students to prepare for careers in Education, Pace developed a Teacher Opportunity Corp (TOC) which offered scholarships to minority students who selected Education as a field of concentration or as a minor. The TOC program included articulation with the Borough of Manhattan Community College. Adults interested in switching to teaching from other careers were able to enroll in a joint Pace-Westchester Community College program created with the assistance of a grant from the Fund for the Improvement of Postsecondary Education. Educators already in the field, as well as those aspiring to careers in Education, could choose from Pace Masters programs in Curriculum and Educational Administration. A specially designed School Business Management Certificate Program was implemented for educators already in service. A Master of Science for Teachers program for liberal arts graduates, early retirees, and individuals changing careers was implemented in 1987. Within two years, it became the largest graduate program in the School of Education. A generous grant from the Carl and Lily Pforzheimer Foundation enhanced minority teacher recruitment in critical subject areas for the Master of Science for Teachers degree.

In the late 1980s, the School of Education positioned the University for Governor Cuomo's Liberty Scholarship program with a $240,000 Liberty Partnership Program Grant (LPP) beginning in the academic year 1989-90. In December 1989 the School of Education received a federally funded Student Literacy Grant. Through these grants (SSPP, TOC, LPP and Student Literacy), the School of Education became the flagship school for urban outreach to at-risk schools and populations, thereby enhancing the University's mission and motto of Opportunitas.

In the 1970s and 80s, teachers from White Plains and other districts in the State of New York enrolled in the Taft Seminars on the Two-Party System. These seminars were held first on the New York campus and then in Westchester, in conjunction with the Social Sciences departments, the School of Education, and the Institute for Sub/Urban Governance, which was headed by former Westchester County Executive Edwin G. Michaelian from 1974 until his death in 1983.

University College

Like the School of Education, University College was striving to meet the needs of adult learners in the seventies and eighties. With activities ranging from non-credit self-help courses to certificate programs in Business and the Liberal Arts, Continuing Education was indeed lively in the 1970s. On all campuses of the University, adults could enroll in either regular or special courses. Some programs were designed for specific constituencies, such as the Associate Degree program for employed minority persons sponsored by Pace and the National Council of Negro Women. Another special program was the Pace Active Retirement Center (PARC), headquartered on the New York campus.

Lectures, workshops and a week-long summer retreat at Pace Pleasantville were regular features of PARC in the seventies when Pace's adult education division was known as the School of Continuing Education.

Following the appointment in 1979 of Dr. James Hall as Dean of the School of Continuing Education, the School became University College. Five years later, University College was replaced by the Division of Continuing Education and Evening Studies. At that time, Dean Hall was appointed Associate Professor in the Lubin School of Business. Associate Dean Joseph Dumbra was named head of the Division of Continuing Education and Evening Studies in New York and Associate Dean Dr. M. Berchmans Coyle, R.D.C., became head of the new division in Westchester. The Division continued to administer the B.A. in Liberal Studies, B.S. in General Studies, and A.A. (A-STEP) in General Liberal Arts.

Lienhard School of Nursing

Like Continuing Education, the Lienhard School of Nursing experienced reorganization in the 70s and 80s. Founded in 1966 and named for Pace trustee and alumnus Gustav O. Lienhard in 1975, the School of Nursing was reorganized four years later with the aim of consolidating its undergraduate and graduate programs. At that time, Dean Marjorie Ramphal, who had previously administered the graduate and baccalaureate programs, was named Dean of the unified Lienhard School of Nursing. A year after the reorganization, a Generic Master's program, one of only two in the United States, was introduced to prepare students lacking an undergraduate degree in nursing for professional nursing careers. A Generic Baccalaureate Nursing degree was also offered to undergraduates on the New York campus in 1980. The following year a Specialty Master's program was introduced, designed for registered nurses possessing a baccalaureate degree in nursing. The three-track program enabled students to choose teaching of nursing care, provision of nursing care or administration of nursing care as well as a clinical specialty in the adult, maternal/child, psychiatric, community or gerontologic areas. In 1983 a Center for Continuing Education in Nursing was established within the Lienhard School.

In 1986 Dr. Marilyn Jaffe-Ruiz was named Dean, to succeed Dr. Beverly Bonaparte who had served in that position since 1981. The following year the School was offering a Bachelor of Science degree in Nursing and a combined B.S.N./M.S, the latter to replace the Generic Master's program. In addition to curricular innovations, the Lienhard School of Nursing was justifiably proud of its success in obtaining major grants, which included awards from the Robert Wood Johnson Foundation, a grant of $l.3 million from the Kellogg Foundation for the establishment of a model program of primary health care within the University, and an award in excess of $500,000, made in 1988 by the United States Department of Health and Human Services to enable the School to deliver health care to the growing number of homeless families in Westchester County.

THE EIGHTIES: A PERIOD OF TRANSITION

Despite the quality of its programs, enrollment in the Lienhard School of Nursing declined in the 1980s, as did enrollment in nursing schools nationwide, for reasons which ranged from the perceived status and compensation of nurses to far greater opportunities in fields not formerly pursued by women. Other schools of the University were also concerned about enrollment in the eighties as the number of high school seniors dwindled. Not surprisingly, even in an institution which saw an increase in enrollment in the 1970s, enrollment management became a priority issue, along with faculty governance and the abolition of mandatory retirement.

For a time, enrollment seemed to be the top priority, and various recommendations were made concerning enrollment management. In addition to an enhanced advertising program, which included television commercials, the University derived favorable publicity from such

diverse events as the Smithsonian at Pace program in the spring of 1987, and the relocation of the Hastings Center, a prestigious think tank, to the Briarcliff campus in 1986. The unified commencements held at Madison Square Garden from 1983 through 1987 also generated publicity for Pace. With such celebrated figures as Chief Justice Warren Burger, Senator Alfonse D'Amato, and actress Ruby Dee as guest speakers, the commencements annually filled the Garden with 15,000 people, attracting considerable media attention. But by the late eighties, the University had reverted to the more personal approach of having separate commencements for the different campuses. In 1989 the New York commencement was held at Radio City Music Hall, while the White Plains and Pleasantville commencements took place at the refurbished Westchester County Center. Law school commencements continued to be held on the White Plains campus.

How the type and location of commencement affects enrollment defies measurement, but there were other innovations of the eighties which had a more direct impact on enrollment. These included the flat tuition rate and innovative scheduling to attract new students and boost retention. A May term took the place of the January Winterim for the period from 1985-87. Many Pace students who enrolled in May courses did so to accelerate, while others took advantage of the late April conclusion of the spring semester to get a head start on summer jobs. To attract new adult students to Pace, selected courses, both credit bearing and non-credit, were offered at an off-campus Northern Westchester location in 1986.

Fluctuations in enrollment provided faculty and administrators with interesting challenges throughout the decade. Especially concerned with this issue was Dr. Dorothy Blaney, Executive Vice President for Planning, Personnel and Academic Support Services, who had come to Pace in 1983 from the New York State Education Department, where she had been Deputy Commissioner of Higher Education and the Professions, to serve as Dr. Mortola's Executive Assistant and Vice President for Strategic and Long-Range Planning. As Executive Vice President until her resignation in 1989 to accept the presidency of Cedar Crest College, Dr. Blaney coordinated the University's enrollment management efforts. Working closely with Dr. Blaney was Dr. Miriam Moran, Vice President for Enrollment Management.

Dr. Joseph Pastore, Jr., who relinquished the position of Dean of the Lubin Schools in 1980 to become Academic Vice President, and who was named Executive Vice President for Academic Affairs in 1984 and Provost in 1985, labored throughout the decade to enhance the quality of courses and offerings in the belief that by making what was good even better, superior students would be attracted to the University. Dr. Pastore was in an excellent position to judge the effectiveness of what went on in the University's classrooms because, like many other Pace administrators over the years, he continued to teach one course at Pace and, while on leave in the fall of 1988, was a visiting faculty member at Columbia University's School of Business.

Historically, the emphasis has been on teaching at Pace, going back to the days of the Institute. For that reason, many Pace administrators have been recruited from the ranks of the faculty, to which they often return in the twilight of their careers. Dr. Edward Kenny, Dean of The College of White Plains, and Dr. Thomas Robinson, Academic Vice President of Pace University, both returned to the classroom in 1980 before retiring a few years later. In 1973 Dr. Joseph Sinzer, Academic Vice President and corporate Secretary, relinquished that position to become University historian and C. Richard Pace Professor of History.

Sometimes men and women who had acquired teaching and administrative experience elsewhere joined Pace in key administrative positions. Dr. Arthur Antin, Superintendent of Schools for the City of White Plains, became Dean of Students at The College of White Plains in 1981. Three years later, Dr. Antin was named Vice President of The College of White Plains when Dr. Frank Falcone, formerly Provost of Ithaca College, Vice President of CWP and Executive Vice President for the Westchester campuses of

"Jack Schiff was a key figure. They were a doubles team. That was a beautiful operation. Jack took care of the inside and Ed the outside."
(Richard Matthews, March 9, 1990)

Pace from 1983, left to become President of Springfield University. Prior to Dr. Falcone's assumption of the reins in Pleasantville as well as in White Plains, Dr. Robert E. Christin, formerly President of Marymount College, Tarrytown, had served as Vice President and Dean of the Pleasantville/Briarcliff campus since 1979.

In 1984 the Chairman of the Department of Literature and Communications at Pleasantville, Dr. Richard Podgorski, was named Dean of Studies for the Pleasantville campus, and in 1988 also became Pleasantville Vice President. In 1984 Dr. Louise Cutler, Professor of Chemistry, was named Dean of Studies of The College of White Plains, and in 1987, Dr. Margaret R. Gotti, Chairman of the Department of Public Administration, was appointed Vice President for White Plains.

Some of the administrative changes occurring at Pace in the 1980s resulted from the untimely death of Dr. Jack Schiff in January 1984. He had served as Executive Vice President of Pace from 1970 until 1982, and thereafter as University Provost. Going back to the 1960s, Dr. Schiff, who had been a Professor and Chairman of Marketing, Dean of the Lubin School, and Provost, was a key person on an administrative team whose members included Dr. Joseph Pastore, Dr. George Knerr, Dr. Joseph Sinzer and Dr. Thomas Robinson. The growth of the University was in no small measure attributable to the genius and dedication of Dr. Schiff. With the assistance and support of a dedicated executive management team, the Schiff-Mortola "partnership" guided Pace through a period of unprecedented growth in the 1970s and 80s. Management expert Peter Drucker discussed the Pace style of management in his book *Innovation and Entrepreneurship*, published in

1986. In the same section of the volume in which he analyzed the innovative management styles of the Polaroid
corporation and McDonald's restaurants, Drucker said,
"Dr. Edward J. Mortola built up the institution from nothing in 1947 into New York City's third-largest and fastest-
growing university....In the university's early years he was a
radical innovator. But when Pace was still very small
(around 1950), Mortola built a strong top management
team. All members were given a major, clearly defined
responsibility, for which they were expected to take full
accountability and give leadership. A few years later, Mortola then decided what his own role was to be and con-
verted himself into a traditional university president, while
at the same time building a strong independent board of
trustees to advise and support him."[80]

Following Dr. Schiff's death, Dr. Edward J. Mortola
assumed the new role of Chancellor in September 1984,
and Dr. William Sharwell, Senior Vice President of AT&T,
became President of the University.

Before joining AT&T, Dr. Sharwell, who possesses a
doctorate from Harvard, was a faculty member, department chairman, and dean at Seton Hall University. While
at AT&T he had been Chairman of the Board of Trustees
of Westchester Community College and after serving as a
Pace trustee for eleven years, he was named Chairman of
the Board in 1983, a position he relinquished at the time
he became President of the University. When Dr. Mortola
reached the mandatory retirement age of 70 in 1987, Dr.
Sharwell became Chief Executive Officer of the University.

Other administrative changes occurring in the late
eighties were the appointments of Dr. Joseph Houle, Dean
of Dyson College since 1971, as Vice Provost in 1987
and of Dr. John Mc Call, Associate Dean of the Lubin
Schools since 1976, as Vice Provost for Academic Administration in 1988.

Quite aside from the enrollment and other challenges
facing Pace administrators and faculty in the decade of the
eighties, the University's students were embracing new
challenges, both inside and outside the classroom. Pace's

*"In 1985 we had an Executive Vice President for
Planning; in 1965 the scheduler did the planning... You
could write letters in answers to state queries but now
reports are required. So many things became
professionalized and when that happens, it takes on a
life of its own."*

(Dr. Joseph E. Houle, April 6, 1990)

Co-Op program, guided by Alice Korngold, had its mod-
est beginnings in 1980, placing students in corporate and
other paid positions. This program became the tenth
largest in the nation before the end of the decade. The University's Leadership Development Program, administered
by Dr. Grace Lamacchia-Paris, exposed a select group of
students to experiences and people capable of actualizing
the undergraduates' potential for leadership. Ongoing
study abroad programs and the Pace Opportunity Program, designed for minority students and administered by
Dr. George Mims, served numerous undergraduates in the
eighties.

Every Pace student benefitted from ISIS, the Integrated
Student Information System. Implemented under the leadership of University Registrar Phyllis Mount, ISIS comput-
erized registration, scheduling, and student records. Pace
students also benefitted from the establishment of Student
Service Centers on the various Pace campuses. A form of
"one-stop shopping," the Centers were strategically
located in heavily trafficked buildings, and provided students with answers and referrals for a variety of academic
and non-academic questions. Graduates of the University
were able to stay in closer touch with alma mater thanks
to an Alumni Federation established in 1982, while faculty, staff and administrators of Pace and other non-profit
institutions in the New York area benefitted from the Academic Federal Credit Union, established in 1980 through
the efforts of Dr. James Holmes, Chairman of the Department of Social Sciences at Pleasantville, and colleagues
from Westchester and New York. An offshoot of the

WILLIAM G. SHARWELL

Dr. William G. Sharwell, fourth President of Pace University, was born in Newark, New Jersey in 1920. A graduate of Bloomfield High School, he received a B.A. degree in accounting from Seton Hall University in 1941 before joining the accounting firm of Brief, Linn and Brief in Newark. During World War II, Dr. Sharwell was a fingerprint analyst for the Federal Bureau of Investigation. Following the war, from 1945 until 1950, he was a faculty member and department chairman at Seton Hall University. While at Seton Hall, Dr. Sharwell earned an M.B.A. in Accounting and Finance at New York University. In 1952 he received an M.B.A. in Administration from Harvard University and in 1960 Harvard awarded him a D.C.S. in Corporation Finance. Dr. Sharwell's long and distinguished career at Bell and AT&T had begun in the meantime.

Commencing in 1953 when he joined the Personnel Department of Bell Telephone Laboratories, Dr. Sharwell quickly advanced through a series of increasingly demanding positions at Bell Labs and AT&T where he became Personnel Research Supervisor in 1955. After serving as Director of College Employment at AT&T from 1959 until 1961, Dr. Sharwell became Division Manager and subsequently General Manager of New York Telephone's Northern Area in Upstate New York. In 1962 he was appointed General Manager of New York Telephone in Westchester. From 1965 until 1966 a series of Vice Presidencies followed and in 1971 Dr. Sharwell became Executive Vice President of Operations of the New York Telephone Company. Five years later, he joined AT&T as Vice President of Planning and Administration. In 1980 he became Vice President of Staff, and two years later as Vice President of Divestiture Implementation and Staff, he played an important role in the reorganization of the world's largest corporation. Before retiring from AT&T to join Pace in 1984, Dr. Sharwell was named Senior Vice President-Staff.

Hardly a newcomer to either Pace or the management of higher education when he was named President of Pace University in 1984, Dr. Sharwell had served on the University's Board of Trustees since 1973 and was Chairman of the Board since 1983. He had also been a trustee of Westchester Community College. As Pace President from 1984 and President and Chief Executive Officer from 1987 until 1990, Dr. Sharwell applied his considerable business expertise to stabilizing enrollment and funding both existing and new programs. The Graduate Center in downtown White Plains was completed during his tenure. Graduate law programs were expanded and the University's newest component, the School of Computer Science and Information Systems, achieved international recognition. Despite these considerable attainments, Dr. Sharwell will probably be best remembered for his unwavering support of student activities, ranging from theatrical productions to proms. Above all, he was a sports fan who rarely missed games of Pace's men's and women's championship basketball teams. A strong supporter of feminism, Dr. Sharwell served on the board of the National Organization for Women/Legal Defense and Education Fund both before and during his tenure as Pace CEO. During his years at Pace he was also co-chairman of the National Conference of Christians and Jews. Leisure time activities include collecting and flying unusual kites, producing videotapes and films and enjoying music, especially jazz.

The creativity exhibited by Dr. Sharwell in his avocational pursuits was reminiscent of Homer and Robert Pace's strong interest in photography. Dr. Sharwell's abiding concern for the institution he headed for six years was also in keeping with the example set by previous Pace Presidents. In an interview with the Pace Press a year before his retirement from the University, Dr. Sharwell spoke about the Pace tradition and the institution's special niche in higher education. "You know," he said,"there are eighty universities in New York, but wherever I go people come up to me and say 'my kids go to Pace,' or 'my uncle went to Pace,' or 'I work with Pace people.' This university touches an awful lot of lives; and it touches them very well. Pace is a human institution that serves a great purpose very well" (Pace Press, May 11, 1989, p. 8.).

Credit Union, the Consumers Energy Cooperative, a fuel co-op, became an independent organization.

Although the University was concentrating on enroll-ment and the delivery of academic services to students in the 1980s, it did not neglect co-curricular and extra-curric-ular activities. In the eighties, plans were formulated for a new sports stadium and Life Fitness Center at Pleasantville to be financed, along with other projects, by funds derived from the $100 million Capital Campaign, launched in 1987. Even without the athletic facilities envisioned for the nineties, Paceites were enjoying sports and other extra-cur-ricular activities in the eighties. Whether it was the New York campus's Pace Pageant, at which a Mr. and Ms. Pace were selected, a dance-a-thon at Pace New York to raise money for UNICEF, or a Pleasantville Beach Party, featur-ing ice cream, soft drinks and other non-alcoholic refresh-ments, students were enjoying their leisure time. The twenty-fifth anniversary of the Pleasantville campus, in the fall of 1988, was also a grand occasion.

Throughout the eighties and into the nineties, on all Pace campuses, spring was an especially busy season for student activities, whether those sponsored by fraternities, such as the Nu Zeta chapter of the national fraternity Delta Kappa Epsilon, or by Student Activities, an increas-ingly important area which was overseen by Edward Zanato, Vice President for Student Personnel Services. Assisting the Vice President were Emanuel Heller, the beloved Dean for Students in New York until his death in 1987, Maryanne DiMarzo, named Dean for Students in Westchester in 1987, and Dr. Terrell V. Kolodzinski, who became Dean for Students at Pleasantville and Briarcliff in 1990. Geoffrey Harter, Dean for Students at White Plains, and Salvatore J. Turchio, Dean for Students at New York, were also appointed in 1990.

Outdoor events, such as the annual PIPNIC at Pleas-antville, attracted students from all Pace campuses, as did the consistently outstanding theatrical productions at White Plains, New York and Pleasantville. That there was unity despite Pace's incredible diversity was evident from

PATRICIA O'DONNELL EWERS

Chicago native Dr. Patricia O'Donnell Ewers, the fifth President and first female chief executive officer of Pace University, was educated at Mundelein College, where she was awarded a B.A. degree summa cum laude and at Loyola University, Chicago, where she earned the M.A. and Ph.D. in English and received the Outstanding Alumna award.

Dr. Ewers' career in higher education began in 1966 when she became an assistant professor of English at DePaul University in Chicago. Three years later, Dr. Ewers became director of the Humanities Division of De Paul's General Education Program. In 1973 Dr. Ewers became chairperson of the University's Department of English. In 1976 she was named Dean of DePaul's College of Liberal Arts and Sciences.

As Vice President and Dean of Faculties at DePaul for a decade commencing in 1980, Dr. Ewers was responsible for initiating and administering a comprehensive enrollment management program. Her other achievements included the successful coordination of an NCA accreditation visit and participation in a $40 million capital development campaign. As a member of DePaul's Budget Committee, Dr. Ewers authored the University's Budget Committee Report. Her lengthy list of publications also includes articles and monographs on subjects ranging from the role of women in higher education to the mission of liberal arts colleges.

An effective public speaker as well as an author, Dr. Ewers has addressed conferences and meetings of professional associations throughout the United States. In view of her national reputation as an educator and the varied and increasingly responsible administrative positions she held at DePaul University, Dr. Ewers was elected President of Pace University in December 1989. She assumed office on July 1, 1990, and was inaugurated as Pace's fifth President at Avery Fisher Hall, Lincoln Center, in New York City on November 3, 1990.

CARL H. PFORZHEIMER III

Carl H. Pforzheimer, III, a trustee of Pace University since 1981 and Chairman of the Board of Trustees beginning in 1990, was born in 1936. Educated at Harvard University, where he received an A.B. in 1958 and an M.B.A. in 1963, Mr. Pforzheimer is Managing Partner of Carl H. Pforzheimer & Co. and director of Petroleum and Trading Corporation.

Mr. Pforzheimer's association with Pace University is the next step in an established connection between his family and the University. Carol Pforzheimer, Carl's mother, was a trustee of the University from 1973 to 1979.

In addition to his service on the Pace University Board of Trustees, Mr. Pforzheimer is a trustee of the Horace Mann-Barnard School, the Hoff-Barthelson School of Music, the Visiting Nurse Service of New York and the Volunteer Urban Consulting Group. He is also a member of the Scarsdale Union Free School District Board of Education, and Vice President and Treasurer of the Carl and Lily Pforzheimer Foundation.

the cross-campus attendance at sporting events. Particularly outstanding in the eighties was the women's basketball team, which included one two-time All-American, Jennifer DiMaggio, and one two-time Academic All-American, Amy Acker.

The decade also saw the completion of a number of capital projects. Under the guidance of Dr. George Knerr, Vice President for Facilities Planning, the Mortola Library, a striking contemporary building overlooking Choate Pond, was erected on the Pleasantville campus. Named in honor of Doris and Edward Mortola, the library was dedicated in October 1983. Townhouse dormitories and new

science laboratories were also built on the Pleasantville campus in the eighties, and the athletic field was refurbished. In New York the University sold 150 Nassau Street and erected an addition to the Civic Center Building to provide more classroom and office space. The tower of the Civic Center Building was renamed Maria's Tower in 1983, in honor of culinary entrepreneur Maria Lee of Hong Kong, a benefactor of the University.

The urban renewal area of downtown White Plains became the home of Pace's Graduate School when the Evelyn and Joseph I. Lubin Graduate Center was dedicated in 1987. Occupying four floors of a high-rise office condominium building in the Westchester Financial Center, the Graduate School houses programs in Business, Education, Computer Science and Information Systems, and Public Administration.

That the University is a dominant presence, a stone's throw from the new Transportation Center in the heart of Westchester County's premier urban area, seems very fitting for despite the bucolic charm of its Pleasantville and Briarcliff campuses, Pace is quintessentially an urban educational institution. Many of the students lounging around in springtime under century-old trees on the Westchester campuses view their time in the "country" as preparation for careers in the Big Apple and other cities in the United States and abroad. On November 3, 1990, when Dr. Patricia O'Donnell Ewers was inaugurated as the fifth president of Pace University at an impressive ceremony held at Avery Fisher Hall, Pace's mission as an urban university was reaffirmed.

In the future, as the University prepares for its centennial in the year 2006, our country and our world will have to come to grips with countless problems resulting from the increasing urbanization of planet earth. If the past is any guide, Pace graduates are likely to be in the forefront of the search for innovative solutions to seemingly insurmountable problems and not just in the fields of Accounting, Management, Marketing and Finance for, on the eve of its second century, Pace University is a vital, comprehensive

JOHN C. HALEY

Like the founders of Pace, John C. Haley, who served as chairman of the University's board of trustees from 1984 to 1990, is a Midwesterner. An Ohio native, born in Akron in 1929, Mr. Haley received his B.A. from Miami University in that state. His graduate work was done at Columbia University where he earned a master's degree in 1951. Two years later Mr. Haley joined the Chase National Bank, serving initially in its Special Development Program and by 1955 in the bank's International Department. In 1959 Mr. Haley became assistant treasurer of Chase. By 1962 he was second vice president of the bank and two years later he was named senior vice president. From 1970 until 1973 he served as chief executive officer of the Orion Bank Group, Chase's London affiliate. In 1973 Mr. Haley became executive vice president of Chase.

Following his retirement from the Chase Manhattan Bank in 1984, Mr. Haley, who received an honorary doctorate in Law from Pace that year, joined Dr. Henry Kissinger as Deputy Chairman of Kissinger Associates, Inc. From 1986 until 1988 Dr. Haley was Chairman and CEO of Business International Corporation. Over the years Dr. Haley served as director of numerous corporations and nonprofit institutions, including the International Executive Service Corp, Ernst Von Siemens Stiftung, Armco, Inc., the German American Chamber of Commerce, of which he was twice Vice Chairman, the Egypt-U.S. Business Council of which he was Vice Chairman, the U.S.-U.S.S.R. Trade and Economic Council, the Japan Society, and the Pacific Basin Economic Council. While serving as chairman of the Pace University Board of Trustees, Dr. Haley was also chairman of the Advisory Committee of the Emerging Eastern European Fund.

For Homer, New York City, at the beginning of the twentieth century, meant OPPORTUNITAS. At the end of the century, a thorough education combining the theoretical with the practical, the contacts made while in the University and the networking afforded alumni, in addition to the degrees earned at the University, add up to Pace's motto, OPPORTUNITAS, for tens of thousands of students. As a recent University advertising slogan states, "You Can Get There from Here." Goals are indeed attainable. Homer discovered that to be true, and, hopefully, Paceites will continue to find this to be so well beyond the twentieth century.

At some point in the twenty-first century, a number of the University's buildings acquired or erected in the previous century may no longer stand. Conceivably Pace may have branched out in ways its founders never envisioned. Perhaps there will be orbiting educational stations, but if a great University's spirit is found in its mission, namely to provide educational and career opportunities to men and women of promise, no matter what their backgrounds, the dynamic, continuously evolving institution known as Pace University is likely to be alive and well and functioning in New York, Westchester, internationally, and maybe even inter-galactically. Stranger things have happened. After all,

President Patricia O'Donnell Ewers delivering her inauguration address

educational institution, the sort of place Homer St. Clair Pace would be proud to have bear his family's name.

> *"A human entity has only one life. An artificial entity has several biographies."*
> (Dr. John Flaherty, March 9, 1990)

who would have ever thought that a Midwestern farm boy would revolutionize accounting education and, in the process, lay the foundation for a full-fledged university? OPPORTUNITAS and PEOPLE: that's what Homer Pace, the man, was all about and that is what the school he founded continues to value, for, even in the space age, some things are timeless.

One Pace Plaza — Student Activity Notices

The Campus Center, Pleasantville

Sculpture Garden, NY

NOTES

Chapter 1

1. Homer S. Pace to Casper Ramsby, November 10, 1899.
2. Loc. cit.
3. H.S.P. to Elmira Pace, May 25, 1904.
4. H.S.P. to C.R., May 26, 1904.
5. H.S.P. to Lewis A. Carman, August 4, 1938.
6. H.S.P. to Cousin David, February 20, 1883.
7. Pere Marquette Account Book, March 9, 1893.
8. H.S.P. to Ivan D. Cole, February 5, 1937.
9. H.S.P. to C.R., November 1, 1899.
10. Loc. cit.
11. Loc. cit.
12. Loc. cit.
13. Loc. cit.
14. Loc. cit.
15. Loc. cit.
16. H.S.P. to C.R., September 16, 1898.
17. Loc. cit.
18. Loc. cit.
19. Loc. cit.
20. Loc. cit.
21. Loc. cit.
22. Loc. cit.
23. Loc. cit.
24. Loc. cit.
25. Loc. cit.
26. H.S.P. to C.R., October 2, 1898.
27. Loc. cit.
28. Loc. cit.
29. H.S.P. to C.R., October 25, 1898.
30. H.S.P. to C.R., November 4, 1898.
31. Loc. cit.
32. Loc. cit.
33. Loc. cit.
34. Loc. cit.
35. Loc. cit.
36. Loc. cit.
37. C.G. Wing to J.S. Stearns, January 2, 1899.
38. C.G. Wing to R. H. Downman, January 2,1899.
39. C.G. Wing to University Steward, Ann Arbor, January 2, 1899.
40. H.S.P. to C.R., September 14, 1899.
41. H.S.P. to C.R., February 27, 1900.
42. H.S.P. to C.R., September 14, 1899.
43. H.S.P. to C.R., February 27, 1900.
44. Loc. cit.
45. Loc. cit.
46. Loc. cit.
47. H.S.P. to C.R., September 14, 1899.
48. H.S.P. to C.R., October 8, 1899.
49. H.S.P. to C.R., October 24, 1899.
50. H.S.P. to C.R., October 17, 1899.
51. H.S.P. to C.R., November 10, 1899.
52. Loc. cit.
53. Loc. cit.
54. H.S.P. to C.R., October 19, 1900.
55. Loc. cit.
56. Loc. cit.

57. H.S.P. to C.R., February 2, 1904.
58. Loc. cit.
59. H.S.P. to C.R., May 12, 1904.
60. Loc. cit.
61. H.S.P. to C.R., March 31, 1904.
62. H.S.P. to C.R., April 8, 1904.
63. H.S.P. to C.R., May 12, 1904.
64. Loc. cit.
65. H.S.P. to Elvira Pace, May 25, 1904.
66. Loc. cit.
67. Loc. cit.
68. Loc. cit.
69. Loc. cit.
70. H.S.P. to C.R., May 26, 1904.
71. Loc. cit.
72. Loc. cit.
73. Loc. cit.
74. Loc. cit.
75. Loc. cit.
76. Loc. cit.
77. Loc. cit.
78. Loc. cit.
79. Loc. cit.
80. Loc. cit.
81. Loc. cit.
82. Loc. cit.
83. Loc. cit.
84. Loc. cit.
85. Loc. cit.
86. Loc. cit.
87. Loc. cit.
88. H.S.P. to C.R., July 8, 1904.
89. Loc. cit.
90. H.S.P. to C.R., August 22, 1904.
91. Loc. cit.
92. H.S.P. to C.R., December 17, 1904.
93. Loc. cit.
94. H.S.P. to C.R., September 12, 1905.
95. Loc. cit.
96. Charles Pace to Mother, September 18, 1898.
97. Loc. cit.
98. H.S.P. to W.S. Gillette, June 3, 1907.
99. Loc. cit.
100. Charles A. Pace to James F. Hughes, October 1, 1909.
101. Loc. cit.
102. Loc. cit.
103. Bulletin of the New York Institute of Accountancy and the Accountancy Institute of Brooklyn, October 22, 1908, p. 1.
104. Loc. cit.
105. Loc. cit.
106. The Accountancy Student (October 1907), p. 4.
107. H.S.P. to James F. Hughes, August 20, 1910.
108. Loc. cit.
109. H.S.P. to James F. Hughes, July 17, 1908.
110. Loc. cit.
111. H.S.P. to J.F.H., August 10, 1908.
112. H.S.P. to J.F.H., May 14, 1909.
113. H.S.P. to J.F.H., June 2, 1910.

114. H.S.P. to J.F.H., October 16, 1908.
115. Loc. cit.
116. Loc. cit.
117. Loc. cit.
118. Loc. cit.
119. Loc. cit.
120. H.S.P. to J.F.H., September 21, 1909.
121. Loc. cit.
122. *World Almanac* (1911). Pace University Advertising Collection
123. *The Journal of Accountancy* (March 1914) Pace University Advertising Collection
124. *The Journal of Accountancy* (June 1916)
125. *The Journal of Accountancy* (December 1915)
126. *The Journal of Accountancy* (August 1914) Pace University Advertising Collection
127. *Collier's*, December 2, 1916.
128. *Collier's*, July 7, 1917.
129. *System* (May 1916).
130. *Detroit Young Men*, January 11, 1913.
131. H.S.P. to J.F.H., March 11, 1911.
132. Loc. cit.
133. *Men of Buffalo*, (February 1912), p. 1+
134. *Pace Student*, I (March 1916), p. 56.
135. Loc. cit.
136. *Pace Student*, II (May 1917), 101.
137. *Pace Student*, III (August 1918), 142.
138. Loc. cit.
139. Loc. cit.
140. Loc. cit.
141. H.S.P. to Daniel C. Roper, February 26,1919.
142. Daniel C. Roper to H.S.P., March 27, 1919.
143. Loc. cit.
144. H.S.P. to C.R., November 10, 1899.
145. *Pace Student*, I (March 1916), p. 57.

Chapter 2

1. "Horatio Nelson Drury," *Pace Student*, VI, No. 6 (May 1921), p. 82.
2. Loc. cit.
3. Loc. cit.
4. *Pace Student*, May 1921, p. 89.
5. *New York American*, March 24, 1929. Pace Newspaper Scrapbook.
6. *The Brooklyn Standard Union*, August 21,1927.
7. *New York Telegram Magazine*, April 27, 1929.
8. "Interesting Field Trips at Pace Institute," *Pace Student*, IX, No. 8, (July 1924), p. 128.
9. Loc. cit.
10. "Dinner Talk to Freshmen," *Pace Student* (February 26, 1926, p. 13.)
11. Loc. cit.
12. Loc. cit.
13. Loc. cit.
14. Loc. cit.
15. "Pace Institute Holds Song Week," *Pace Student* (December 1923), p. 16.
16. "Speak in Public and Have a Good Time,"

Pace Student (May 1926), p. 21.

17. Loc cit.
18. "Business Needs Women," *Pace Student* (October 1924), p. 168.
19. Loc cit.
20. *New York American*, September 25, 1927.
21. Loc cit.
22. Pace University Advertising Inserts: 1924.
23. Loc. cit.
24. Loc. cit.
25. Pace Secretarial Practice Course Brochure 1926.
26. Loc. cit.
27. *Pace Student* (February 1922), p. 46.
28. *Pace Student* (April 1922), p. 75.
29. Loc cit.
30. Loc cit.
31. These articles appeared in the following issues of the *Pace Student*: March 1926, November 1923, December 1924, March 1925.
32. These articles appeared in the following issues of the *Pace Student*: August 1926, September 1924, January 1924, November 1923, April 1922.
33. These articles appeared in the following issues of the *American Accountant*: September 1927, November 1927, March 1933, April 1933.
34. American Accountant, September 1927, p. 2
35. Homer S. Pace to J.B. Scholerfield, January 8, 1934.
36. Loc cit.
37. Loc cit.
38. C.D. Giles to H.S.P., December 28, 1933.
39. H. Geist to H.S.P., December 27, 1933.
40. Atlee L. Percy to H.S.P., January 8, 1934.
41. C.P.A. Bulletin, III, No. 10 (February 1934)
42. James F. Hughes to H.S.P., December 28, 1933.
43. Loc. cit.
44. H.S.P. to J.F.H., December 29, 1933.
45. H.S.P. to J.W. Hooper, January 8, 1934.
46. H.S.P. to Walter C. Wright, January 12, 1934.
47. The New York American, April 20, 1930.
48. Brooks Atkinson, ed. *The Pace Report* (New York: Pace College, 1966), p. 91.
49. Atkinson, p. 92.
50. *Hudson Dispatch* (Union City, N.J.), February 6, 1936.
51. "From High School to Business" (1931), p. 6.
52. Loc cit.
53. "From High School to Business," p. 14.
54. The New York American, August 15, 1937.
55. *Forbes*, July 15, 1937.
56. Charles Dyson, Oral History Memoir, April 20, 1983, p. 15.
57. Atkinson, p. 102.
58. Alfreda Geiger, Oral History Memoir, pp. 19-20.
59. Walter W. Nissely to State Education Department, January 10, 1935.
60. Charles T. Bryan to Harlan Horner, May 30, 1935.

61. H.H. to C.T.B., May 31, 1935.
62. H.S.P. to H.H., June 6, 1935.
63. H.S.P. to H.H., June 25, 1935.
64. H.S.P. to H.H., October 29, 1935.
65. Loc cit.
66. H.H. to H.S.P., October 31, 1935. To differentiate the C.P.A. program from the rest of the accounting offerings, the Institute had two separate schools,the School of Accountancy Practice and the School of Accountancy and Business Administration.
67. Loc cit.
68. H.S.P. to H.H., November l, 1935.
69. Announcement of November l, 1935, in Pace Newspaper Scrapbook & State Ed. Dept. Charter Correspondence, July December 1935.
70. *The Brooklyn Citizen*, January 14, 1936.
71. *The Sun*, August 16, 1930.
72. Loc cit.
73. *The Standard Union*, February 20, 1932.
74. Press Release, August 17, 1935 in State Ed. Dept. Charter Correspondence.
75. H.S.P. to Irwin Conroe, January 31, 1941.
76. Loc. cit.
77. Loc. cit.
78. Loc. cit.
79. Loc. cit.
80. Loc. cit.
81. "Professional Photography," 1938, p. 382. Loc. cit. The photography program was phased out in the 1940s as was the School of Shorthand Reporting, a graduate program for secretarial students. In 1939 the School of Credit Science was eliminated.
82. Loc. cit.
83. Charles T. Bryan to Herman Cooper, June 22, 1937.
84. Memorandum Respecting Conference with Dr. Herman Cooper on October 11, 1938.
85. Lillian Smith to Frederick Schaeberle, October 13, 1938.
86. Loc. cit.
87. Loc. cit.
88. Loc. cit.
89. Charles B. Heisler to H.S.P., September 7, 1938.
90. Loc. cit.
91. H.S.P. to C.B. Heisler, September 10, 1938.
92. Loc cit.
93. H.S.P. to J. Hillis Miller, May 4, 1942.
94. Charles A. Brind, Jr. to H.S.P., May 18, 1942.
95. Trustee Minutes, May 28, 1942.
96. *New York Sun*, May 22, 1942.
97. *Brooklyn Eagle*, May 23, 1942.
98. R.S.P. to Thomas F. Paskell, July 6, 1942.

Chapter 3

l. Minutes of the Pace University Board of Trustees, August 27, 1942.
2. "Pace Institute: The Acme of Education's Best," The Compass, June 15, 1943, p. 1+
3. William C. Carpenter to Pace & Pace, August 26, 1943.

4. *New York Journal-American*, January 17, 1943, Pace Newspaper Scrapbook.
5. Loc. cit.
6. *Accredited News*, February 1943, Pace Newspaper Scrapbook.
7. Loc. cit.
8. Loc. cit.
9. *New York City Weekly Underwriter*, January 13, 1945, Pace Newspaper Scrapbook.
10. *Mamaroneck Times*, January 23, 1948, Pace Newspaper Scrapbook.
11. *Newsday*, October 20, 1943, Pace Newspaper Scrapbook.
12. Loc. cit.
13. Loc. cit.
14. Irwin J. Conroe to Robert Pace, July 25, 1946.
15. Loc. cit.
16. Robert S. Pace to Irwin Conroe, August 6, 1946.
17. Trustee Minutes, June 22, 1948.
18. Trustee Minutes, December 3, 1946.
19. Charles A. Brind, Jr. to Charles T. Bryan, December 20, 1948.
20. Robert S. Pace, Special Announcement to Alumni, December 23, 1948.
21. Robert S. Pace to Carroll V. Newsom, February 28, 1951.
22. Trustee Minutes, May 18, 1951.
23. C.V. Newsom to R.S.P., June 22, 1951.
24. Irwin J. Conroe to R.S.P., June l, 1949.
25. Loc. cit.
26. Loc. cit.
27. Loc. cit.
28. R.S.P. to Irwin J. Conroe, June 23, 1949.
29. Loc. cit.
30. Loc. cit.
31. *New York World-Telegram*, February 28, 1950, Pace Newspaper Scrapbook.
32. Loc. cit.
33. Trustee Minutes, March 15, 1950.
34. C.V. Newsom to Edward J. Mortola, April 13, 1950.
35. E.J.M. to C.V. Newsom, April 15, 1950.
36. R.S.P. to H.L. Field, March 10, 1950.
37. Loc. cit.
38. E.J.M. to H.L. Field, March 20, 1950.
39. Loc. cit.
40. C.V. Newsom to R.S.P., May 24, 1950.
41. Loc. cit.
42. E.J.M. to R.S.P., June 2, 1950.
43. Loc. cit.
44.. Loc. cit.
45. E.J.M. To C.V. Newsom, October 3, 1950.
46. Loc. cit.
47. D.S. Otis to R.S.P., January 17, 1951.
48. Loc. cit.
49. E.J.M. to Charles T. Bryan, June 9, 1952.
50. Loc. cit.
51. E.J.M. to Ewald B. Nyquist, November 6, 1952.
52. Loc. cit.
53. E.B. Nyquist to R.S.P., February 27, 1953.
54. Bulletin to the Schools, April 1953, p. 237.

55. Speech by C.T. Bryan on the Purchase of 41 Park Row.

56. Loc. cit.

57. *Pace Alumni Magazine*, September-October 1951, p. 3.

58. Robert S. Pace's Remarks at Luncheon Meeting of the Board of Trustees and the Advisory Board on Real Estate, May 20, 1959.

59. Loc. cit.

60. Margaret Kelly to R.S.P., February 26, 1954.

61. Loc. cit.

62. Loc. cit.

63. E.J.M., The Function of Pace College in Teacher Education, May 17, 1956.

64. Loc. cit.

65. "Evaluation Report," Pace College, May 16-17, 1956, p. 16.

66. E.B. Nyquist to R.S.P., June 7, 1956.

67. Loc. cit.

68. Trustee Minutes, June 24, 1954.

69. Trustee Minutes, September 22, 1954.

70. Loc. cit.

71. Pace College Evaluation Report for the Commission on Institutions of Higher Education of the Middle States Association of Colleges and Secondary Schools, January 6-9, 1957, p. 12

72. Loc. cit.

73. Ibid., p. 11

74. Simon L. Ruskin to Charles T. Bryan, June 19, 1953.

75. Trustee Minutes, August 25, 1954.

76. Loc. cit.

77. Trustee Minutes, July 19, 1951.

78. Loc. cit.

79. R.S.P.: Address at the Downtown Athletic Club, December 15, 1955.

80. Loc. cit.

81. Announcing of the Semicentennial of Pace College, 1906-1956.

82. Loc. cit.

83. Loc. cit.

84. Pace College: Semicentennial Symposium, October 6, 1956.

85. Loc. cit.

86. Loc. cit.

87. Loc. cit.

88. Loc. cit.

89. Loc. cit.

90. Loc. cit.

91. Pace College News Release, October 4, 1956.

92. Committee on College Teaching Methods and Examinations, "Effective Teaching," 1950-52.

93. Loc. cit.

94. Joseph Sinzer, "Why I Teach," *Pace Alumni Magazine*, January 1955, p. 10+.

95. Report of the Chairman of the Faculty Council for the Academic Year 1950-51.

96. Minutes of the Faculty Council, February 9, 1953.

97. Sabbatical Leave Committee, Report to Faculty Council, March 11, 1957.

98. Loc. cit.

99. Loc. cit.

100. Trustee Minutes, January 22, 1958.

101. *Strictly Confidential*, December 15, 1950.

102. *Strictly Confidential*, August 11, 1953.

103. *Pace Newsletter*, October 15, 1954.

104. "Mr. Schaeberle Retires June 30," *Pace Alumni Magazine*, July 1954, p. 5+.

105. Minutes of the Administrative Council, February 19, 1958.

106. Minutes of the Administrative Council, October 30, 1957.

107. Loc. cit.

108. *Strictly Confidential*, April 19, 1951.

109. Loc. cit.

110. Loc. cit.

111. *Strictly Confidential*, March 7, 1950.

112. Loc. cit.

113. Loc. cit.

114. Loc. cit.

115. *Pace Newsletter*, April 1, 1960.

116. "Careers for Women," *Bulletin of Pace College*, XXV, No. 1, November 1952.

117. Loc. cit.

118. Loc. cit.

119. *Strictly Confidential*, March 11, 1960.

Chapter 4

1. *Pace College Newsletter*, VII-1 (September 12, 1960), p. 1.

2. *Pace College: A Story of Growth* (1961), p. 4.

3. Edward J. Mortola, "Inaugural Address," *Pace Student*, XXX, No. 2 (March 1961), p. 1.

4. Ibid., p. 2.

5. Ibid., p. 3.

6. Edward J. Mortola, "Comments on Adult Education," February 24, 1960.

7. Edward J. Mortola, "Address to Alumni Volunteers," November 8, 1962.

8. Dinner Program, Tribute to Edward J. Mortola, October 20, 1965.

9. Edward J. Mortola, "Remarks", October 20, 1965.

10. Loc. cit.

11. J. Lubin, Oral History, October 5, 1982, p. 76.

12. Absolute Charter of the Pace College Foundation, February 25, 1962.

13. Edward J. Mortola to John J. Toomey, November 13, 1968.

14. Trustee Minutes, November 21, 1962.

15. Progress Report to the Middle States Association, September 30, 1965, p. 2.

16. Edward J. Mortola to Edwin G. Michaelian, April 12, 1965.

17. Loc. cit.

18. Trustee Minutes, May 5, 1965.

19. Press Release, November 27, 1968.

20. *Pace Alumni News*, III, No. 10 (June 1972), p. 1.

21. Edward J. Mortola, Annual President's Report to the Trustees (November 1960).

22. *The New York Times*, December 20, 1966.

23. *New York Construction News*, December 26, 1966.

24. *Pace Alumnni Magazine*, XII, No. 1 (January 1960).

25. *Pace Alumni News*, III, No. 8 (April 1972), p. 1.

26. Trustee Minutes, November 20, 1963.

27. Edward J. Mortola, Annual Report to the Board of Trustees, November 26, 1968, p. 9.

28. Trustee Minutes, November 17, 1965.

29. Loc. cit.

30. *The Pace College Letter*, XXI, No. 1 (September 12, 1972), p. 5.

31. Faculty Self-Evaluation Report for the Commission on Institutions of Higher Education of the Middle States Association of Colleges and Secondary Schools (January 1967), p. 14.

32. Loc. cit.

33. Abstract of Recommendations Contained in Middle States Evaluation Report to Pace College, June 1967, p. 6.

34. Loc. cit.

35. Ibid., p. 7.

36. Ibid., p. 11.

37. Edward J. Mortola to Colleagues, September 7, 1967.

38. Pace College Long-Range Planning Guidelines and Procedures, March 1968.

39. Walter E. Joyce to Edward J. Mortola, April 26, 1966.

40. Trustee Minutes, May 8, 1968.

41. Edward J. Mortola to Faculty, October 28, 1965.

42. Loc. cit.

43. Pace College Westchester Faculty Council Meeting, April 1, 1968.

44. *The Pace College Press*, XXXIII, No. 7 (November 10, 1966), p. 5.

45. Edward J. Mortola to Faculty, Administration and Students, March 24, 1969.

46. Trustee Minutes, July 1, 1969.

47. Senate of Pace College: A Commemorative Report: 1969-1970, p. 1.

48. *Pace Press*, May 15, 1970, p. 3.

49. Loc. cit.

50. Loc. cit.

51. Loc. cit.

52. Edward J. Mortola to Students, Faculty and Staff, May 9, 1970.

53. Trustee Minutes, Development & Executive Committees, February 9, 1965.

54. Trustee Minutes, October 3, 1967.

55. Loc. cit.

56. Trustee Minutes, November 16, 1966.

57. Edward J. Mortola to Joseph I. Lubin, April 3, 1967.

58. G.F. Knerr to E.J.M., June 13, 1972.

59. John V. Thornton to David R. Breien, August 10, 1973.

60. Charles Dyson to E.J.M., July 31, 1973.

61. E.J.M. to Edwin G. Michaelian, October 6, 1967.

62. Edwin G. Michaelian to E.J.M.,
October 16, 1967.

63. Gustav Lienhard to E.J.M.,
February 2, 1973.

64. Agreement Between Pace College and the
American Academy of Dramatic Arts,
August 12, 1971, p. 2.

65. O.A. Knorr to E.J.M., October 8, 1965.

66. Loc. cit.

67. Trustee Minutes, March 28, 1972.

68. Loc. cit.

69. T. Edward Hollander to E.J.M.,
July 25, 1972.

70. Loc. cit.

71. Ewald B. Nyquist to E.J.M.,
September 7, 1972.

72. *The New York Times*, March 29, 1973,
51:1

73. Loc. cit.

74. Loc. cit.

Chapter 5

1. Sister Mary Basel Hayes has written the
definitive history of The College of White
Plains. Her book-length manuscript is in the
Archives of the Sisters of the Divine
Compassion. The story of the founding and
early history of the order is recounted in
Sister Teresa Brady's *The Fruit of His
Compassion* (New York: Pageant
Press, 1962).

2. Minutes of the Board of Trustees of The
College of White Plains, March 8, 1975.

3. Loc. cit.

4. Loc. cit.

5. Minutes of the CWP Executive Committee,
April 16, 1975.

6. CWP Trustee Minutes, April 18, 1975.

7. Loc. cit.

8. Outline of the Material Features of a Plan of
Consolidation Between Pace University and
The College of White Plains.

9. Loc. cit.

10. Loc. cit.

11. Faculty Council Minutes, Pace University,
Pleasantville, May 2, 1975.

12. Loc. cit.

13. Charles Dyson and Edward J. Mortola to
the Board of Trustees, May 20, 1975.

14. Memorandum of Law Submitted by Cuddy
& Feder, Attorneys for The College of
White Plains, June 25, 1975.

15. Loc. cit.

16. Robert D. Stone to J. Robert Bleakley,
Bleakley, Platt, Schmidt & Fritz (Attorneys
for Pace University), June 27, 1975.

17. Robert D. Stone to E. A. Dominianni,
Coudert Brothers (Attorney for the Sisters),
September 12, 1975.

18. A Proposal by Pace University for the
Establishment of a Law School in
Westchester County - Prepared for the Joint
Conference on Legal Education,
May 12, 1973.

19. Edward J. Mortola to Michael H. Cardozo,
June 20, 1973.

20. E.J.M. to Morris Lasker,
February 16, 1974.

21. Trustee Minutes, February 26, 1974.

22. Loc. cit.

23. Trustee Minutes, June 25, 1974.

24. Minutes of the Executive Committee,
April 22, 1975.

25. Loc. cit.

26. *Pace World*, II, No. 3 (October 20, 1976),
p. 1.

27. University Administrative Committee,
January 25, 1980.

28. Loc. cit.

29. *Pace World*, III, No. 7 (March 22, 1978),
p. 1.

30. E.J.M. to Law School Faculty,
March 2, 1979.

31. Loc. cit.

32. E.J.M. to Paul D. Polidoro, April 17, 1979.

33. "Problems Gnawing at Growth of Pace
University Law School," *New York Law
Journal*, May 7, 1979.

34. Nicholas A. Robinson to Charles F. Kiley,
May 17, 1979.

35. Loc. cit.

36. Trustee Minutes, May 18, 1981.

37. Charles Dyson to E.J.M.,
November 13, 1973.

38. Loc. cit.

39. Thomas B. Hogan, "A Brief Glimpse of
Briarcliff College," December 13, 1976.

40. Loc. cit.

41. Loc. cit.

42. Loc. cit.

43. Minutes of the Long-Range Planning
Committee, January 5, 1977.

44. *The New York Times*, March 23, 1977.

45. *Newsweek*, April 11, 1977, p. 96.

46. *Pace World*, 1, No. 5 (November 19, 1975),
p. 1.

47. Ruth Fischer, "Pace University: How to
Ignore the Steady State," *Change Magazine*
(November 1977), p. 33.

48. Ibid., p. 36

49. Ibid. cit., p. 37

50. Trustee Minutes, January 17, 1978.

51. Edwin G. Michaelian, "Governing
Westchester County," *Westchester County:
The Past Hundred Years 1883-1983*
(Valhalla: Westchester County Historical
Society, 1984), p. 177.

52. Report to the Faculty, Administration,
Trustees, and Students of Pace University by
an Evaluation Team Representing the
Commission on Higher Education of the
Middle States Association Prepared after
Study of Pace University's Self-Evaluation
Report and a Visit to the Campus on April
17-20, 1977, p. 19.

53. Loc. cit.

54. Howard L. Simmons to E.J.M.,
February 28, 1983.

55. Report to the Faculty, Administration,
Trustees and Students of Pace University by
an Evaluation Team Representing the
Commission on Higher Education of the
Middle States Association of Colleges and
Schools Prepared after Study of the
Institution's Self-Study Report and a Visit to
the Campus on 13-17 March 1988, p. 19.

56. Loc. cit.

57. Pace University Press Release No. 243,
April 7, 1981.

58. Pace University Press Release No. 375,
October 6, 1981.

59. Pace University Press Release No. 369,
October l, 1981.

60. A Report from the President's Commission
on the Core Curriculum: The Nature,
Purposes and Objectives of the Core
Curriculum at Pace University,
October 1981.

61. Loc. cit.

62. Minutes of the Executive Session of the
Board of Trustees, October 8, 1974.

63. Loc. cit.

64. Loc. cit.

65. *Pace Press*, XLII, No. 1
(September 24, 1974), p. 1.

66. *Pace Alumni News*, VI, No. 1
(September 1974), p. 1.

67. Pace Press Release, No. 87/88-48,
November 30, 1987.

68. Report of Dr. E. Nyquist, Minutes of the
Trustees Committee on Educational Policies,
June 29, 1981.

69. J.M. Pastore to Members of the Trustees
Educational Policies Committee,
October 7, 1982.

70. Loc. cit.

71. Ibid., p. 5.

72. Ibid., p. 6.

73. Loc. cit.

74. Loc. cit.

75. *Pace Press*, LXVIII, No. 5, October 30,
1980, p. 5.

76. NewsPace, March 7, 1984.

77. Ewald B. Nyquist, Question for Discussion:
What are the Reasons for Retaining or
Abolishing the School of Education at Pace
University, March 20, 1981, p. 2.

78. Ibid., p. 3.

79. Ibid., p. 8.

80. Peter F. Drucker, *Innovation and
Entrepreneurship* (New York: Harper &
Row, 1986), pp. 201-202.

APPENDIX

Pace Chronology

1906	Homer St. Clair and Charles Ashford Pace open a school of accountancy in the Tribune building opposite City Hall
1908	The school moves to larger quarters in the Hudson Terminal complex
1910	Increased enrollment requires a move to Church Street
1913	The Pace brothers admit Frederick M. Schaeberle to their partnership
1919	A day school division is established
1921	Charles T. Bryan is admitted to the partnership
1927	Increased enrollment leads to a move to the new Transportation Building at 225 Broadway.
1933	Charles Ashford Pace retires
1935	Pace Institute is incorporated as a non-profit institution of higher education in New York State; the New York State Board of Regents grants the Institute a provisional charter; the Institute becomes a stock corporation
1940	Charles Ashford Pace dies
1942	Pace Institute is granted an absolute charter by the New York State Board of Regents; Homer St. Clair Pace dies; Homer's son, Robert Scott Pace, Secretary of the Institute, becomes President; another son, C. Richard Pace, becomes Secretary
1947	Pace Institute becomes Pace College, a non-profit, non-stock corporation; Dr. Edward J. Mortola comes to Pace as Assistant Dean
1948	Board of Regents approves Pace's application for college status and permits the awarding of B.B.A. degrees
1951	Pace College acquires the New York Times building at 41 Park Row\
1953	New York State Education Department authorizes Pace College to grant B.A. degrees; the college moves to the newly renovated 41 Park Row building
1954	New York State Education Department authorizes Pace College to confer the honorary degrees of Doctor of Commercial Science and Doctor of Civil Law
1956	A convocation marks Pace's fiftieth anniversary
1957	Pace is authorized to confer A.A. and A.A.S. degrees
1958	Graduate division is established; Pace is authorized to grant M.B.A. degrees
1959	Pace is authorized to confer honorary degrees of LL.D and L.H.D
1961	Dr. Edward J. Mortola is inaugurated as Pace's third President
1962	Wayne and Helen Marks donate property for Pleasantville campus; Pace is authorized to confer A.A. and A.A.S. degrees in Pleasantville and B.S. in New York; first Man in Management dinner (renamed Leaders in Management in 1976) held at the Waldorf-Astoria Hotel
1964	Graduate Division of Business becomes the Graduate School of Business Administration; the School of Liberal Arts becomes the School of Arts and Sciences
1965	Pace is authorized to confer B.B.A. in Pleasantville in evening division and A.S. in Pleasantville and New York
1966	Business school named for Joseph Lubin; School of Arts and Sciences, School of Education, and undergraduate School of Business Administration are established; School of Nursing is established; ground breaking for Pace Plaza building; Pace is authorized to confer B.A. and B.S. in Pleasantville and B.B.A. in Pleasantville in day division
1968	Pace is authorized to confer M.A. in New York and M.B.A. in Pleasantville
1969	Pace is authorized to confer M.S. in Education and M.A.T. in New York
1970	Pace Plaza building opens
1973	State Education Department accords Pace university status
1974	The School of Arts and Sciences becomes the Charles H. Dyson College of Arts and Sciences
1975	The College of White Plains consolidates with Pace University
1976	The School of Law opens on the White Plains campus; a Midtown Center is established
1977	Pace University acquires the assets of Briarcliff College

1979	Pace becomes the first school in New York State to offer the Doctor of Psychology degree in school/community psychology; Municipal Law Resource Center is established; Lienhard School of Nursing receives National League for Nursing accreditation for its baccalaureate program
1980	Pace student Sally Hoffman receives highest score in the U.S. on the Uniform Certified Public Accountancy Examination; scientists from the Haskins Laboratories and Biology Department on the New York campus are recognized for pioneering research on African sleeping sickness
1981	Pace celebrates its seventy-fifth anniversary
1982	IBM establishes International Finance, Planning and Administration program at Pace; this is the only IBM program of its kind in the U.S.
1983	U.S. Department of Education selects the Lubin School of Business Administration to develop one of six programs nationwide in international business studies for undergraduates; the library at Pleasantville is named in honor of Edward and Doris Mortola; School of Computer Science and Information Systems is established; west wing addition to Pace Plaza building is completed
1984	Dr. Jack Schiff, Provost, dies; Dr. William G. Sharwell becomes President; Dr. Edward J. Mortola becomes Chancellor and Chief Executive Officer; Schaeberle Chair in Accounting is established
1985	American Chemical Society awards first prize for undergraduate research to a Pace student; a Pace accounting student achieves the highest New York State score on the national C.P.A. examination for the sixth year in a row; Master's degree program in Publishing is established; Pace University is ranked in highest 11 percent of American colleges and universities with alumni in executive positions in leading corporations; first townhouse dormitory opens at Pleasantville
1986	Lubin Schools of Business are ranked largest private business schools in U.S.; J.D./M.P.A. and M.S. in Information Systems are established; B.S. in Computer Science is accredited by the Computing Sciences Accreditation Board, making Pace one of only 22 accredited schools nationwide
1987	Dr. William G. Sharwell becomes President and Chief Executive Officer of Pace; Lubin Graduate Center in downtown White Plains is completed; Hastings Center moves to Briarcliff campus; addition to Dyson Science Building at Pleasantville is completed; second townhouse dormitory is opened at Pleasantville; Peat Marwick Main Professorship in Accounting is established
1988	Athletic field at Pleasantville is named for Peter X. Finnerty, retired athletic director
1989	Dr. Patricia O'Donnell Ewers is named President of Pace University
1990	Dr. Patricia O'Donnell Ewers is inaugurated as fifth President of Pace University

Chairs of the Board of Trustees

Leaders in Management Award

1962	Henry C. Alexander, Chairman of the Board, Morgan Guaranty Trust Company
1963	Roger M. Blough, Chairman of the Board, United States Steel Corporation
1964	Monroe J. Rathbone, Chairman of the Board, Standard Oil Company (NJ)
1965	Frederick R. Kappel, Chairman of the Board, American Telephone & Telegraph Company
1966	Thomas J. Watson, Jr., Chairman of the Board, International Business Machines Corporation
1967	George Champion, Chairman of the Board, the Chase Manhattan Bank
1968	James A. Linen, President, Time, Inc.
1969	Charles H. Dyson, Chairman of the Board, the Dyson-Kissner-Moran Corporation
1970	Arthur Levitt, Comptroller of the State of New York
1971	David Rockefeller, Chairman of the Board, the Chase Manhattan Bank
1972	Donald T. Regan, Chairman of the Board, Merrill Lynch, Pierce, Fenner & Smith
1973	Walter B. Wriston, Chairman of the Board, First National City Bank
1974	John B. M. Place, Chairman, President, and Chief Executive Officer, the Anaconda Company
1975	Rawleigh Warner, Jr., Chairman, Mobil Oil Corporation
1976	Frank T. Cary, Chairman of the Board and Chief Executive Officer, International Business Machines Corporation
1977	John D. deButts, Chairman of the Board and Chief Executive Officer, American Telephone & Telegraph Company
1978	Joseph F. Cullman 3rd, Chairman of the Executive Committee, Philip Morris Incorporated
1979	Thomas A. Murphy, Chairman of the Board and Chief Executive Officer, General Motors Corporation
1980	John F. McGillicuddy, Chairman of the Board, President and Chief Executive Officer, Manufacturers Hanover Corporation and Manufacturers Hanover Trust Company
1981	Thomas M. Macioce, President and Chief Executive Officer, Allied Stores Corporation
1982	Robert M. Schaeberle, Chairman and Chief Executive Officer, Nabisco Brands, Incorporated
1983	John R. Opel, Chairman of the Board and Chief Executive Officer, International Business Machines Corporation
1984	James E. Burke, Chairman of the Board and Chief Executive Officer, Johnson & Johnson
1985	Leonard H. Goldenson, Chairman of the Executive Committee and Director, Capital Cities/ABC, Inc,
1986	Edward J. Mortola, Chancellor and Chairman of the Executive Committee of the Board of Trustees, Pace University
1988*	Delbert C. Staley, Chairman and Chief Executive Officer, NYNEX Corporation
1989	John L. Weinberg, Senior Partner and Chairman of the Management Committee, Goldman, Sachs & Co.
1990	Willard C. Butcher, Chairman of the Board and Chief Executive Officer, the Chase Manhattan Corporation, The Chase Manhattan Bank, N.A.
1991	Maurice R. Greenberg, President and Chief Executive Officer, American International Group, Inc.

*Due to a year adjustment, there is no listing for 1987

Honorary Degree Recipients of Pace University

T. Coleman Andrews, '21, Commissioner of Internal Revenue D.C.S. June 1954

Jacob L. Holtzman, Regent of the University of the State of New York D.C.L. June 1954

John Edgar Hoover, Director of the Federal Bureau of Investigation D.C.L. June 1954

Frederick Martin Schaeberle, '14, Incorporator and Retired Treasurer of Pace College D.C.S. June 1954

Charles T. Bryan, '14, Incorporator and Retired Chairman of the Board of Trustees of Pace College D.C.L. June 1955

William B. Franke, '17, Secretary of the Navy D.C.L. June 1955

John A. Krout, Vice President and Provost of Columbia University D.C.S. June 1955

Aloysius A. Lally, '25, Certified Public Accountant D.C.S. June 1955

Joseph I. Lubin, '21, Certified Public Accountant, Chairman of the New York State Board of Certified Public Accountant Examiners D.C.S. June 1955

Chester A. Allen, '15, President of the Kings County Trust Company D.C.L. June 1956

Elliott V. Bell, Chairman of the Executive Committee, McGraw-Hill Publishing Co., Inc. D.C.S. June 1956

Ernest A. Johnson, President of Lake Forest College D.C.S. June 1956

Carroll V. Newsom, President of New York University D.C.L. June 1956

Peter F. Drucker, Professor of Management, Graduate School of Business Administration, New York University D.C.S. October 1956

Edward H. Litchfield, Chancellor of the University of Pittsburgh D.C.S. October 1956

Charles F. Noyes, Chairman of Charles F. Noyes Company, Inc. D.C.S. October 1956

Theodore S. Repplier, President of The Advertising Council, Inc. D.C.L. October 1956

Emanuel Saxe, Dean of the Bernard M. Baruch School of Business and Public Administration, the City College of New York D.C.S. October 1956

Margaret Chase Smith, United States Senator from Maine D.C.L. October 1956

Dwayne Orton, Editor of "Think" Magazine and Educational Consultant, International Business Machines Corporation D.C.S. April 1957

William F. Albright, W.W. Spence Professor of Semitic Languages, the Johns Hopkins University D.C.L. June 1957

John F. Brosnan, Chancellor of the Board of Regents, the University of the State of New York D.C.S. June 1957

Clarence Michalis, Chairman of The Seaman's Bank for Savings D.C.S. June 1957

C. Richard Pace, Incorporator, Retired Member of the Faculty, Retired Member of the Board of Trustees, and Secretary of Pace College D.C.L. June 1957

The Very Rev. Laurence J. McGinley, S.J., President of Fordham University D.C.L. June 1958

Everett J. Penny, Regent of the University of the State of New York D.C.S. June 1958

Jacob K. Javits, United States Senator from New York D.C.L. June 1958

Joseph Gruber, Director of Business Education, Board of Education of the City of New York D.S.C. June 1959

Richard C. Patterson, Jr., Commissioner, Department of Commerce and Public Events of the City of New York D.C.L. June 1959

Carl H. Pforzheimer, Jr., Regent of the University of the State of New York D.C.S. June 1959

Edward L. Steiniger, '25, Chairman of the Board of Sinclair Oil Corporation D.S.C. June 1959

Malcolm Wilson, Lieutenant Governor of New York LL.D. June 1959

Helen Pace Bowen, Retired Member of the Board of Trustees of Pace College L.H.D. November 1959

Thomas R. Horton, Director of University Relations,
International Business Machines Corporation LL.D. June 1976

Richard M. Matthews, Dean, Lubin School of Business
Administration, Pace University D.C.S. June 1976

Reverend Gordon G. Powell, Minister, Christ Church on Quaker
Hill, Pawling, New York LL.D. June 1976

Jean Ray, President of SOFINA, Belgium D.C.S. June 1976

John C. Sawhill, President, New York University L.H.D. June 1976

Lowell Thomas, Author, Cinerama and TV Producer, Radio and TV
Commentator L.H.D. June 1976

Hugh L. Carey, Governor of the State of
New York LL.D. October 1976

Bessie Gerber Glass LL.D. October 1976

C.P. Snow, Author, Scientist, Philosopher,
Commentator L.H.D. April 1977

Frank T. Cary, Chairman of the Board and Chief
Executive Officer, International Business Machines
Corporation D.C.S. April 1977

John D. deButts, Chairman and Chief Executive Officer,
the American Telephone & Telegraph Company D.C.S. May 1977

Alfred B. DelBello, County Executive of
Westchester LL.D. May 1977

Arthur P. Antin, Superintendent of Schools, White Plains
City School District L.H.D. May 1977

George W. Bonham, Editor-in-Chief,
Change Magazine LL.D. June 1977

Leonard M. Greene, President, Safe Flight Instrument
Corporation D.C.L. June 1977

Timothy S. Healy, S.J., President, Georgetown
University L.H.D. June 1977

Franklin A. Thomas, President and Chief Executive Officer,
Bedford Stuyvesant Restoration Corporation LL.D. June 1977

Robert Greene, Chairman of the East Hudson
Parkway Authority D.C.L. April 1978

Jane Cahill Pfeiffer, Management Consultant L.H.D. May 1978

William Vincent Cuddy, Attorney, Cuddy & Fedder LL.D. May 1978

Harry E. Ekblom, Chairman and Chief Executive Officer,
European American Bank D.C.S. June 1978

Leon Finley, Senior Painter, Finley, Kumble, Wagner,
Heine & Underberg LL.D. June 1978

Kenneth W. Fraser, Honorary Trustee,
Pace University D.C.S. June 1978

Theodore M. Black, Chancellor, New York State
Board of Regents L.H.D. June 1978

Michael N. Chetkovich, Managing Partner, Deloitte,
Haskins, & Sells LL.D. June 1978

Thomas P. Hawe, '68, Treasurer, Norton
Simon, Inc. D.C.S. June 1978

Daniel Patrick Moynihan, United States
Senator LL.D. January 1979

Joseph F. Cullman 3rd, Chairman of the Executive
Committee of the Board, Philip Morris
Incorporated D.C.S. April 1979

Mother Mary Dolores Hayes, R.D.C., '29, General Treasurer,
Sisters of the Divine Compassion L.H.D. May 1979

Frank Joseph Shakespeare, President, RKO General
Incorporated D.C.S. May 1979

Louis S. Auchincloss, Novelist, Partner, Hawkins,
Delafield and Wood L.H.D. June 1979

Malcolm S. Forbes, President and Editor-in-Chief, Forbes
Magazine, Incorporated LL.D. June 1979

Virginia A. Henderson, Research Assistant Emeritus, Yale
University School of Nursing L.H.D. June 1979

William H. Mulligan, Circuit Judge, United States Court of
Appeals for the Second Circuit LL.D. June 1979

William G. Sharwell, Vice Chairman, Pace University
Board of Trustees, Vice President, American Telephone &
Telegraph Co. LL.D. June 1979

Thomas A. Murphy, Chairman of the Board and Chief Executive
Officer, General Motors Corporation D.C.S. April 1980

Lawrence H. Cooke, Chief Judge, New York State
Court of Appeals LL.D. June 1980

Harry B. Helmsley, President and Chief Executive Officer,
Helmsley-Spear, Inc. D.C.S. June 1980

Arthur Levitt, Jr., Chairman, American Stock
Exchange LL.D. June 1980

Felice N. Schwartz, President, Catalyst L.H.D. June 1980

Stansfield Turner, Director of the Central
Intelligence Agency D.C.L. June 1980

John F. McGillicuddy, Chairman of the Board, President and
Chief Executive Officer, Manufacturers Hanover Corporation
and Manufacturers Hanover Trust Co. D.C.S. March 1981

Basil A. Paterson, Secretary of State of the State of
New York D.C.L. May 1981

Robert B. McKay, Esq., Director, Institute of Judicial
Administration Senior Fellow, Aspen Institute of
Humanistic Studies LL.D. May 1981

Alan Greenspan, President & Chief Executive Officer,
Townsend-Greenspan & Co., Inc. D.C.S. June 1981

William S. Lasdon, Director, Warner-Lambert
Company D.C.S. June 1981

Dorothy Melville, Community Leader, Trustee Emerita of
Bennett College L.H.D. June 1981

Liv Ullman, Actress, Vice President of the International
Rescue Committee L.H.D. June 1981

John C. Whitehead, Senior Partner, Goldman, Sachs
and Company LL.D. June 1981

Colleen Dewhurst, Actress L.H.D. June 1981

Stephen C. Eyre, Senior Vice President - Secretary,
Citibank, N.A. D.C.S. June 1981

Barbara Goldsmith, Author L.H.D. June 1981

Henry Viscardi, Jr., President, Human Resources
Center LL.D. June 1981

Edward J. Hurley, Architect L.H.D. November 1981

Thomas M. Macioce, President and Chief Executive Officer,
Allied Stores Corporation D.C.S. March 1982

Peter K. Warren, President of PepsiCo
International D.C.S. June 1982

Lewis N. Branscomb, Vice President and Chief Scientist,
International Business Machines
Corporation L.H.D. June 1982

Margaret Hennig, Dean of the Graduate School
of Management, Simmons College D.C.S. June 1982

Anne Jardim, Dean of the Graduate School of Management,
Simmons College D.C.S. June 1982

Edgar M. Bronfman, Chairman, Joseph E. Seagram & Sons,
Inc. L.H.D. June 1982

Jose Papa, Jr., President of the Federation of Commerce of the
State of Sao Paulo D.C.S. June 1982

Warren H. Phillips, Chairman and Chief Executive Officer of the
Wall Street Journal L.H.D. June 1982

Mark A. Schubart, Director of Education at Lincoln Center
Institute L.H.D. June 1982

Edward I. Koch, Mayor of the City of New York D.C.L. June 1982

Dave Marash, Anchorman and Correspondent,
CBS News L.H.D. June 1982

Recipients of the Kenan Award for Outstanding Teaching

1960	Prof. Gunner Ekberg	1984	Dr. Philip A. Fulvi
1961	Dr. Harold Lurier		Prof. Dudley Nearing, Jr.
1962	Prof. Rolph Marsh		Dr. Barnard Seligman
1963	Mr. William Shinn		Dr. Richard Podgorski
1964	Dr. Gilbert Rubenstein		Dr. Bronislaw Wisniowski
1965	Dr. Benjamin Ford		Dr. Edward Kenny
1966	Dr. Kenneth Morgan	1985	Dr. Paul Echandia
1967	Dr. John Walsh (posthumous)		Prof. Marie Casciano
			Prof. Richard Turshen
1968	Prof. Peter Fingesten		Prof. Hubert Dwyer
1969	Prof. William Welty	1986	Dr. Cyrus Bacchi
	Prof. Nishan Parlakian		Prof. M. Peter Hoefer
1970	Prof. Oscar Kriegman		Prof. Wesley L. Jordan
	Prof. John Buchsbaum		Prof. Joan Magratten
1971	Prof. Brenda Bettinson	1987	Prof. Fred Hauser
	Dr. Richard Gill		Prof. Anthony Sallustio
1972	Prof. Ruth Eisenberg		Prof. Helena Brady
	Dr. John Flaherty		Dr. Michele Newman
1973	Prof. Henry Rubenstein	1988	Prof. Carl Crego
1974	Prof. Margaret E. Nix		Dr. John Raftery
	Prof. Ivan Fox		Prof. Cathleen Carmody
	Prof. Kate Schachter		Dr. John Sharkey
	Prof. Emmanuel Heller		Dr. Gerard Vallone
1975	Prof. Melvin Swartz	1989	Prof. Celesta Kelley
	Prof. Louis Quintas		Prof. Jordan Young
	Prof. George Shanker		Prof. Jack Yurkiewicz
	Prof. Lillian Katz		Prof. Bertram Kessler
1976	Prof. Jay Scott Arrance		Prof. Martin Kotler
	Prof. Elizabeth Plummer	1990	Prof. Blanche Abramov
	Prof. Elizabeth Wesman		Prof. Philip Young
	Prof. Muriel Shine		Dr. Lawrence F. Hundersmarck
1977	Prof. Marie Eckert		Prof. Lewis Schier
	Prof. Marygold Nash		Prof. David Bickimer
	Prof. Gerald Wohl		Sr. M. Teresa Brady
	Prof. Anthony Salotto	1991	Harlan P. Wallingford
1978	Prof. William Adams		Rita Silverman
	Prof. John Norman		William J. Coffey
	Sr. M. Teresa Brady		Rudy A. Jacob
1979	Prof. Jane Philips		Charlotte Rotkin
	Dr. Robert Oliver		
	Dr. Louise Cutler		
1980	Prof. Carol Gartner		
	Prof. Walter Joyce		
	Prof. Anthony Pustorino		
	Prof. James Holmes		
	Prof. Paul Numerof		
1981	Sr. Helen Coldrick		
	Dr. Joan G. Roland		
	Prof. Irene Nebens		
	Prof. Albert Kalter		
1982	Prof. J.J. Miranne		
	Prof. Carol H. Stix		
	Dr. Marilyn Weigold		
	Prof. Richard Matthews		
1983	Prof. Rudolph Mondelli		
	Prof. Michael Szenberg		
	Prof. Robert Dell		
	Dr. Mojmir Bednarik (posthumous)		

New York Undergraduate Pace Alumni Association Presidents

Henry E. Mendes '10	1925-26
Arthur S. Swenson '23	1926-27
Oscar J. Youngberg '23	1927-28
Joseph Sussman '25	1928-29
George H. Coppers '25	1929-30
Chester A. Allen '15	1930-31
Max E. Solomon '25	1931-32
William C. Talley '24	1932-33
Paul E. Clark '17	1933-34
James P. Smith '28	1934-35
Walter E. Davis '29	1935-36
Edward J. Koestler '25	1936-37
Lynn A. Cook '28	1937-38
Jerome J. Kern '28	1938-39
Lewis H. DeBraun '20	1939-41
C.E. Brotherton '27	1941-42
Thomas E. Scanlon '36	1942-43
Eli Hurwitz '33	1943-44
William A. McCormack '22	1944-45
Henry G. Fissell '37	1945-46
William A. McCormack '22	1946-47
Edward T. Farrell '43	1947-48
Alvin C. Hirsch '26	1948-50
Charles H. Dyson '30	1950-51
Chris L. Roscher '21	1951-52
Marshall M. Thomas '17	1952-53
Malcolm S. Kerr '39	1953-54
Thomas F. Mowle '28	1954-55
Robert F. Gurrin '32	1955-56
Joseph L. Golucci '51	1956-57
William E. Jacoby '34	1957-58
Rudolph Lindstrom '24	1958-59
Edward W. Stack '56	1959-60
Richard J. Reynolds '51	1960-61
Kenneth E. Monaghan '51	1961-62
Ernest Goldhirsch '53	1962-63
Colin Park '47	1963-64
R. Palmer Hollister '37	1964-65
Howard Wolpin '53	1965-66
Barney C. Alfano '50	1966-67
Allan M. Rabinowitz '57	1967-68
Arthur W.J. Beeney '39	1968-69
William E. Humphreys '41	1969-70
Michael A. D'Angelico '54	1970-71
Gustave A. Reh, Jr. '30	1971-72
Stanley C. Anderson '49	1972-73
Thomas P. Hawe '65	1973-74
Robert Plattner '56	1974-75
Fred Turek '55	1975-76
Ralph Scarpa '59	1976-77
Charles Lindsey '73	1977-78
Harry Mayo III '68	1978-79
Joseph Rourke '59	1979-80
Anthony R. Conti '66	1980-81
Barbara Ann Evensen '74	1981-83
Louis Cappellini '70	1983-85
Stuart J. Speck '59	1985-87
Nathan Perlmutter '71	1987-89
Stephen Ellis '63	1989-90
Leonard Weiss '67	1990-

College of White Plains Alumni Association Presidents

Frances M. Kelly, '57	1967 - 1970
Virginia Curry, '59	1970 - 1972
Cynthia Schwanderla, '56	1978 - 1980
Joanne Stack, '49	1980 - 1983
Barry Kennedy, '80	1983 - 1985
Carolyn Dzurka, '65	1985 - 1991
Christine Cavallucci-Meininger, '84	1991 -

Pleasantville Alumni Association Presidents

George Oros	1976-1977
Charles Lindsay '73	1977-1978
Marianne Baggini '77	1978-1979
Richard Gros '76	1980-1983
Patricia Brown '75	1983-1984
Barbara Treadwell '69	1984-1987
Mary Lang Farrell '70	1987-1988
Salvatore Barrese, Jr. '83	1988-1990
Aaron Soury '80	1990-

Past Presidents of the Lubin Graduate School of Business Alumni Board

Charles J. DeLorme, '70	1980-82
John R. Manak, '72	1982-84
Kevin Brown, '73	1984-85
Joseph Paladino, '80	1985-87
G. Wilson Hager, '82	1987-89
Michael E. Guerrasio, '75	1989-

Members of the Pace University 20 Year Club

Blanche W. Abramov	James "Patrick" Costello
William J. Adams	Dudley Cox
Dan Ailloni-Charas	Sr. Mary Berchmans Coyle
Harry C. Alexander	Richard F. Creedy
Jean Alleyne-Graves	Louise M. Cutler
Blanche Amelkin	Ida E. Daggett
Frank Antinucci	Harold Danenberg
Vincent Aprigliano	Michael D'Angelico
Jay Arrance	Bela Danville
Arlene B. August	Nina Dayan
Cyrus Bacchi	Frances M. Delahanty
Josephine M. Bacchi	Frances Dell
John R. Bailey	Robert M. Dell
John B. Barcia	Mary A. DeSalvo
Leonard E. Bart	Steven R. Diner
Richard W. Beglin	Kathleen M. Doke
Paul F. Bellins	Bryan Donabie
Michael Bernkopf	Margaret E. Donnelly
Brenda Bettinson	Matthew F. Donohue
Henry Birnbaum	Douglas M. Doty
Gordon L. Bishop	Emma L. Dromshouser
Percy Black	Alfred J. Dumais
Donald Blankenship	Joseph V. Dumbra
Ruth Bogin	James Duncan
James O. Boisi	Delores Dwiggins
Anthony S.E. Bono	Edward R. Easton
Sr. M. Madonna Bradshaw	Paul Echandia
Helena Real Brady	Sr. Marie Eckert
Sr. M. Teresa Brady	Mary Efthimion
Robert S. Breitbart	Barbara A. Egidi
Bernard P. Brennan	Ruth E. Eisenberg
Louis Brignoll	Kathryn L. Ekirch
Bertram Broder	Alfred Ellis
Harold Brown	Csaba Elthes
Julius I. Brown	Charles E. Elting
Sidney Brown	Sune Engelbrektson
Frederick B. Bunt	Anatole Epstein
E. Gifford Burnap	Carl B. Erdberg
Raymond S. Burns	Richard Fabrizio
Lynne Byrne	Frank X. Fallon
Janet Calace-Mottola	Peter W. Fazzolare
Gerard Cannon	Sr. Mary Leona Fechtman
James A. Cannon	Luke Feeney
David E. Carl	Charles Feit
Kathleen M. Carty	Mary Felice
Marie Casciano	Ruth Ferguson
Carmine Casella	Peter X. Finnerty
Alma Cassidy	Sr. Deborah B. Flaherty
Nicholas Catalano	John E. Flaherty
Daniel Caust	Austin Fowler
Leonard Chalmers	Ivan Fox
Daniel Chasanoff	Jesse J. Frankel
Laura Chunosoff	Theodore Fried
Vito M. Cifichiello	Susan R. Gannon
Sondra E. Cohen	Efrain Garcia
Robert M. Congemi	Lulu Garcia
William A. Clary	Herbert Garfinkel
Frank Colbourn	J. Philip Gass
Helen F. Coldrick	Alfreda J. Geiger
John F. Collins	Abe Gershowitz
William J. Collinson	Carmine Gibbia
Joseph V. Connors	Anthony Gioffre

Marvin Glasser
Norman Gluss
Margaretta Goerlitz
Myron H. Goldberg
Mary Goldman
Richard Gonzalez
Thelma K. Gorham
Alvin Grant
Martin Greene
Leo Greenfest
Louis Greenspan
Joseph J. Gross
Rachel Gross
Ronald R. Gruberg
Charles Guccione
Richard T. Guerin
Theodore B. Gussak
Jeffrey C. Hahner
Nancy Lynch Hale
Sr. Mary Joan Haley
Hannah Hall
Barbara J. Harris
Peggy Hayek
Sr. M. Basil Hayes
David Hecht
Janet E. Heinrichs
Joseph A. Hoehlein
Robert Hoffstein
William Hollock
James H. Holmes
Joseph E. Houle
Aldona S. Iannace
Margaret Ivers
Marcia Jacques
Irving Jankowitz
Frank A. Janus
Heinz Jauch
Stanley Jeffrey
Helena Jioia
Eileen V. Johnsmeyer
Rosealie Johnson
Wesley L. Jordan
Harriet Joseph
John S. Joy
Walter E. Joyce
Albert Kalter
Edwin Kassoff
Dolores E. Keller
Sr. M. Celesta Kelley, R.D.C.
Thomas H. Kendall
Edward B. Kenny
Jerome J. Kern
Francis S. King
Max Kirschbaum
George F. Knerr
Terrell Kolodzinski
Anthony J. Konde
Richard J. Kraus
Martin Kotler
David Krell
Oscar M. Kriegman
Estelle Kulick

Irene Lenczner
Michael Levandowsky
George Levine
Saul S. LeVine
Walter Levy
Joan Lichtenberger
Josef Lichvar
Howard F. Livingston
Joseph Lizzio
Juliana Lochowitz
Henry C. Lodge
Stephen T. Lofthouse
Sylvia LoGiudice
Gina Logomarsino
Raymond H. Lopez
Milton Lowe
Harold E. Lurier
Almond Mackie
Mary E. Maney, R.D.C
John Marchisin
John Markey
Sr. Mary Alocoque Marshall
Charles D. Masiello
Richard M. Matthews
Elizabeth M. McBride
June W. McCauley
George B. McLaughlin
Thomas J. McShane
Herbert Millington
George L. Mims
Herbert Minot
Sr. M. Liguori Mistretta
John J. Mitchell
Rudolph J. Mondelli
Josephine Monforte
Miriam L. Moran
Edward J. Mortola
Phyllis Mount
John Mulgrew
Stanley H. Mullin
Byung H. Nam
Bronius Nemickas
Joseph Newman
Michele O. Newman
Margaret Nix
German Noas
John Norman
Charles L. North
J. William Nystrom
Harold Oaklander
Peter A. O'Brien
John J. Ogie
Sr. Mary Therese O'Hearn
Robert C. Oliver
Melvin Jay Oremland
Alice Ottun
Curtis Owens
Albert M. Panariello
George R. Pappas
Nishan Parlakian
Brian Pasby
Mary Pasles

John P. Pasquariello
Donald Phillips
Henry M. Platt
Richard Podgorski
Barbara Potter
Gordon A. Potter
John C. Powers, Jr.
Carmelo Prestifilippo
Lillian P. Puleo
Sandra M. Pulver
Anthony R. Pustorino
R. Irving Pyatt
Linda G. Quest
Thomas Quinn
Louis V. Quintas
Allan M. Rabinowitz
John V. Raftery
Joseph Ragus
Robert Raphael
Sherman Raskin
George J. Rauth
Eva L. Reiman
Herbert E. Robb
Norbert Robbins
Thomas P. Robinson
Joan C. Roland
Saul Rozinsky
Robert I. Ruback
Jeffrey P. Rubens
Gilbert M. Rubenstein
Henry Rubenstein
Teddy Ruiz
Sr. M. Felicitas Russell
Joseph Russo
Donald Ryan
Stanley Salmond
Anthony W. Salotto
Anthony T. Sallustio
John V. Saly
Jay G. Samsky
Thomas Edward Sayles
Thomas E. Scanlon
Richard A. Schaake
Kate Schachter
Lewis Schier
R. Schmalzbach
Louis J. Schmitt
Jerome M. Schwartz
Martin F. Schwartz
Vic Sciacca
Irwin Sears
Barnard Seligman
Irving Settel
George Shanker
John B. Sharkey
Ernest Sherman
William H. Sievert
Vernon Simpson
Harvey Singer
Joseph F. Sinzer
Ellen J. Skinner
Glenn Slade

Donald C. Smith
Eldred Smith
Margaret O'Brien Smith
William C. Smith
Martin Sokoloff
John H. Spillner
Walter Srebnick
Marcel Stein
Sidney Stein
Christine Stephens
Carol H. Stix
John R. Swanson
Melvin B. Swartz
William J. Swift
Edward Talvensaart
Gerard Tarpey, Jr.
Robert Taylor
Bryce Thomas
Elizabeth Torrance
John G. Troiano
Richard S. Turshen
Gerard Vallone
Martin Van Blarcom
Mary A. Vanderpeyl
Andrew Varanelli, Jr.
Robert Vexier
Gabriel Vitalone
Dorothee von Huene-Greenberg
John M. Waldman
John R. Ward
George E. Warner
Marilyn Weigold
Robert Weingard
Leo Weitz
William M. Welty
Ivan Wentworth-Rohr
Elizabeth M. Wesman
Marilyn T. Williams
Valentine R. Winsey
Bronislaw L. Wisniowski
Lillian O. Withers
Gerald Wohl
Jean Fagan Yellin
Jordan M. Young
Stanley Young
Edward C. Zanato
George P. Zimmar

216

Administrators: 1906 - 1991

ARTHUR P. ANTIN — Vice President and Dean, the College of White Plains of Pace University: 1984-1987

DAVID AVDUL — Dean, School of Education: 1984-

NATHAN M. BECKER — Dean, School of Business Administration: 1967-1969

ANIELLO BIANCO — Treasurer: 1984-1988

HENRY BIRNBAUM — University Librarian: 1963-

DOROTHY G. BLANEY — Vice President for Strategic and Long Range Planning: 1983-1984 Executive Vice President for Institutional Planning Management and Support Service: 1984-1985; Executive Vice President for Planning and Personnel: 1985-1989

BEVERLY H. BONAPARTE — Dean, Lienhard School of Nursing: 1982-1986

TONY H. BONAPARTE — Dean, Graduate School: 1975-1983; Vice Provost for Corporate and International Programs and Dean, Lubin Schools of Business: 1983-1986

DAVID R. BREIEN — Treasurer: 1955-1965; 1975-1977 Vice President for Administration and Treasurer: 1977-1984

VINCENT BRENNAN — Vice President for Career Planning: 1985-1988

CHARLES T. BRYAN — Comptroller: 1935-1938

ARON BUKSPAN — Director of Development: 1983-1985; University Director of Development: 1985-1989

FREDERICK P. BUNT — Dean, School of Education: 1967-1983

JOSEPH BURKHART — Executive Vice President for University Relations: 1983-1989

ARTHUR P. CENTONZE — Dean, Lubin School: 1990-

ROBERT E. CHRISTIN — Vice President, Pleasantville/ Briarcliff: 1980-1983; Vice President and Managing Editor for Publications: 1983-1984

FRED COUEY — Dean of Students: 1961-1963

LOUISE CUTLER — Dean of Studies, The College of White Plains: 1984-

MARYANNE DIMARZO — Dean for Students, The College of White Plains: 1987-1988; Dean for Students, White Plains, Pleasantville/Briarcliff: 1988-1990

KATHRYN L. EKIRCH — Dean of Women, Pace College Westchester: 1970-1974; Assistant Vice President for University and Community Relations: 1974-1983; Assistant Vice President and Editor for Publications: 1983-1986; Assistant Vice President for Community Relations: 1987

PATRICIA O'DONNELL EWERS — President: 1990-

FRANK FALCONE — Vice President and Dean, The College of White Plains: 1981-1983; Executive Vice President for Westchester and Dean, The College of White Plains: 1983-1984; Executive Vice President for Westchester: 1984-1985

PETER W. FAZZOLARE — Vice President for Institutional Services: 1978-1982

PETER FINNERTY — Vice President for Athletics and Recreational Facilities: 1981-1984; Vice President for Athletics and Recreational Planning: 1984-1985; Vice President for Athletics and Recreational Facilities: 1985-1988

JOHN E. FLAHERTY — Dean, Graduate School: 1968-1971

ROBERT B. FLEMING — Dean, School of Law: 1977-1981

FRANCES J. FLYNN — Vice President for Management and Computer Information Systems: 1985-1990

ROBERT A. FRANKEL — Executive Vice President for Management and Computer Information Systems: 1984-1985

ANGELA M. GIARDINA — Librarian: 1945-1963

STEVEN GOLDBERG — Dean, Law School: 1989 -

WARREN F. GOODELL — Vice President and Dean of Pace University Westchester: 1973-1977; Vice President and Dean of Pace University Pleasantville: 1977-1978

MARGARET GOTTI — Vice President, The College of White Plains: 1987-

JOSEPH GRUBER — Dean, School of Continuing Education: 1968-1973

JAMES C. HALL — Dean, School of Continuing Education: 1979-1984

GEOFFREY HARTER — Dean for Students, White Plains: 1990-

EMANUEL HELLER — Dean for Students, New York: 1986-1987

ROBERT M. HOFFSTEIN — Vice President, Planning and Research: 1984-1988

JOSEPH E. HOULE — Dean, School of Arts and Sciences: 1972-1990; Vice Provost: 1987-1990

MARCIA JACQUES — University Registrar: 1980-

MARILYN JAFFE-RUIZ — Dean, Lienhard School of Nursing: 1987-

JANET A. JOHNSON — Dean, School of Law: 1983-1989

W. MERRITT JONES — Financial Vice President: 1968-1977

WALTER E. JOYCE — Dean, Student Personnel: 1967-1975

MARGUERITE KAKOSH — Dean, Graduate School of Nursing: 1974-1975

FRANCES A. KEEGAN — Vice President for University Communications: 1981-

EDWARD B. KENNY — Vice President and Dean, The College of White Plains: 1977-1980

JOHN I. KERPATRICK — Financial Vice President and Treasurer: 1966-1968

GEORGE KNERR — Dean of Admissions: 1961-1963; Dean of Student Personnel: 1963-1965; Vice President for Student Personnel: 1968-1969; Vice President for Planning: 1970-1974; Vice President for Planning and Administration: 1974-1980; Vice President for Facilities Planning and Development: 1980-1985; Vice President for Facilities Planning: 1985-

TERRELL KOLODZINSKI — Dean for Students, Pleasantville/ Briarcliff: 1986-1987; Dean for Students, New York: 1987-1990; Dean for Students, Pleasantville/Briarcliff: 1990-

LEO KORNFELD — Vice President, Enrollment Planning: 1990-

PAUL MAGALI — Vice President and Chief Financial Officer: 1977-1983; Executive Vice President for Finance and Administration: 1983-

WILLIAM E. MAHER — Financial Vice President: 1983-1985; Vice President for Finance: 1985-

CHARLES MASIELLO — Dean, Dyson College: 1990

RICHARD MATTHEWS — Dean, Joseph I. Lubin School of Business Administration: 1970-1971; Dean, Lubin School of Business Administration: 1972-1977

WILLIAM F. MCALOON — Dean, Pace College Westchester: 1966-1969; Vice President and Dean, Pace College Westchester: 1970-1973

WALTER A. MCCADDEN — Treasurer: 1968-1975

JOHN T. MCCALL — Vice Provost: 1987-1990

SUSAN M. MERRITT — Dean, School of Computer Science and Information Systems: 1984-

MIRIAM L. MORAN — Vice President for University Admissions: 1980-1983; Vice President for Enrollment Management: 1983-1991

C. EUGENE MORRIS — Dean of Students: 1958-1961

EDWARD J. MORTOLA   Provost: 1949-1956; Vice President and Provost: 1956-1961; President: 1961-1984; Chancellor: 1984-90

PHYLLIS MOUNT   Registrar: 1961-1963; Secretary and Registrar: 1973-1979; Secretary of the University: 1980-1983; Assistant Provost for Management Information Systems: 1983-1984; Vice President, Students Information Systems: 1984-1988

STANLEY H. MULLIN   Vice President for Development: 1966-1968; Vice President for College and Community Relations: 1968-1981; Vice President for University Alumni Relations: 1981-1982

DOROTHEA MURPHY   Dean, New Directions: 1974-1975

EWALD B. NYQUIST   Vice President for Academic Development: 1978-1985

J. WILLIAM NYSTROM   Vice President for Administration: 1981-1985; Vice President for Academic Development: 1985-1987; Executive Vice President - University Projects: 1987-1990; Executive Vice President, Enrollment Management, Planning and Personnel: 1990-1991

ALICE OTTUN   Dean of Admissions and Instruction: 1937-1949

C. RICHARD PACE   Secretary: 1942-1958

HOMER ST. CLAIR PACE   President: 1906-1942

ROBERT S. PACE   Secretary: 1937-1941; President: 1942-1961

GEORGE M. PARKS   Dean, Lubin Schools of Business: 1986-1990

JOSEPH M. PASTORE   Dean, Lubin School of Business Administration: 1977-1980; Vice President for Academic Affairs: 1980-1985; Provost: 1985-1991

OWEN F. PEAGLER   Dean of Evening Administration: 1970-1977; Dean, School of Continuing Education: 1977-1979

RUTH K. PELL   Dean, School of Nursing: 1972-1979

GLENN PERRONE   Vice President for Alumni Relations: 1983-1991

RICHARD PODGORSKI   Vice President for Pleasantville/Briarcliff: 1985-

SAL J. PREZIOSO   Vice President, Public Service Programs: 1984-1986

MARJORIE RAMPHAL   Dean, Graduate School of Nursing: 1975-1979; Dean, Lienhard School of Nursing: 1979-1981

RUTH C. REARDON   Vice President for Development and Alumni Relations: 1978-1979

THOMAS P. ROBINSON   Dean, School of Arts and Sciences: 1967-1971; Dean, Graduate School: 1972-1975; Vice President for Development: 1975-1978; Vice President of Pleasantville/Briarcliff Campus: 1978-1979; Vice President for Academic Affairs: 1979-1980

ADRIAN N. RONDILEAU   Dean of Liberal Arts: 1949-1954

ROBERT RUBACK   Corporate Secretary and Legal Counsel: 1983-

FREDERICK SCHAEBERLE   Treasurer: 1935-1954

JACK S. SCHIFF   Dean, Graduate School of Business Administration: 1966-1968; Provost: 1968-1969; Executive Vice President: 1970-1983; Provost: 1983-1984

WILLIAM G. SHARWELL   President: 1984-1990

JOSEPH F. SINZER   Dean of Faculty: 1955-1959; Dean of Academic Affairs: 1959-1965; Academic Vice President: 1966-1969; Vice President and Secretary: 1970-1973

EDWARD F. SMITH   Vice President for Budget Management: 1973-1974

LILLIAN M. SMITH   Dean of Admissions and Instruction: 1937-1941

VINCENT SPINELLI   Executive Vice President for Institutional Advancement: 1991-

SALVATORE TURCHIO   Dean for Students, New York: 1990-

JULIUS YOURMAN   Dean of Business: 1950-1953; Dean of Accountancy Practice and Business: 1953-1956

EDWARD C. ZANATO   Dean of Students, Pace College Westchester: 1970-1979; University Dean for Students: 1979-1981; Vice President for Students Services: 1982-1983; Vice President for Students Personnel Services: 1983-